F
1034.3
.M377
B57

Bissell, Claude Thomas

The young Vincent
Massey.

DATE DUE			

THE YOUNG VINCENT MASSEY

CLAUDE BISSELL

The
Young Vincent
Massey

UNIVERSITY OF TORONTO PRESS

Toronto Buffalo London

© University of Toronto Press 1981
Toronto Buffalo London
Printed in Canada

ISBN 0-8020-2398-3

Canadian Cataloguing in Publication Data
Bissell, Claude T., 1916–
The young Vincent Massey
Includes index.
ISBN 0-8020-2398-3
1. Massey, Vincent, 1887–1967. 2. Statesmen –
Canada – Biography. I. Title.
FC611.M37B57   971.063'3'0924   c81-094651-3
F1034.3.M37B57

This book has been published
with the assistance of the Canada Council
and the Ontario Arts Council
under their block grant programs, and with
the help of a generous gift to the
University of Toronto Press from the
Herbert Laurence Rous Estate.

Contents

Preface

The years from 1906, when Vincent Massey entered the University of Toronto, to 1935, when he left Canada to take up his appointment as high commissioner to the United Kingdom – the years from age 19 to age 45 – are, in terms of his whole career, the youthful ones. They are the years during which individual initiative was at its strongest, when he questioned received opinions and attitudes and set out on his own course. It was a period of youthful protest against his family inheritance. The element of protest during these years may seem slight to those who have lived through the sixties, but to the young Vincent Massey it was real and formidable. For a legalistic and pietistic religion he substituted a relaxed and Laodicean faith; from a tough, entrepreneurial tradition he moved towards an emphasis on social and cultural responsibilities; beginning with a cautious interest in the arts as an adjunct to religion, he put them at the centre of his life; in the place of the political conservatism of his family he adopted a 'new liberalism' shaped by progressive thought in the United States and Great Britain.

To the Canadian public, Vincent Massey in his early forties still seemed like a young man. The slight, boyish figure reinforced the impression of youthfulness, and the features, which tended in subsequent years to settle into a solemn mask, could support a cheerful vivacity. He seemed youthful, too, by contrast with many of his associates. Mackenzie King, R.B. Bennett, Joseph Flavelle, and Howard Ferguson – to mention some of the principal ones – were all at least a decade older; Vincent Massey had a contemporary flavour, whereas they seemed to be Victorians or Edwardians propelled by an innate vigour into a later age.

The book follows a chronological scheme. But I have at the same time tried to be selective and analytical. This has often required a thematic organization of material with, from time to time, a departure from a simple linear chronology and a re-examination of periods already given a general treatment. This kind of organization is particularly necessary in the early chapters when Massey's ideas and attitudes are in the process of formulation and he has not yet fixed upon his formal role. To ease the way, a brief chronology is appended to the preface.

The book is based largely on manuscript material, but I have benefited also from conversations with a number of people. The following have given me impressions and information that were helpful in writing this volume: Mr and Mrs Geoffrey Andrew, Mr Hunter Bishop, Professor Michael Bliss, Mrs F.H. Cundhill, Dr Robertson Davies, Dr James S. Duncan, Professor Robert Finch, Senator Eugene Forsey, President Goldwin French, Mrs Lee Gossage, Professor George Glazebrook, Miss Charity Grant, Professor George Grant, Dr and Mrs George Ignatieff, Professor Douglas LePan, Mrs L.C.V. Massey, Mr Hart Massey, the Hon. Paul Martin, Mr Andrew S. Mathers, Professor Charles Stacey. I am grateful to the Dominion Archivist, Dr W.I. Smith, and his associates for their prompt and generous assistance during my various visits to the Public Archives of Canada. Mrs D.F. MacDermaid, the university archivist, and her associates greatly facilitated my examination of Massey material at Queen's University. The manuscript was typed by Mrs Audrey Douglas, and I am grateful for her care and patience. Dr Desmond Neill, the librarian of Massey College, was responsible for the administration of the Massey Papers, and his informed advice greatly eased my task.

I am especially grateful to Hart Massey, who gave me permission to use the Massey papers in the Public Archives of Canada, and to Mrs C.H.A. Armstrong, a daughter of George Wrong, who gave me many insights into the young Vincent Massey and permitted me to quote from letters in her possession written by her brother, Hume, to his mother. A grant from the Social Sciences and Humanities Research Council of Canada was of great assistance. The grant enabled me to obtain the services of Mr Murray Barkley, a graduate student in history at the University of Toronto, who was helpful in many ways, in particular in dredging up the references to Vincent Massey from the vast sea of the Mackenzie King diary. Miss Kirsty Boyanoski, an art historian, prepared an architectural analysis of the Massey tomb which I found valuable. I am grateful also to the Rockefeller Foundation which invited me and my wife to be scholars-in-residence at the Study and Conference Centre, Bellagio, Italy, from 22 August to 28 September 1978. There, in that most beautiful of all academic retreats, I plotted this volume and wrote the first two chapters. My wife has lived patiently and philosophically with the Massey project, which became far more complex and demanding than I had ever imagined; she also transcribed and analysed the early Massey diaries. Dr Robertson Davies, master of Massey College from 1961 to 1981, invited me to write this biography, and he and the senior fellows of Massey College gave me sole access to the Vincent Massey papers that are deposited in the college. I regret that this book, which is only the first part of my task, was not published before Dr Davies retired as master.

Massey College
19 June 1981

A Chronology of the Young Vincent Massey

20 February 1887	Birth of Charles Vincent Massey at Toronto
1887–1911	Resides at family home at 519 Jarvis Street
20 February 1896	Death of Vincent's grandfather, Hart Almerrin Massey
30 August 1896	Birth of Vincent's brother, Raymond
11 November 1903	Death of Vincent's mother, Anna
1903–1906	Attends St Andrew's College
1906–1910	At University College, University of Toronto
1910–1911	Works on plans for Hart House
September 1911 – September 1913	At Balliol College, Oxford
1913–1926	Resides at 71 Queen's Park Crescent, Toronto
October 1913 – June 1915	Dean of residence at Victoria College and special lecturer in modern history at the University of Toronto
4 June 1915	Marries Alice Parkin
1915–1918	Staff officer in Military District No. 2 in charge of musketry; final rank, lieutenant-colonel
2 July 1916	Birth of Lionel Massey
18 December 1917	William Grant installed as principal of Upper Canada College
30 March 1918	Birth of Hart Massey
January 1918	Appointed associate secretary to the war committee in Ottawa
November 1918	Appointed secretary of repatriation and employment committee of the cabinet
24 January 1919	First meeting of the Massey Foundation

May 1919	Establishes commission on the secondary schools and colleges of the Methodist Church of Canada
11 November 1919	Opening of Hart House
January 1920	Appointed governor of the University of Toronto
1920–1926	Active as actor and director in Hart House Theatre
October 1921	Burgon Bickersteth appointed warden of Hart House
December 1921	Elected president, Massey-Harris Company
April 1923	Elected president, National Council of Education
March 1924	Formation of Hart House String Quartet
July – August 1924	Visits Russia
January 1925	Appointed trustee of the National Gallery
September 1925	Enters Liberal cabinet as minister without portfolio
October 1925	Resigns as president of Massey-Harris Company
28 October 1925	Liberals defeated in federal election; Massey defeated in Durham
2 July 1926	Death of Vincent's father, Chester
14 September 1926	Liberals win federal election; soon after, Vincent Massey appointed first Canadian minister to Washington
October 1926	Member of Canadian delegation to Imperial Conference in London; confirmed in the Anglican Church by the Archbishop of Canterbury
January 1927	Takes up residence in Washington
September 1928	Country home, Batterwood, near Port Hope, completed
May 1930	Appointed high commissioner to London by Mackenzie King
28 July 1930	Liberals defeated in federal election; R.B. Bennett becomes prime minister
September 1930	Resigns as high commissioner
1930–1931	Extensive travels in Europe and Far East
October 1932	Elected chairman of Dominion Drama Festival
May 1932	Elected president of the National Liberal Federation
September 1934	Purchase of David Milne pictures
3 February 1935	Death of William Grant
14 October 1935	Liberals win federal election; Mackenzie King returns to office
31 October 1935	Reappointed high commissioner to London
7 November 1935	Leaves Canada to take up post of high commissioner

The Massey tomb as it is today

Vincent's parents: Anna Vincent
and Chester Massey (with the infant Vincent)

OPPOSITE Vincent, aged five. In the top photograph
he is with his grandfather Hart, builder of the
family fortune, and his cousin Ruth

Chester and Raymond Massey at home on Jarvis Street

OPPOSITE Vincent as a cadet at St Andrews
(he is the leftmost figure in the front row), and
clowning at Dentonia Park about 1905

TOP Vincent in his early twenties, with a young
friend in Muskoka. BELOW The reception after the wedding of
Alice and Vincent Massey, 3 June 1915. From the left: Raymond Massey,
Margaret Grant, Hume Wrong, Vincent Massey, George Wrong, Alice Massey,
Charity Grant, William Lawson Grant, Harold Tovell, Mrs Wrong

Alice Parkin Massey about the time of her marriage

Wartime family snapshots: Vincent and Alice, with Lionel

BELOW Hart and Lionel Massey, with their parents, at
Hart House, 1920

Vincent, as a cockney burglar, is taken in hand in
The Point of View at Hart House Theatre, 1923

George Wrong, relaxed with his family on the porch
of Durham House, his summer home near Port Hope

The Hart House String Quartet performs at Batterwood
in the 1920s

Burgon Bickersteth with Hart and Lionel at Batterwood

The 1925 style in election posters: in the original
the portrait is in colour

OPPOSITE The first Canadian minister to the United States
and Mrs Massey with Lord Willingdon, the governor general, and
Lady Willingdon, December 1927

William Lyon Mackenzie King, flanked by Sir Esme Howard,
the British ambassador to the United States, and the Canadian
minister, outside the Canadian legation in Washington,
November 1927

The minister's library in the legation

The minister on the dinner circuit, on this occasion as speaker
to the American Institute of Steel Construction

His Majesty's Envoy Extraordinary and Minister Plenipotentiary
for Canada with Alice in 1928 and, OPPOSITE, on a restorative canoe trip
in Muskoka after the defeat of the Liberals in 1930

A portion of the living room of Batterwood House

Batterwood, the Masseys' country home

OPPOSITE
Three views of life at Batterwood:
Alice, Hart, Vincent, and Lionel at the rock pool;
a scene from the filming of 'Durham Darling';
the Christmas house party in 1930 (with Lady Parkin in the centre)

At the Port Hope Conference, September 1933: Vincent
with Raymond Moley (immediately to his left) and a Canadian delegate

Lionel and Hart Massey

THE YOUNG VINCENT MASSEY

The Family Inheritance

In the city of Toronto the best known cemetery is called Mount Pleasant. When it was established in 1873 it lay well beyond the northern outskirts of the town, and continued to do so long after the town had become a city and had begun to break out of the little pocket by the lake to which it had been confined. Now the cemetery occupies a great tract of land in the heart of the metropolitan area. It is not, like many urban cemeteries, a bleak stretch of densely packed headstones and monuments. It is a place of little valleys and gently rolling hills, and nowhere in a city that seems at times to vanish into a forest are the trees more various and splendid.

The oldest section of the cemetery lies just to the east of Toronto's main north-south thoroughfare, Yonge Street. Important citizens – those who served both themselves and their fellows well – are buried there; and a short walk beyond the entrance gates will yield the grave of a prime minister, a lieutenant-governor, a university president, and a great company of men who made their mark in the world of business and public affairs. The names on the monuments have a solid British ring – English and Scottish primarily, with an occasional Irish name of clear Protestant provenance. The graves here are marked by monuments, most of them of a modest height with discreet embellishment. But in certain areas the monuments become tombs, usually of neo-classical design, and form little avenues of dignified opulence.

The most conspicuous of these tombs is not on a fashionable avenue. It stands in the centre of an ample triangle of ground, on a gently rising slope. In the years since it was erected – now close to a hundred – trees have obscured the massive grey-stone structure. Above the main facade, surmounting a central tower on a hipped pedestal, a life-size figure rises above the trees and gazes out westward across the field of monuments far below. It is an enigmatic figure – female, clothed in billowing robes, the left hand reaching down to hold and balance an upright anchor, the right hand covering her heart, the expression on her face intense and serious. The figure was meant to represent 'hope' anchored securely in 'faith.' But to the uninstructed observer the maiden has a brisk, secular quality, part Britannia, part Columbia, the spirit of liberty.

This is the Massey family tomb, commissioned by Vincent's grandfather, Hart Massey, in 1894. It was designed and built by Edward Lennox, the most prominent contemporary Toronto architect, who was responsible for two enduring city landmarks, the formidable old city hall and Sir Henry Pellatt's vast castle *cum* residence, Casa Loma. Although the sepulchre dominates the surrounding area, it is, in some respects, reticent and unassertive. It is with some difficulty that one discerns the word 'Massey' on the lintel above the central doorway. The letters have been simply incised in the stone without any clarifying outline (although the thought occurs that this may be the splendid reserve of those who have no doubts about their own importance).

Vincent Massey is not buried in the family tomb. He disliked it intensely, and had no wish to join his forebears in this Methodist fortress. He would find his resting place in the cemetery of the little Anglican church at Port Hope, Ontario, near his country home, and would thereby underline quietly his rejection of much in the family tradition.

No one, of course, frees himself from a family tradition by a declaration of independence or even by the sedulous pursuit of a different way of life. An intellectual repudiation may still leave room for admiration and affection, and ancestral ways may subtly affect new patterns. When Vincent was a young married man establishing himself in Toronto society, he engaged a genealogist in England to explore his English roots. This yielded little except a cluster of names, disjointed records of marriages and property changes, and some stories of stubborn, Protestant independence. He fell back on the relatively firm basis of his North American inheritance – two centuries in New

England, and a century or so in Canada. The New England years provided a connected narrative, but with few details; only by the middle of the nineteenth century did a clear picture begin to appear. In a brief sketch of the family history that Vincent wrote for his sons, he dealt fondly on the legacy of homespun integrity and practicality. Integrity and practicality were there indeed, particularly during the early pioneer period. But by the time Hart had commissioned the building of the family tomb, a much more complex family pattern had emerged; and in the tomb that pattern found a not unfitting embodiment.

In his later years Vincent Massey returned again to the exploration of his family's past, but this time he was concerned with the early Canadian years. In a remote churchyard near the little Ontario village of Grafton, thirty miles or so from where he himself had by this time built his country home, he found the graves of some of the first Canadian Masseys. They belonged to the family of Daniel Massey, the sixth American generation of the family, and Vincent's great-great-grandfather. He had crossed into Canada from northern New York state in 1802, and had begun once more a cycle that his forebears had already passed through several times south of the border. The area he came to was pioneer land, heavily forested, with very few recognizable roads. Cobourg was the nearest settlement of any size; it was essentially an isolated little port that was an entry point into Canada of Americans coming across the lake from Sackets Harbor. Daniel was not a loyalist: the U.E. Loyalist wave of immigrants had subsided, and there was nothing in the Massey record of these early years to indicate an attachment to the British crown. Indeed, Daniel's father, Jonathan, had identified himself so thoroughly with the fledgling republic that he had served as a lieutenant with the Continental army in the Revolutionary War. Merrill Denison speculates that the motive for immigration into Upper Canada was religious, and that Daniel followed 'Bishop Leckie, the famous Methodist divine' across the border.[1]

The original Massey hegira from England had been in pursuit of religious freedom; but there could have been no question of such a cause in 1802. The Methodists were still a small sect in the United States but they were expanding rapidly, and no restraints had been imposed upon them. Methodism in the United States had moved away from the original Wesleyan conservatism – its authoritarian centralism, its loyalty to constituted government. It had become a faith congenial to the frontier, with its emphasis on the individual's power to achieve salvation, its summons to a world of Christian action, its buoyant optimism: the scriptures said 'Let us go on to perfection,' and, to the devout, perfection beckoned as a goal potentially attainable in this world. Methodism had adapted itself with ease to wilderness conditions. Although the emphasis on centralized control remained, vitality and growth belonged to the small unit. The 'circuit,' the parish of the preacher on horseback, could adjust itself easily to the sudden eruptions of the frontier. Whether or not the exigencies of his faith did in fact play a part in Daniel's decision to cross the border, there can be no doubt about the centrality of Methodism in his life, and in the lives of his nineteenth-century descendants. The three Massey patriarchs, Daniel (1766–1838), the second Daniel (17██–1856), and Hart Almerrin (1823–1896) were Methodists, first a█d foremost, and men of action only as exemplars of the faith.

On the whole, Methodism on the North American frontier was an expansive and liberating faith. It also constituted an emotional release, especially when it incorporated the camp meeting, with its excitement and its invitation to self-examination and self-expression, as an integral part of its program. Yet along with the contempt for ritual and elimination of any intermediary between God and man went a relentless emphasis on the good life conceived of in strictly legalistic terms. The Methodists inherited in full the Puritan insistence on avoidance of any activity that might distract the mind from concern with salvation. Compromise and tolerance were unthinkable in matters of conduct. The quest for perfection must be constant and unremitting. It could be best carried on in the home, a 'sacred asylum' which should be an earthly foretaste of the heavenly home, with the father, a stern but just deity, the mother, the spirit of compassion and affection, and the children, bound to both, dependent, obedient, and adoring.[2] Methodism thus was to become associated with a sullen negativism, a proscription of whatever threatened sobriety and a concentration on the spiritual life – from drinking alcoholic beverages to supporting public transportation on the Sabbath.

The legalistic flavour of the Massey Methodism was strong and pervasive. It continued into the fourth Canadian generation, although by then the family was far removed from frontier and small town. Thus Hart's third son Walter, embarked in 1887 on a round-the-world trip, praised a resort in California as 'an especially desirable spot for health seekers. No spirituous liquors can be sold or given away, all amusements of a doubtful character are prohibited, and all must be quiet after ten thirty P.M.'[3] The youngest son, Fred Victor, carried the warfare against sin aggressively into the camp of the enemy. He wrote home from Boston, where he was a student at the Massachusetts Institute of Technology, about an encounter with a fellow boarder who attacked 'Christianity, temperance, morality and poured out such unbearable, intolerable rot about art and its influence.' Fred Victor concluded in a tone of savage unction. 'I have downed him and others admit it. I hold him in derisive contempt, and I think I have made the others despise his views too.'[4]

It was the Methodists who had a major responsibility for fashioning the grim Toronto Sunday, a distinguishing mark of the city until only a few decades ago. Towards the end of the nineteenth century a Toronto visitor recorded this impression: 'Altogether Sunday is as melancholy and suicidal a sort of day as Puritan principles can make it.'[5] But to the devout this 'suicidal' day was an earthly foretaste of the heavenly kingdom. 'A sacred silence,' wrote a devout contemporary, 'falls upon the land, the whirling wheels of machinery stand still, the countless chimneys of myriad factories cease to pour forth their volumes of smoke, the air becomes pure, and the blue sky is seen, unstained by a cloud, a symbol of the holy influence of the Lord's Day.'[6]

It is tempting to place a great emphasis on the deadening effect of Methodist moral strictures. The expenditure of so much spiritual energy by serious and solemn people on seemingly minor matters invites ridicule. But too much emphasis on Methodist narrowness can give a distorted picture. The Masseys, except for the occasional individual sally, were not noted proselytizers; they did not lead the forces of righteousness into holy combat. The Massey household was not subject to the arid rigidities and the cold formalism of evangelical Anglicanism, such as Samuel Butler portrayed in *The Way of All Flesh*. There was room for humour and genial relaxation. The reading and study of the Bible was, of course, at the heart of family life; it was 'the book of books.' Yet other books were important too, particularly books that helped to develop natural aptitudes or widened knowledge of people and places. Victoria, the Methodist college at Cobourg, where Hart attended classes in the forties, became for him, as for many Methodists, a central bastion of the faith.

The Masseys fully realized the Methodist concept of the close-knit family. The first Daniel's family was small – three children – and we know little about them, but the second Daniel and Hart had families of a comfortable Victorian size: seven in Daniel's, five in Hart's. Daniel's wife, Lucina Bradley, is a shadowy figure, but Hart's wife, Eliza Ann Phelps, emerges clearly as the strong, ideal mother of the Methodist family. Hart had met her in 1846 when he was attending the wedding of a relative in Gloversville, New York, and had returned in June of the following year to win and marry her. It was an arduous three hundred miles from Gloversville to the Massey farm and the bride must have had a chilly thought or two about the life that awaited her on the Canadian frontier. It was to be, as only a few years began to reveal, a life of rapid change and increasing comfort, of intense happiness and great sorrow.

Hart's remarkable career as entrepreneur and industrialist had had a prologue in his father's business initiative. Breaking from the repetitive routine of the frontier farmer's life, Daniel had first become an agricultural developer, buying uncleared land, clearing and selling the timber, then selling the improved land to a new settler, then repeating the process, with mounting profits. Then in 1830, on a trip to Watertown, New York, which was an external headquarters for Masseys who had emigrated to Canada, he saw a mechanical thresher and was fascinated by it. A clever mechanic, he brought back the parts, reassembled them, and began to think of reproducing the machines for the Canadian market. By 1847 he was prepared to make the leap from agriculture to manufacturing. He moved to Newcastle, set himself up in modest quarters, and in 1849 founded 'The Newcastle Foundry and Machine Manufactory, C.W.' In 1851 Hart, who shared his father's interest in machinery, left the farm at Grafton to become factory superintendent, and gradually assumed control. The growth of the business in the last half of the nineteenth century is one of the great stories of entrepreneurship: the securing of Canadian patents from American inventors; the formation of the Massey Manufacturing Co. in 1870 with a capitalization of $50,000; the move in 1879 to the 'largest and best equipped factory ever built in Canada,'[7] in an area in Toronto shrewdly chosen to take advantage of railway facilities, and to provide an enclave for the workers well removed from the demoralizing distractions of the city; the internationalization of the company so that by the end of the century it had become the leader in the British Empire in the manufacture of agricultural machinery. A series of mergers in the 1890s, the major one between the Massey Company and its great rival, A. Harris, Son & Company of Brantford, finally assured the indisputable primacy of the new organization.

Throughout this whole period of rapid expansion and of intensive, unremitting concern with the 'works' (the word that Hart continued to use as a general designation for both factory and office, indicating thereby the merging of the two in his mind), Hart remained a stout Methodist, both active in the church and munificent in its financial support. For him there was no conflict between religious belief and success in material affairs. Indeed, success was an indication of the movement towards 'perfection' enjoined upon Methodists, and if it were gained, as was Hart's, by hard and unceasing labour, it was an armour against all worldly attractions of a cheap and enervating nature. Methodism, indeed, was an economy as well as a faith. When in 1871 Hart left Canada to live in Cleveland, the ostensible reason was ill health. But during his absence for a little over ten years, he kept in touch with the company and with its president, Charles Albert, his oldest son. And in Cleveland, where he had many relatives and Methodist associates, he moved into new business enterprises and acquired the education in corporate finance that enabled him to conduct the subsequent Massey mergers with skill and boldness.

No doubt Hart was sustained in his labour by the knowledge that he was contributing to human welfare directly and substantially, that he was supporting the human activity that was the greatest source of a nation's strength and the nursery of its moral stamina. In his history of Massey-Harris, Denison argues that the introduction of the self-binder – the mechanism that did away with hard labour for the tying of the sheaves – 'exerted a more profound influence on the world's economy than any other of man's technical accomplishments, save possibly the locomotive.'[8] (Ironically, the self-binder hastened the shift from farm to city, for it greatly reduced the number of men required for harvesting.)

The Massey firm was not technologically innovative, except in so far as it recognized the importance of new developments and quickly acquired patent rights. To sustain its competitive position it depended on the excellence of its materials and the skill and devotion of its workers. The Massey product would rarely be first in the market, but when it appeared there would be no doubt of its durability and efficiency. It bore upon it, so to speak, the stamp of Hart's integrity, his striving for perfection.

From his return to Toronto in 1882 until his death in 1896 Hart was the dominating figure within the firm. The presidency was occupied by his sons, but nothing could take place without his approval. The firm had been recapitalized; the family was in complete control, with Hart in possession of the majority of the stock. In the eighties and nineties he became a symbol of capitalist enterprise. His correspondence for this period of ascendancy has been preserved, and it provides an insight into a strong and dominating personality.

The bulk of the correspondence is concerned with financial transactions, many of them involving small sums. In business Hart did not tolerate casualness or sentiment. Agreements must be rigidly observed, and money given only for service precisely and faithfully performed. He presided over his business affairs, whether they concerned the firm or a personal enterprise, like the God of the Old Testament, vigilant for signs of backsliding, punishing weakness and inefficiency, always exacting the full measure of the bond. A great many of the letters written to him about financial matters are shrill and combative in tone. They were written by men who felt that they had a justifiable grievance, but had scant hope of getting an understanding and generous response. Thus a lawyer wrote about the cost of a fence separating his Cleveland property from a property owned by Hart – one of many secured during his Cleveland years, and rented out until real estate values rose to a satisfactory height. Hart had refused to accept any responsibility for the expense. The letter begins with a reference to 'your *insulting* and I am told characteristic letter' and continues 'I don't think I know you personally – you have lived here and you have left a reputation. I was told I would have trouble with you – It has come.'9 Hart pressed his creditors hard, even when failing health must have warned him that his own days were numbered. One creditor, threatened by Hart with a lawsuit, replied: 'Mr Massey should not forget that he was poor once himself, that it is a glorious thing to have a giant's strength but tyrannous to use it like a giant, that in a few short years he and I and all concerned, like poor E.B. Harper who was consigned to his mother earth a week ago to-day, will have passed away, and it will be poor satisfaction to him that he did what he could to crush, worry and vex poor Cameron who whatever his faults that of not being willing to pay his honest debts is not one.'10 No financial detail escaped Hart's attention. His letters pointing out inadequacies in workmanship had a brutal directness that was in sharp contrast to his thin, spidery handwriting. To a local firm that had done some work on his house, Hart sent a cheque for $165 in payment for a bill of $185, and to the resultant protest he replied as follows: 'I am in receipt of yours of the 12th in which you acknowledge receipt of my cheque for $165 which you are aware was in full of ac. as my letter stated and if you do not accept it as such you will return the cheque at once. You are well aware I have not accepted the work as at all satisfactory nor completed and it was only to save trouble and annoyance that I sent what I considered more than your due that I might be in full of account.'11

Hart took a stern and unbending attitude towards his workers. A worker was hired to do a specific job, and it was his responsibility to do it well; the inevitable and just consequences of inefficiency and laziness were dismissal and poverty. Labour was a commodity to be purchased in accordance with the needs of the firm, and if at a given time the commodity was not needed, the firm had no further responsibility. Hart kept a close watch on his branch managers, and was ruthless about suspected inefficiency or neglect. On one occasion he employed the Canadian Service Agency, an organization 'prepared to do all kinds of legitimate detective work,' to bring in a report on a manager. The consequent report, which cost the Massey company $12.50 for two and a half days' work, emphasized those details of taste and character that would have a special significance for a puritan Methodist. 'He [the Massey branch manager] does not dress extravagantly, nor does he sport much jewellery. He wears only a plain watch chain, and a gold pin (an old one). He does not seem particularly fond of cards, but he is fond of a glass of whiskey. He was at the Albion Hotel bar, from 1 to 3 p.m. Saturday, when he had several glasses of whiskey and soda.'[12]

Trade unions were incomprehensible. To Hart, they were blatant disrupters of normal business procedures. When the Massey firm was subjected to strike action, he asked for support from fellow manufacturers and received from one an assurance that it would give him 'all the assistance in our power to fill the places of your strikers with men independent of this order [the Knights of Labor] and will positively refuse to employ any of the men who are or have been on strike at your works.'[13]

If financial success did not modify Hart's simple, rigid ideas about business, he none the less quickly acquired something of the style and many of the attitudes of wealthy Torontonians. His purchase in 1882 of a home of conspicuous opulence on fashionable Jarvis Street gave him a setting appropriate to his importance and power. The house was an example of high Victorian exuberance in its wildest flight – battlements, towers, cupolas, clusters of chimneys all thrust together in a hectic striving for the picturesque. The house, however, did not reflect any deep personal taste; it was simply an imposing pile, and its desperate transmogrifications in this century emphasized its inherent formlessness – from antique gallery to exotic and fashionable restaurant to one of a chain of popular eating places.

Hart also abandoned his Liberalism and became a devout Tory. In political and social affairs Methodism was unpredictable: the English Wesleyan tradition was conservative and instinctively loyalist, but the hardier American offshoot could acquire a populist tinge. The second Daniel, for instance, was a Mackenzie supporter in the troubles of the thirties, and there is a tradition that in 1839 he was associated with the Cobourg conspiracy to bring back the fiery rebel from exile in the United States.[14] As a young man Hart continued the tradition, but in a solid, circumspect manner. In Newcastle he was a member of the central committee of the West Durham Reform Association, and in the sixties and seventies he supported Edward Blake and the Liberal party. But in 1878, with the launching of Macdonald's National Policy of protection, he saw a great light, and later frequently mentioned that date as marking his conversion to Conservatism. By the late eighties his allegiance was so widely recognized that Sir John A. Macdonald could peremptorily request his financial aid for the party. In a letter Sir John congratulated Hart on the excellence of a recent Toronto display of Massey agricultural machinery, then added balefully, 'However you manufacturers are not out of the wood yet.' The prime minister went on to make his hard political point: 'Commercial Union is having a run now throughout Canada and should be arrested. This can only be done by getting a first class newspaper to fight the battle of the National Policy. I must ask you to take a lot of stock in the newspaper. I don't offer it to you as directly a profitable investment but you can look upon it as a most valuable kind of insurance.'[15] There is no reply in Hart's correspondence, but shortly afterwards a meeting was arranged in the Queen's Hotel in Toronto, and Hart no doubt responded to Sir John's request.

As the Massey firm grew in size and power, Hart, by nature a plainspoken, undemonstrative man, could not be altogether blind to his rise to national eminence. In London, England, following the triumphant reception of Massey products at an exhibition, he was invited to a dinner given by the Canadian high commissioner, Sir Charles Tupper, and was duly called upon to speak. He wrote home to his son, Chester, about the sudden onrush of the spirit as he rose in reply to the invitation, like a devout Methodist witnessing to the power of grace: 'I had not taken wine with the others to inspire me but had a glass of ginger ale and so I got up and went at it. I felt quite at home and spoke for some 15 minutes with much freedom and cheered all the way through.'[16]

Late in life Hart set down unapologetically the nature and intent of his achievements. In the early part of 1893 he wrote a series of letters to leading political figures – to the prime minister of Canada, Sir John Thompson, to senior cabinet ministers in the federal government, to the Canadian high commissioner, Sir Charles Tupper, and to prominent Methodists – urging his appointment to the Senate: a fruitless campaign as it turned out. The letters made the same points with variations in detail and language. In one letter he gave a brief summary of his career, expressed in terms of the classic rise from poverty to riches: 'I am a Canadian-born subject of his Majesty, have risen from a farm laborer to my present situation, was a Justice of the Peace for something over 20 years while residing in the United Counties of Northumberland and Durham, have been a manufacturer for about 50 years, and am now the employer of a greater number of men than any other Canadian manufacturer.'[17] In a letter that he wrote on the same day to the Hon. Mackenzie Bowell, minister of trade and commerce, Hart was much more specific and boastful, with a heavy-handed assertion about the easy convertability of economic into political power: 'I believe that in my position I can control and influence more voters than any other business man in Canada, and as you are aware, my influence and support has been with the Government since 1878. The companies that I represent as President now employ directly and indirectly from fifteen to twenty thousand persons, and they are doing a business to the extent of about five million dollars annually – I feel that few men have done more for advancement of Canada's industrial enterprise and prosperity than I.'[18]

Hart's rigidities in business practice, his uncompromising attitude towards trade unions, and, above all, the monopolistic position of the Massey-Harris Co. in the agricultural machinery market aroused sustained and bitter criticism, especially in the radical press. Hart honestly believed that the criticism was unjust; he contended that he was acting in the interests of the farmer. 'For some reason or other,' he wrote, 'it does seem that people are using every means possible to vent their spite on the Massey-Harris Co. on account of its consolidation. Why they should do this when they are actually getting their machines at a lower price than they did before, seems strange to us.'[19] In this letter Hart contemplated a libel action against a western paper that had attacked the family firm; but caution stayed his hand, for he knew the futility of such a move. Three years before he had brought a libel action against W.F. McLean, the editor of the muck-raking newspaper *The World*. That suit had its origins in a slashing attack on Hart (referred to contemptuously as 'Hayfork Massey') for acting hypocritically in his proclaimed benefactions. McLean referred specifically to an offer by Hart of $100,000 to Victoria College providing it could guarantee its independence by raising a total of one million dollars; the implication was that Hart was acting in the spirit of Leacock's 'whirlwind campaign,' making his pledge contingent on the obtaining of a total subscription so large as to make it worthless. Hart lost the case.

It was ironical that Hart should lose a lawsuit in which he had been accused of hypocrisy in his benefactions, for no Canadian of wealth of his day gave more generously and more wisely. In his own mind he felt no need to defend his business practices; he had always acted, he believed, with integrity and honesty, and skill, assiduity, and foresight had brought him success. He thought of his worldly success as conferring an inward assurance of the presence in his life of the Holy Spirit. But assurance from this source was not enough. To gain full assurance he must do good works; he must see that this wealth was devoted to good causes. In one of his senatorial letters he had announced that 'I am preparing for the distribution of my means to the best advantage in the interests of Canada, and am desirous of doing what I can during the remainder of my days towards the advancement of these interests and the giving of my time largely to the benefit of the public.'[20] When Hart wrote this he had already emerged as a major benefactor. He had given away over $300,000: $40,000 to Victoria College for a chair in religious education; two major buildings in the city of Toronto, $62,000 for a mission named in memory of his youngest son, Fred Victor, and $144,000 for a music hall in memory of his oldest son, Charles; and a number of smaller gifts to Methodist colleges in various parts of Canada. These benefactions were a prologue to the will by which Hart disposed of his estate. Of the total value of the estate, between $2,100,000 and $2,200,000, only a little over ten per cent went to relatives. (Presumably the three surviving children, Chester, Lillian, and Walter, already possessed substantial holdings of Massey stock.) There was a long parade of small benefactions, from $5,000 to $10,000, for religious and charitable purposes, but the major bequests were to Methodist universities: $200,000 for Victoria College, $100,000 for Mount Allison College, and $50,000 for the American University in Washington, DC. The residue of the estate, over a million dollars, was to be distributed by the executors over the next twenty years in accordance with the model of the will. During his last years Hart had occasionally responded to appeals from Methodist groups planning to erect a parsonage, or to launch a church in a new community poor in natural wealth but rich in human souls; but he had resisted most of these appeals, as well as those coming from evangelistic entrepreneurs (one persistent suppliant had suggested that a fair division of labour would be between material supplied by the Masseys and satisfaction of spiritual needs by the suppliant). His will was the declaration of a devout Methodist, but of a Methodist who believed that religion would flourish best in institutions devoted to the liberal arts.

The Methodist environment in which Hart formed his ideas and tastes during the eighties and nineties was a far cry from the pious austerities of his Newcastle days. In Toronto, the headquarters was Metropolitan Church, the 'cathedral of Methodism'; the new building had emerged from a competition in which the use of the Gothic style was a condition of entry. Outside Toronto, the headquarters was the Methodist centre for adult education situated at Fair Point on Chautauqua Lake, New York. It had been founded in 1874 by Bishop John Heyl Vincent of the Methodist Episcopal Church, a close friend of the Masseys, and a virtual member of the family after his half-sister married Chester in 1886. Chautauqua was conceived as a non-denominational summer program for Sunday School teachers; but it grew into a centre for extended programs and the idea spread into other places, Chautauqua becoming a movement as well as a place. It had, of course, a stout religious core, but it welcomed an alliance with music, literature, and, in a general inspirational way, with science. Chautauqua was the old Methodist camp meeting of Chester's youth transformed by a more liberal and less introverted age. Its influence was duly noticed in university circles. Professor David R. Keys of the department of English, University of Toronto, writing in the *University of Toronto Monthly*, commented: 'Since Bishop Vincent made Browning the hero of the Chautauqua clubs, his vogue on this continent has been extending in ever-widening circles.'[21]

Bishop Vincent's concept of Chautauqua was broad, democratic, and visionary. It was a combination of the Methodist striving for perfection and the American revolutionary dream of a free, equal, and enlightened republic. 'Self-improvement in all our faculties, for us all, through all times, for the greatest good of all people – this is the Chautauqua idea, a divine idea, a democratic idea, a millennial idea.'[22] Chautauqua, its supporters declared, was a fusion of 'paradise and Athens.'

It was in the Chautauqua atmosphere of optimism and intellectual curiosity that Hart formulated his will. Under Chautauqua influence, too, he had earlier accepted a concept of broad workers' education in the Massey firm. The refining effect of music was recognized in the establishment of the Massey Cornet Band, which was trained and led by a musician brought from Germany especially for this purpose. Literature was recognized by the establishment of a Workmen's Library Association, and by the publication of a succession of magazines in which the firm was celebrated and the muse discreetly invoked. One of the magazines, the *Trip Hammer* (thirteen issues published from February 1885 to February 1886), might have been a Chautauqua publication. In its prospectus, the *Trip Hammer* declared that it was 'the first literary magazine published by the employer of any business concern, and was established with a view to increasing the interest of the working public in literature and learning, being devoted to "Labour and Knowledge".' The most famous of the Massey magazines appeared in January 1896, the month preceding Hart's death. It was called *Massey's Magazine* and was a principal vehicle for the expression of literary nationalism. Almost every contemporary English Canadian writer of any distinction appeared in its pages, among them Charles G.D. Roberts, Bliss Carman, Duncan Campbell Scott, Archibald Lampman, Wilfred Campbell, John McCrae. It was absorbed in July 1897 by the *Canadian Magazine*, which was a purer literary medium for nationalism.

For the literary and cultural activities in the Massey firm, Hart's third son, Walter, had a large responsibility. He had succeeded to the presidency on the death of his oldest brother, Charles, in 1884, and he was, by nature, expansive and outgoing, eager to win public approbation for himself and his company. Hart was, however, until his death in 1896, still a dominant and autocratic figure. He had few close associates in the business world, or outside it, and even with these he had a disposition to quarrel. More and more he retreated into his family, which now formed an enclave on Jarvis Street – Chester immediately to the north of the patriarch's house, Walter in another large house across the road. Hart's affections were now concentrated on the most recent family arrivals, Charles Vincent, Chester's son, born in 1887, and Ruth, Walter's daughter, born two years later. When, at the age of four, Vincent, with his parents and his Aunt Lillian, made the first of many transatlantic trips, he received six letters from his grandfather during his three-month absence. The letters are typed, and most of them bear the official heading 'From Head Office of the Massey Manufacturing Co.' (Even the affairs of the heart Hart attended to with business-like precision.) But the letters are warm and affectionate. The old man, at that time contemplating how best he could extend his influence beyond the grave, could still enter the world of his four-year-old grandson. Here is one of the letters to the young traveller:

Dear Vincent: Your Grandpa is so anxious to see you, as he knows you are growing to be quite a little man, and understands that you can now talk German. We will have a good time when you come home riding out after the grey horse in the cart. He goes nicely now, and it will be so fine for you to ride out in the morning with grandpa while your papa and Uncle Walter are getting ready.

I was over to Erie Villa for a while yesterday and saw a lot of your playthings upstairs. They are all nicely put away there and they made me think of you a good deal. Little Ruth looks at your picture, as she knows who it is, and I know she would like to see you. You must be a good boy, and when you come home tell your Grandpa all you have seen. Good Bye.

from Grampa

Vincent carefully preserved these letters. He would later recall how each morning before the official departure to the 'works,' he and his grandfather would take a short ride and he would be permitted to hold the reins.

Vincent was destined to be the principal agent by which Hart's final wishes were realized, although with an amplitude and boldness that Hart had not envisaged. Hart had bound Vincent, both by example and by directive, to a life of public service, and this essential part of the Massey inheritance Vincent gladly accepted. Other parts of the heritage he repudiated. The Mount Pleasant mausoleum became, for him, a symbol of much that he disliked: ostentation and deference to fashionable taste. But the mausoleum also stood for other things that Vincent could not easily cast aside: a passion for power and a delight in its exercise, an accommodation of the spiritual to the secular, and a sense of a peculiar calling.

Chester Daniel Massey, Vincent's father, was born in 1850, the second child of the family. Of the four Massey boys, he was the only one to survive well into the twentieth century. (Walter lived until 1901, but for Vincent he existed only in memory as the fabulous uncle of his early years). Chester lacked the energy and drive of Charles and Walter, who both became influential officers in the Massey enterprise, helping to shape and direct it. In a family where the male position was defined by service to the firm, Chester moved shadowily in the background. He did, at various times, occupy high executive positions, but always, it would seem, by survival rather than by positive election. After Charles' death, he became treasurer; after Hart's, vice-president; after Walter's, president for a brief period. From 1903 until his death in 1926 he was honorary president and chairman of the board.

In one respect he resembled both his father and grandfather: he was tall – well over six feet – and thin. In manhood he wore a short beard and side-whiskers, and the resemblance to Abraham Lincoln, portrayed later with such striking realism on the stage by his younger son, Raymond, must have been noted. But Chester was a delicate and withdrawn Lincoln: the eyes have nothing of his grandfather's gimlet sharpness, or of Hart's level, intense gaze; they have a slightly melancholy cast, a suggestion of langorous introspection. Chester had a serious illness in his youth (like so many Victorian maladies its precise nature was never recorded, nor, one suspects, known) and much of his adult life was directed to a search for health, frequently abroad. Valetudinarianism turned into melancholy. Vincent refers in his diary to the 'brooding tendency that [his father] inherited from grandmother.'[23]

The melancholy and self-pity were relieved by gentleness and a delicate sense of humour. Vincent has preserved the first letter he received from his father. It was written on 15 July 1887 when Chester was away on business in England. (Since Vincent was then not quite five months old, his father was really writing a piece of humorous fantasy for the amusement of the family.)

My Darling Little Son:

I hope you will not think I have forgotten you because I have not written you. You must remember that you have not written me. Your dear little mama has been telling about your doings and sent me some of your pictures. I wonder what the artist gave you for keeping so still. Your photograph astonishes the natives and I think it is wonderfully good. I hear that your grandmama has been teaching you how to shake hands so I expect you will be reaching out your hand to me when I get back. She will be making a regular monkey of you teaching you so many tricks. But you have no better friend have you?

How do you like your rations these days. If you like I will bring you over some English Bacon, Fried Soles, and Mutton Chops.

All being well when you get this I will be on the ocean where I can cascade just as easily as you can. Can't you bring your mother down to New York to meet me? Give her and Grandmama my love and remember me to Emily,

From your loving Papa

I am crazy to see you.

The gentle humour so charmingly shown in this letter could sharpen into mimicry – a skill that reappeared in his two sons. Chester was more a gentleman and dilettante than a man of affairs. In his autobiography Vincent recalls how his father's greatest pleasure was to sit alone in his picture gallery, dressed in velvet jacket, contemplating his treasures, 'nearly all the works of minor painters of the Barbizon school, or of Dutch artists of his day.'[24] But the delight in mimicry and interest in art did not ruffle the surface of Chester's serene Methodist orthodoxy. An incident related by both Raymond and Vincent illustrates this beautifully. When Raymond made his shattering decision to go on the stage, and informed his father of his intention, the old gentleman, with remarkable powers of accommodation, gradually recovered, and saw even a pagan career in the theatre in a redeeming Methodist light. Father and son knelt in prayer asking God's blessing on the career Raymond had chosen. Chester then expressed the hope that Raymond would not 'practise' on Sunday.[25]

In family affairs, Chester had a particular responsibility for benefactions, which became more substantial and more numerous as the firm expanded and prospered. One of these was to the Chautauqua movement, in which the family was actively involved. This involvement had led to Chester's meeting with Anna Vincent, half-sister of the Chautauqua's founder. She and Chester were married in 1886. Vincent was born on 20 February 1887; Raymond, nine years later in 1896.

Anna Vincent had been born in Chicago on 19 July 1859. The family was of Huguenot descent and, like the Masseys, had become devout

Methodists. Anna studied 'literature and music' at Centenary Colle-giate Institute in Hackett's Town, New Jersey, an institution under the control of the Methodist Church and devoted to preparing young ladies for their responsibilities in a Christian home. But about Anna Massey there was not a trace of the severe or the sanctimonious. She was petite and beautiful, dark-haired, with delicate features; her face mirrored intelligence and warm feeling. She had a cultivated interest in art and music and demonstrated that devoutness did not mean dullness. Nathanael Burwash, the chancellor of Victoria College, paid tribute after her death, in a privately printed memorial, to 'the rich beauty and the harmony and good taste' she brought to the big house on Jarvis Street. Vincent recalled how, during a visit to London, she persuaded her husband to take her to a performance of an opera at Covent Gardens; Chester insisted, however, on one condition – that a net should cover the bodice of the formal low-cut dress prescribed for such occasions.

Vincent preserved a little bundle of letters she wrote to him just before the turn of the century when she was away with Chester on his business trips. Vincent was then a young boy, aged eleven, whose range of activities aroused motherly interest and concern. Raymond was an infant. The letters brim with affection. 'Oh! to feel my arms around you and Raymond would I think be the greatest joy I could have this moment'; and with solicitude: 'Papa and I both think it better that you take *no* part in the games as long as we are away and I would feel so anxious about it.'[26] Two days later she added, 'I wonder if you are in church and if you will go to Sunday School.'[27] She told Vincent amusing stories that have an adult sophistication: 'I wish you could have seen Papa this morning. We were going down to breakfast. I was a little way ahead of him when I heard a great noise. I looked back and here was Papa trying to pick himself up. His hat had gone about six feet ahead of him – I asked what is the matter? he said I have only two legs, it is a little hard to stand up when they go from under you.'[28]

Vincent – for an eleven-year old – was a good correspondent. He recounted family events, repeatedly sent his love, and commented on his sadness at his parents' absence. He echoed his mother's solicitude about his activities: 'Mama may Grandma get me a baseball. She was a little uncertain whether you would aprove write me what you think in next letter.'[29] A peremptory note appears only when his literary interests are involved: 'I got the beautiful paper you sent me but was disappointed to find that it was the same number that Uncle Charles sent me, I gave one to Ruth. Please send me some more cartoons from different papers and if you can, another "Truth".'[30]

Ruth was Walter Massey's oldest child. In Vincent's memoirs, she is the relative he recalls with the greatest affection. 'As very small children – she was a couple of years younger than I – we were constant playmates. We created a world of our own out of the large and shaggy garden in which our grandfather's house stood.' He then notes with approval that in later life, as Mrs Harold Tovell, she became 'an able historian of art.'[31] Vincent preserved the letters that she wrote to him as a young school girl. He is addressed as 'Bim,' and the letters, full of detail about the animals at her father's farm and the athletic club organized by the children to preside over the games, occasionally sound a more personal and affectionate note. 'Thank you very much for your valentine. I would have sent you one but you said last year that you did not care anything about them. I have received seven so far.'[32] 'If you missed me half as much as I missed you I pity you from the bottom of my soul.'[33] She was pleased by Vincent's faithfulness as a correspondent. 'It was very kind of you to write me 40 minutes after leaving Toronto at the Waldorf and after leaving the dock.'[34] Occasionally she tried to impress him with her scholarly interests: 'I am reading "In Memoriam" by Tennyson now. It is great.'[35]

Dentonia Park, about which Ruth wrote, was a farm owned by her father and named after his wife, Susan Denton. Its two hundred and forty acres have long since been absorbed in greater Toronto, but in 1897, when Walter built his summer home there, it lay to the northeast beyond the city. Chester also built a summer house there, so that Dentonia Park became a family enclave. It was, in a sense, a private Chautauqua where sport, scientific experiment, and cheerful piety blended. Walter was the presiding spirit, exuberant, endlessly inventive, a great hero to his own children and to his nephews and nieces. His death in 1901 was a particularly severe blow to Vincent, who found him a more fatherly figure than his own gentle and withdrawn father.

An even more bitter blow was the sudden death of Anna Massey in November 1903, in London, during a European trip with her husband

and the two boys. Just before the return sailing date, Anna became ill. The illness was diagnosed as appendicitis and, in accordance with the medical knowledge of the day, the doctor prescribed the following treatment: 'fluid diet, glycerine and bella donna to be painted on the tender spot of the abdomen, olive oil and enema, followed by two pints of warm boracic lotion, night and morning.' Anna became ill on 20 October; an operation was not performed until 10 November. By then it was too late. The nurse in attendance, Margaret Osmond, described Anna's last hours in a letter to Mrs Hart Massey. It is a moving tribute to Anna's selfless courage in the face of approaching death, and a tender picture of the last meeting between mother and her sixteen-year old son.

Then Mr Dean and Dr Head came, and upon a consultation they decided to perform transfusion in the hope of stimulating the heart, which was getting rapidly weaker with each attack of sickness. They, therefore, injected six pints of saline solution in a vein in the left arm, and all this Mrs M. bore without a complaint. She knew it was all for her good and she said to Mr Dean: 'I am going to get better.' I do not think she realized how ill she was, though when the night nurse appeared, she clutched my hand and implored me not to leave her, and I promised her I would not, I would stay with her all night. After the transfusion her pulse certainly improved for a time, and Mrs M. said herself she felt better and she was so thankful that the sickness was better. She had asked for appolonaris water a little while before and she said it was doing her good. She was still having oxygen.

The improvement in the pulse did not last long, and then her breathing got very bad and distressed her a good deal, and she kept asking what was the matter with her breathing ... all her thoughts were for others up to the very last, and when Dr Brown brought Vincent to say 'Goodnight' to her she was very sweet and thanked him for the roses he had sent her in the day, and said good-night to him quite naturally. Soon after this she became unconscious and passed away after two.

It is quite impossible for me to tell you in writing how brave, bright and heroic Mrs M. was. She never once complained and her thought for everyone was most wonderful and touching.[36]

The deaths so close to each other of the two people in his immediate world whom he most admired – his Uncle Walter and his mother – had the effect of isolating Vincent increasingly from his family. His father remarried four years after Anna's death, and Vincent never accepted the second Mrs Massey, a cousin of his father, as a member of the family. When the marriage was imminent Vincent quarreled violently with Chester. 'Had an awful talk with father over the situation concerning Margaret P.' He brought himself to attend the wedding, which was a 'devilish hard ordeal.'[37] In subsequent diary references the second Mrs Massey is conspicuously uncharacterized; she appears only as Madame. Anna's influence was preserved, however, by one of her cousins, a southerner who had been brought up on a pre-Civil War plantation in Alabama and had, Vincent wrote, 'all the graces of a Southern lady – charm, dignity, and sweetness of character.'[38] She was known as 'Cousin Kate'; she was over ninety when she died and, to the very last, Vincent faithfully called upon her whenever he was in Toronto.

From 1903 until 1913 when he took his degree at Balliol, Vincent's personal life was bound up with schools and universities. He had been to a number of schools before 1903 – a small kindergarten; an ordinary public school; the provincial Model School, a special school designed as a 'model' for student teachers, which Vincent recalled with satisfaction for the tough 'fiber' of its curriculum; and, briefly, the local high school, Jarvis Collegiate Institute, which was distractingly co-educational. The important pre-university years, 1903–6, were spent at a private school, St Andrew's College. Vincent went there because it was a Presbyterian establishment and, therefore, more acceptable to a Methodist family than the older and more famous Upper Canada College, which had pronounced Anglican leanings. St Andrew's was conveniently near, at first in a large house about a mile to the north of the Massey residence, and for Vincent's last two years in a new building still more conveniently located in Rosedale, which according to a college brochure was 'one of the healthiest and most desirable residential districts in the city.' The new building provided residential accommodation, and during his final year Vincent was a resident, although, as he explained, 'only a weekly boarder, returning home on Fridays and going back to College on Monday.' The family ties were thus carefully preserved, especially on Sundays, which were dominated by church attendance, often in both the morning and the evening, with Sunday School in the afternoon.

Vincent did not chafe at going to church; for a brief period, indeed, he took satisfaction in editing the Metropolitan Church calendar. But there were signs of mild dissidence. On Sunday, 28 May 1905, for instance, when he was eighteen, he recorded: 'church in a.m. as usual. Went to Sylvester's for tea, and I went unwillingly and solitarily to the Elm St Church to hear a young minister at Pater's bidding.' On a subsequent Sunday he 'went to church with Father in a.m. Sparling preached his final sermon, thank the saints.'[39] He began to venture outside Methodist territory. He went to the evening service at St James' Cathedral, which he liked, although he added with a touch of non-conformist arrogance that there were 'very queer people at St. J.'[40]

The church dominated only on Sundays. Evenings during the week were increasingly given to music and the theatre. At the Princess Theatre Vincent heard a number of operas – *Carmen, Lohengrin,* and *Parsifal* – and expressed his unqualified delight, a sharp contrast to later unvaryingly harsh judgment on all opera. He regularly attended concerts at Massey Music Hall, and commented with particular fervour on the violinist Ysaye, and the pianist Paderewski. Many of the great British actors were then bringing the classics or special bravura pieces to Canada – Mansfield in *Beau Brummel* and Mantell in *Hamlet,* for example – and Vincent saw them all.

At St Andrew's College he joined eagerly in the activities of the school, content to give his formal studies only enough attention to assure an orderly progression from form to form. He practised assiduously for the cross-country run, played golf and tennis, and won the school championship in duelling – not a resplendent triumph, since in this event there was only one other competitor. He was secretary of the athletic association, and first lieutenant in the cadet corps. He delighted in the cadets, and particularly in his officer's status. When the corps joined the 48th Highlanders in trooping the colours before the lieutenant governor, he proudly reported that 'we officers went to the House after for refreshments. The Common Soldiers ate on the lawn!'[41]

The real centre of Vincent's interests at St Andrews, however, was literary, and found its expression in debating and in writing for the college magazine. With his inseparable companion Murray Wrong, he took the negative in debating the resolution that 'science is a better course for the average boy than classics.' It was a great occasion for the St Andrew's new boy, just turned sixteen. In his diary he reported triumphantly, 'We won! Got heaps of congratulations. Papa, Prof. Wrong, J.K. Macdonald (a judge of the debate) and lots of masters and boys were there.'[42] In his speech on that occasion he sounded with school-boy stridency a note that was to be gently modulated in hundreds of speeches of the grown man: 'Education is not only a training of the mind but rather of the character. Science deals entirely with matter and things and regards man as an animal, but classics deals with great men and events, beautiful literature and art and regards man as a character. Surely it develops the higher nature of a boy more than science, so mechanical in all its methods.' Another debate, two years later, was phrased to encompass a current political problem, 'Resolved that Canada should contribute to Imperial defence by taking immediate steps to establish a Canadian Navy.' Vincent, speaking for the negative, argued that a separate Canadian navy would deplete resources that should be used to develop the country, and, given the might of the British navy, was unnecessary.

In his final year Vincent became an editor of the *St Andrew's College Review*, which had been founded in 1901. His contributions, both in prose and verse, are competent but undistinguished. They are chiefly about the college – a description of the new building, an account of residential life, school activities: attendance at dramatic productions and the participation of the cadet corps in various ceremonial events. He had acquired the character of the school intellectual, with the suggestion of slightly pompous sophistication. In a selection of the characteristic sayings of prominent students, Vincent's was alleged to be, 'Don't you think it would be a jolly good thing to have a Greek play?' None of his own school-boy letters survive, but two letters from a friend, Edward Wallace, give some evidence of young Vincent's interests. It is the summer of 1903, and Vincent is in Europe on the ill-fated trip that ended with the sudden death of his mother. Young Wallace is at a cottage on Georgian Bay, and, between accounts of canoe trips, inserts a formal record of his reading, in recognition, no doubt, of his correspondent's serious tastes. 'I have done a little reading since I came up. A little Herodotus, which is easy Greek, and in spots funny, everywhere entertaining; for lighter work "The Woman Who Toils" by Miss Van Vorst, a fascinating but terrible picture of women's labour conditions, and "The Newcomes" which I am reading for the second time. You, I suppose, never touch a book unless it be your Baedeker or an art catalogue – you lucky boy ... Do a little hero-worshipping for me at the shrines of Dickens and Thackeray and Tennyson and Shakespeare. I do envy you your visit to Stratford and Anne Hathaway's cottage.'[43] The following summer, Wallace writes to Vincent about a magazine of which Vincent is an editor – presumably the *St Andrew's College Review* – and observes presciently, 'Really, old man, it is credit and it may be that journalism, not High Anglicanism is to be your fate.'[44]

Clearly during the St Andrew's days Vincent was creating a milieu that was a far cry from the Chautauqua exuberance of Dentonia Park, even farther removed from his father's serene piety, or from the atmosphere of Euclid Hall, his grandfather's old house, where his Aunt Lillian's recently acquired husband, John M. Treble, exuded the satisfaction that came from presiding over Treble's Great Shirt House on King Street and from directing various activities of the Methodist Church. The changes that were taking place in young Vincent are reflected in letters of Bishop John Vincent. The bishop was a robust and untroubled Methodist, but he had, like Anna, great vivacity and sensitivity. Vincent was a favourite of his, and he thought of Vincent as inheriting the best qualities of his mother. He wrote to Chester: 'I have had a very delightful letter from Vincent – well written indicating real ability and having more of the Vincent than of the Massey in its tone.'[45] In the years of Vincent's bereavement, he wrote to him as to one steadfast in the faith, confident in the belief 'that all who persevere to the end, and only those, may hope to be saved in heaven for ever.'[46] The bishop could abandon the heavy pastoral note and speak to Vincent as a cultivated man of letters.

I received your pleasant letter. I think you have a gift for letter writing. You conform to the usual laws of polite letter writing, and have a good way of saying what you set out to say. I congratulate you! There is in our day (on our American side of the line) too much carelessness in our correspondence. It comes from the intense and hurried way in which we do things. To be a good letter writer, simple and not stilted, to write as one would talk, to have something to say and to say it, is a gift of no slight value.[47]

The bishop could even join good naturedly in Vincent's playful speculation about becoming a Methodist minister. When Vincent sent him a picture of himself as a senior at St Andrew's, he wrote

Thanks to the 'Curate' for academic reflections and philosophizing, and for the noble photo just received of the classic, reposeful, and self-possessed candidate for the Methodist ministry! It's a good picture. There are 'volumes' in it to one who can read it – who can trace the influence of that sweet mother with her lovely eyes aspiring ambitions and that noble and amiable father with his ideals of character. I am glad and more than glad to have the picture and the kind thought of good will that sent it – and the playful reference to ecclesiastical ideas which the real *Vincent Massey doesn't entertain.*[48]

Then, when Vincent entered university, Bishop Vincent became alarmed and wrote to Chester Massey in an urgent and troubled tone.

I am just a little anxious about Vincent. There is a vein of fight in him. He is critical. He finds fault. He is a gifted fellow but he will have to learn that the great factor in this world that counts and wins is good will. *When the angels sang over Bethlehem their theme was 'Peace on earth, good will to men.' Vincent is a little critical – hypercritical. I am sorry to see it because it means for him enemies and opposition and many an hour of regret, whereas with such ability as he has and as splendid prospects open out before him, he ought to be the most genial, good natured and popular fellow in Canada. Perhaps you had better not say this to him, but I would like to have a frank talk with him about these matters. I foresee trouble that he is bound to encounter in the future. If he were not the son of my sister I should feel that I had no business to say a word on the subject. But I loved his mother with such intensity and knew her so thoroughly and held her in such profound respect that I cannot bear to have her boy fail to fulfill the splendid mission which is easily open before him.*[49]

The bishop had accurately recognized the change that had taken place. The callow sophistication of Vincent's St Andrew's days had developed in the university into a sharp critical sense. At St Andrew's he had encountered only one powerful and critical mind – a young history master, William Grant, who spent two years at the school between teaching at Upper Canada College and studying at Paris. At the university there were a number of men who opened up new perspectives. Vincent was the first member of the Massey family to attend university as a free spirit, without the constant reminder that he was preparing for a position of responsibility in the family firm. The four years at the University of Toronto were the crucial ones during which he resolved his attitude towards the family tradition and began to shape ideas and attitudes that he would hold throughout his life.

CHAPTER TWO

Undergraduate

In 1906, when Vincent entered the University of Toronto, he was a slight young man of nineteen, a little under the average height, the head not square and formidable in the Massey mould but long and narrow with his mother's delicate, dark colouring, and beneath the superior, amused smile a hint of his mother's gentle, warm expression. By every family tradition he should have gone to Victoria, the intellectual citadel of Methodism, which had recently, and somewhat reluctantly, moved from Cobourg to Toronto to become a college in the University of Toronto. The Massey family was closely associated with Victoria. His grandfather had been a student and then a stout supporter, initially opposed to the move to the city and determined to maintain the autonomy of the college. Chester, although not a graduate – his education had been interrupted by illness – was continuing the Massey benefactions to the college; he had recently contributed the money for a men's residence. The pressure on Vincent to attend Victoria from his family and close associates must have been great. 'The few Methodists who still avoided the college,' its president, Nathanael Burwash, reported, were 'mostly lovers of sport or persons to whom the high moral tone of the College is not an attraction.'[1] Vincent was clearly not one of the first group; the secretaryship of the St Andrew's Athletic Association and the besting of a single rival for the school duelling championship were not high athletic credentials. He was closer to Burwash's second group. He had not, however, embraced a loose and pagan outlook. He was still a serious young man, outwardly faithful to his Methodist upbringing. But he was beginning to chafe under the Massey burden of moral earnestness and loyalty to the firm. His choice of University College, the provincial college that had no official religious ties, and about which there still hung a faint aroma of godlessness, was a declaration of independence, a clear indication that he did not intend to follow in the family footsteps.

In 1906 University College was still in large part the University of Toronto – the secular, state-supported university that had emerged from acrimonious debates in the 1840s over the relationship of religion and higher education. The building, completed in 1859, was an amalgam of styles – Norman, Romanesque, Gothic, Renaissance, Byzantine – but it still managed to achieve a sombre unity. To Torontonians – and, for decades, to many Ontario emigrants to Western Canada – it was a symbol of the dignity and splendour of higher learning, set apart from the market place, arousing agreeable associations with cathedrals, monasteries, and ancient seats of learning. It was at this time the administrative centre of the university. The president and his fellow administrators had their offices there; and although University College had its own principal, the distinction, both physically and theoretically, between college and university was not clear. University College was thus, in fact, the embodiment of the university tradition. The great growth of the professional faculties lay ahead, and the newly federated colleges like Victoria were still too conscious of their own traditions to feel part of the University of Toronto.

In 1906 University College had 826 undergraduates. It was by far the largest of the four colleges within the university – Victoria, the second in size, had 380 – and, deprived recently of its men's residence, it appeared to lack coherence. But there were compensations. The University College undergraduate had a sense of being in the main stream. The college had an alumni body to which it could already point with national pride. Stephen Leacock was now happily established at McGill as professor of political economy, but he was better known as a writer of humorous prose: young college journalists looked back upon his years at University College as a golden age. William Lyon Mackenzie King had become deputy minister of labour in the federal government, and at the University College dinner in February 1907, which Vincent in all likelihood attended, he replied to the toast to

'Alma Mater' in a speech that, according to the college reporter, was 'remarkable for refinement of style and gravity of thought.'[2] Henry John Cody was the secretary of a provincial commission that had just published a crucial report on the future of the university, and he was destined for great distinction either in the church or in education, possibly in both.

University College could also draw upon eminent supporters from outside its own graduates. Edward Blake, the former leader of the Liberal party, had been chancellor of the university from 1876 to 1900, and he was a notable and rare example of the intellectual in Canadian public life. Even more influential was Goldwin Smith, at one time Regius professor of modern history at Oxford, the friend and associate of many of the Victorian great in politics and letters, who had taken up residence in Toronto and now for years had directed a fresh stream of thought on the pallid, provincial life of the city. The university, which to Smith was synonymous with University College, was one of his principal interests. He was a member of the recent university commission, and his views on the need for a university that was supported by the state and, at the same time, buttressed against it, shaped the recommendations of the report. To the thoughtful University College undergraduate, Goldwin Smith was a formidable presence – a seer, who led the life of the mind amid genteel affluence, like a Whig aristocrat exerting great influence from a country house. One of the most detailed entries in Vincent's diary is a description of a visit that he and some fellow students made to the Grange, Goldwin Smith's home, where the great man, old and frail, received them with courtesy and captivated them with his talk about literature and politics.

It was an experience I shall never forget. The very sensation of turning in at the gates of 'The Grange' and walking up to the house after so many hundreds of times having passed by and admired from a longing distance – this feeling was sufficient to make me tread on air.

We were shown into a drawing-room at the right hand as you enter the door and shook hands with a very strikingly handsome woman to whose identity our only clue was that she referred to the master of the house as 'Uncle Goldwin.' The drawing-room was furnished on the admirable theory of furnishing – to have your room as comfortable as possible and to have your family possessions from photographs to assegais about you in masses.

Not long after we arrived Mr Goldwin Smith came in. An old, old man he is, with a colourless face, stooping shoulders and a tottering walk. Somehow he had a forsaken, a sad, lonely appearance that perhaps was accentuated by the carelessness in his dress. I noticed that his collar and cuffs although spotlessly clean were badly frayed at the edges and his black suit too looked old and worn. He wore a black skull cap and carried a brown walking-stick.

At lunch we were waited upon by the old butler who has been in the family since Mr Goldwin Smith was a boy. (To be basely material and to sound like a gourmet – the lunch was excellent and the sherry delicious.)

After lunch Mr Goldwin Smith led the three of us into his study in the West Wing. The walls from floor to ceiling were lined with books. A billiard table – used evidently more for literary than for other purposes stood in the centre of the floor – a large mantel-piece occupied the west wall and the three windows opened to the south.

Once seated before the fire with cigars going (Mr Goldwin Smith – I noticed neither smoked nor drank any wine) our host lapsed into a reminiscent vein. The centenary of Gladstone's birth and the general elections in England gave him a theme. I don't think that from my mind will ever fade the picture of that old scholar sitting, quite bent, in his easy chair with his hands on his stick gazing into the fire and wandering from one incident to another in the political life of fifty years ago. Outside I could see the elms in the Grange grounds – a calm unviolated retreat in a region of squalor. Within were the stately Georgian apartments with their lofty ceilings and dignified lines. And in the centre of such a setting was the one man in Canada who could occupy it naturally and as a matter of course. Mr Goldwin Smith personifies the atmosphere of 'The Grange' – he is the spirit of stately and graceful simplicity.

In his conversation to us he exhibited most of those opinions which have always characterized him. His distrust of Home Rule – the only note of sadness we noticed in his talk was the melancholy regretfulness with which he spoke of Gladstone 'going over to Home Rule and leaving us' – his Pro-Boer sympathies – his hatred of Party Government –.

In defiance of literary form I am going to put down some of the pearls this swine remembers from Mr Goldwin Smith's conversation.

He said that he had once talked to a colleague of Pitt's and a Marshal of Napoleon's who had fought at Waterloo.

He said that O'Connell was a blackguard.

He said that the artifice to which Joseph Chamberlain would not stoop has yet to be invented. He thinks that his illness was partly feigned.

He rather sadly lamented the fact that there is no great leader in present-day politics in England and that here is no great poet living. Canadian verse, he said, was rather bad stuff.

He was rather indignant at some of his private letters being published in Lindy St Hilier's 'Reminiscences.'[3]

Within the college halls, the most eloquent spokesman for the values of the university was the principal of the college, Maurice Hutton, who was also acting president of the university during Vincent's freshman year. He was one of a succession of scholars from the United Kingdom, chiefly in the humanities, who developed a new loyalty for the university and for Canada, without abandoning the right to point out the shortcomings of either. Hutton was a classics scholar from Oxford. He helped to give classics at Toronto a special imprimatur, but he exercised a wider influence both in the university and among the general public by his skill and grace as speaker and essayist. During Vincent's undergraduate days, from 1906 to 1910, his was the dominant voice. His style was elaborately rhetorical at times, but always lightened by humour and sharpened by wit. It was in sharp contrast to that of the Rev. Robert Falconer, who was appointed president of the university in 1907, which was measured and serious, with overtones of the pulpit.

Hutton's constant theme was the university as a place of disinterested thought. He did not oppose the establishment of professional faculties, and he knew the value of applied science in turning the natural resources of a new country into economic strength. But, even in a pioneer land, first things must come first. One of his most uncompromising statements in this connection was made in an address to the senate of the University of Saskatchewan, a new institution in a province that was still a frontier: 'a University,' he observed, 'like the Christian church, exists to idealise life, to nourish contemplation, to promote thought.'[4] From this high position Hutton looked sharply at Canadian society.

Like Goldwin Smith, he believed that Canadian society was deeply materialistic, largely immune to ideas, and committed to commercial values. He followed Goldwin Smith too in his condemnation of Canadian politics. In a famous aphorism, which was quoted with approval in undergraduate publications, he declared that 'our annals are dull as ditch-water, and our politics are full of it.'[5] Popular journalism, he thought, was in alliance with a commercialized and vulgarized society and reflected its values. 'But the Press,' he said, 'has all the weakness of omniscient individuals ... There is no one who knows so much – that isn't so, as a newspaper; and this is rather hard on the community that depends on its papers.'[6]

All too often, Hutton thought, the university embodied rather than repudiated the values of society. One example was the wave of 'nativism' (or, as we would say today, nationalism) that had swept over the university and threatened, according to Hutton, to weaken intellectual standards. It manifested itself in a call for the appointment of Canadians to teach 'vital Canadianism,' a vague phrase, said Hutton, that could not be related to the work of the university, which had an international and timeless outlook. Another example of the university's apeing of society was its tolerance of fraternities. They were, Hutton declared, secret societies that made a real community impossible. 'But where there are secret societies, there are suspicions; and if clouds have gathered and relations are strained, whether between students and faculty or students and students, then there is suspicion everywhere.'[7]

Like many scholars with strong convictions and a talent for invective, Maurice Hutton was guilty of malicious exaggeration. His anti-Americanism was persistent and unshaded. When he gave his grudging approval to the establishment of a faculty of education, he observed balefully that it was 'the unhappy hunting ground of American spread-eagleism and American notions.'[8] It was a comment that many American scholars might have made, and did not necessarily show a mean antipathy towards the United States. This could not be said of his gratuitously venomous remarks about the Jews. In an article about France, he ascribed many of the country's woes to Jewish machination. He regretted that the surviving Protestants in France 'have been thrown into the arms of the Jews' and that 'the Jews who have at most times exploited France, have done so since with the greater success.'[9] Later on, he added two observations in the same dark vein. 'The one-eyed, one-idea fanatics who hold intellectual sway here [he was referring to scientists who interpreted psychical phenomena in materialistic terms] ... or share it with the omnipresent Jews.'[10] And again: 'the Dean of the Law Faculty is one of that race of Jews which is running, if not ruining, the University for the rest of France.'[11] At the time, these remarks fell upon unprotesting ears. Few Jews had yet reached university, and few, if any, occupied positions of importance in the city or province. In complacent Anglo-Saxon Toronto, anti-semitism was an accepted, if usually unvoiced, aspect of polite society.

Vincent did not study classics at University College (his only exposure was a few months of swotting in preparation for 'responsions' – an examination in elementary Greek whose successful passing was a condition for Oxford entrance) and he did not, therefore, know Hutton in the classroom. But Hutton's attitudes and ideas had a deep influence, particularly on those who, like Vincent Massey, wrote for college literary publications and were active members of clubs directed to debate and discussion. Hutton's harsh anti-semitism fortunately found no echo in student publications (although it doubtless had its residual effects); his critical attitude towards Canadian society – his distaste for its materialism and cheery nationalism – was, however, enthusiastically endorsed by student intellectuals. In one particular, Vincent followed Hutton's lead. He disapproved of fraternities, and for reasons similar to those of Hutton.[12]

With another principal figure in the university, George Wrong, professor of history, Vincent developed a closer relationship, both in and out of the classroom. Vincent's course was modern history and modern languages, with history the dominating subject. The professor of history was thus his mentor for his entire undergraduate career.

By 1906 George Wrong's place in the university was unquestioned. His academic career had begun shakily. When he was appointed in 1892, his qualifications for teaching history were not self-evident: on graduation from University College he had studied at Wycliffe College, the low Anglican theological college at Toronto, had been ordained, and had subsequently taught church history and apologetics at Wycliffe. But at the university he had built a strong history department by a series of appointments of bright young men, chiefly Oxford graduates, and he had firmly established Canadian history as a major field of scholarship. At a time when a professor occupied a respectable place in the social hierarchy, Wrong had become a considerable public figure. He retained, from his theological days, an interest in good works of an improving nature – the spread of Christian teaching among working men and the redemption of the wayward.[13] And he was always prepared to comment on public affairs, and to offer advice to those in offices of responsibility.

His influence on Vincent was exercised in the home as well as in the classroom. The Wrongs lived close to the Masseys on Jarvis Street. Thanks to the generosity of Mrs Wrong's father, Edward Blake, the Wrong house was of unprofessorial size and elegance, with generous grounds. After the death of his mother, Vincent found his own home increasingly unattractive. The original family mansion next door, now the home of his Aunt Lillian, was even more uninviting. Lillian, the object of her father's solicitous and tyrannical love, had, after his death, married unspectacularly. Her husband, John Treble, a widower of mature years, was a respectable businessman (he owned a large shop that specialized in men's shirts and was known as an innovator in advertising techniques) and an active worker in the Methodist Church. It was not likely that the bookish undergraduate would find much nourishment at the Trebles'. But at the Wrongs', there was a comfortable, relaxed society, where books and literary and political talk formed the substance. The Wrong house at 467 Jarvis Street was not only a retreat; at this period of Vincent's life, it was his salvation. 'I think,' he wrote, 'that if the Wrongs were not here I should become absolutely desolate and should eventually crawl into a sewer-pipe and die.'[14]

As professor and public figure, George Wrong was formal and a little formidable, with pince-nez, and cut-away coat. But in the home he was relaxed and informal, a Victorian squire with aesthetic tastes. Vincent Massey thus recalled the domestic scene:

... the old fashioned drawing room, with the Scottish maid Lizzie putting the oil lamp on the table (Lizzie lived to be one hundred and three); Mrs Wrong reading a volume of Trollope (she herself might have come from the pages of Barchester Towers*), Mr Wrong probably lying in front of the fire, occasionally using his snuff-box, and making remarks that his wife may have regarded as somewhat too frivolous; the children sitting about the room reading.*[15]

Vincent had a special link with the Wrongs through his friendship with their son Murray. They were together at St Andrew's and University

College, and went to Balliol at the same time. Their letters to each other from boyhood on testify to the warmth and depth of their friendship.

George Wrong's influence on Vincent Massey was strong and lasting. He embodied ideas and attitudes far removed from anything that could be found in the Massey family traditions: the scholarly generalist who wanted to play a part in the events of his time; the Canadian proud of his native inheritance, yet glorying in the Empire and at home in the imperial centre; the Christian moralist who was not bound by puritan legalities.

On certain specific issues, the Wrong influence helped to determine Vincent's stand throughout his life. This was true, for instance, on the question of the education of women. In 1909 George Wrong was chairman of a university committee to examine the desirability of establishing a women's college; and the committee, no doubt swayed by the firm views of its chairman, reported that such a college was, indeed, desirable. The committee put forward two practical arguments: first, a women's college would encourage women to diversify their choice of courses instead of concentrating in self-defence on a few, chiefly in language and literature; second, such a college would lead to the employment of women staff. In an article in the *University of Toronto Monthly*, Wrong defended the committee's recommendations on general sociological grounds. It might be described as the argument of superior inequality. In the domestic economy, Wrong declared, men earn the money and women spend it, and each function demands a different form of education. But above such circumstantial differences was the principle upon which male chivalry was based, 'that the chief charm and strength of woman is in her being unlike man.'[16]

The recommendations of Wrong's committee were never accepted; indeed his arguments were attacked as male condescension posing as chivalrous solicitude. But Vincent was impressed, and always thought of co-education as one of those callow doctrines from across the border. On another subject, Wrong's ideas were equally influential and much more enlightened. The Wrongs spent their holidays at Murray Bay on the St Lawrence, deep in French Canada. The area had been given as a seigneury to a Scotsman for service at Louisbourg and the Plains of Abraham. Despite his efforts to foster Protestantism and British customs, the seigneury had remained stubbornly Roman

Catholic and French. Wrong told its story in *A Canadian Manor and Its Seigneurs*, published in 1908. In the final two chapters entitled 'A French Canadian Village' and 'The Coming of the Pleasure Seekers,' he expressed his general attitude towards French Canadians. He admired their 'marvellous tenacity for their own customs,' and their ordered and temperate life. What was more unusual was his admiration for the language of the habitants: 'One would not have them speak any other tongue than their French, preserving her archaic usages, with new words for new things, influenced of course by English, but still the beautiful language of an elder France than the France of today.'[17] Vincent spent several summers with the Wrongs at Murray Bay. He, too, acquired an admiration for French Canadian society, which remained with him through his life. In later years he would become irritated at English Canadian condescension towards the language of French Canada, and he would argue vigorously against the assumption, not uncommon for many years in the French departments of Canadian universities, that the language and literature of French Canada were not proper concerns of the English-speaking universities.

Although Wrong had, certainly in contemporary terms, a generous and liberal attitude towards French Canadians, he still thought of them as a colourful strand in an Anglo-Saxon pattern. The university spokesmen were all convinced of the primacy of the Anglo-Saxon in Canada and in the world, and to them the Anglo-Saxon was at his highest and best in England. In higher education, the Anglo-Saxon tradition tended to narrow down to Oxford – the centre of light and humane learning, where wit and scholarship, it was believed, were intertwined, and from which the materialism of the world had been banished. English politics, largely because of the dominance of Oxford men, was of a superior nature: Asquith, Rosebery, and Balfour were on a higher plane than Laurier, Borden, and Blake. The British moved in a realm of ideas elegantly and forcefully expressed. Nowhere was the worship of England and Oxford more pure and intense than in the university's history department. When the dean and future master of Balliol, A.L. Smith, gave a lecture at Toronto, Kenneth Bell, Brackenbury scholar of Balliol, fellow of All Souls, and a recent appointment to the department, wrote a review of the lecture which was really a celebration of Balliol and Oxford. Smith, wrote Bell, was 'always in the van of the fresh ideals and enthusiasms of young Oxford, the most unconquerably young community in the world'; he spoke in the quintessential Oxford manner, with 'far reaching suggestiveness,' 'quaint, ripe humour,' and 'independent, vigorous and hopeful thought.'[18] A.L. Smith was on an extensive North American tour, which had begun with a series of lectures at Columbia. Two of his daughters accompanied him, and, in a letter to their mother, one of them reported with enthusiasm on the Oxonian flavour of the history department at Toronto, and on the deep attachment they found everywhere to the mother country:

Toronto was ripping for the day and a half we were there, it was like meeting a part of Oxford, so many Past and Future Members of that place were congregated there, the Bells and E.J. Kylie, and we stayed with the Professor of History and his family (Prof. Wrong), all struggling to come to Oxford, so we could tell them lots of things. They were very Canadian, but it was jolly to get back to British soil and hear something more like our pure native tongue spoken.

Canada fascinates me, I felt my heart warm towards it. The country is so lovely and looks somehow like the Land of Canaan (not that I have ever seen it!), full of promise, and then it's so splendidly patriotic, much more so than England is, English and insular to the backbone, only somehow what is insular and absurd and rather petty with us strikes one as rather magnificient in a colony and such a colony as this is. The people look jollier and their manners everywhere are much better than the Americans.[19]

Vincent Massey's undergraduate years corresponded with a period during which the University of Toronto occupied a central position in the life of the city, and, to a considerable degree, of the country as a whole. It was still a compact university, although it grew rapidly from 1906 to 1908 in numbers of students and in diversity of faculties. It finally extricated itself from direct political control, and developed a robust sense of individuality. Physically it was not surrounded and overwhelmed by the city; intellectually and socially it was a dominating voice. Its major spokesmen were humanists like Hutton, Wrong, Falconer, and Goldwin Smith (the last as an unofficial university professor), and they ranged, with a Victorian amplitude, over the whole range of morals and politics, uninhibited as yet by the stern proscriptions of specialized research. The professor, occupying a comfortable place in a society that was not yet choked by affluence, was recognized as an influential citizen.

The best students responded to the atmosphere. They had a sense of belonging to a world of ideas in which they had a part to play. Certainly Vincent was one of this number. Academically, his record was only fair. He began shakily in his first year with an over-all third-class standing, gradually moving into the second-class in his third and fourth years, with a first in history in both those years. The indifferent academic record reflected the heavy investment he made in extra-curricular activities. But those activities constituted in themselves an informal academic program. He was at various times chairman of the Letters Club, president of the Modern Language Club, and vice-president of the Historical Club (the last including among its members at this time the future historians A.L. Burt, Walter N. Sage, Frank Underhill, and Murray Wrong.) His major interest was in journalism, where he could sharpen his critical ideas and exercise his burgeoning talent for light satire. In *Torontonensis: the Annual Year Book of the Students of the University of Toronto,* Vincent's photograph was accompanied by the quotation, 'Rest, rest, perturbed spirit!' – a reference to his perpetual discontent with the ways of the university and his fellow students, from the excessive emphasis on Anglo-Saxon in the English course to student insensitivity to their physical surrounding. He ridiculed aggressive feminism in the university in a masque he, along with Murray Wrong, wrote for *Torontonensis*.[20] He was the editor and chief writer of the *Evening Blast,* an occasional publication that was a broad burlesque of the daily newspapers. One issue, for 9 December 1909, is preserved in his papers: a front-page story recounts the election of the dean of women from among a number of strong candidates, including Mary Baker Eddy, Carrie Nation, Emmeline Pankhurst, and Lydia E. Pinkham. Vincent was also on the staff of *The Varsity,* the undergraduate newspaper, at that time closer to a literary periodical than to the daily press. But his principal labour, and really, one suspects, his chief interest, was another publication, *The Arbor,* which was an undergraduate continuation of the dialogue of their mentors. *The Arbor* was Vincent's brain-child, conceived in his final term at the university. He was never the editor, but he was a major participant, both as contributor and adviser, from the first number in February 1910 to the last, April 1913 (even though he was for most of that time a graduate with no formal status in the university). *The Arbor* was a literary magazine with political and social overtones. When Vincent visited Harvard, he wrote back to Murray Wrong: 'they can teach us nothing in journalism. I have seen all their publications and our little indigo rag overtops them all.'[21] This was not just undergraduate cockiness. *The Arbor* was a very good periodical, with particularly high standards in its critical prose.

It was as uncompromising as Hutton in its commendation of a critical point of view, and in its lament for the apathy and conformity that made Canadian society rigid and dull. 'In Canada, in spite of what our press insists upon saying about "the virility of our young nation," we have characteristics which strongly suggest the decadence of old age. We hate enthusiasm unless it is in a most conventional form.'[22] To Canadians, it declared, criticism is an affront. 'Our people,' an editorial noted ironically, 'embody all the known virtues and several unknown ones.'[23]

On some specific issues, *The Arbor* was more presciently outspoken than its elders. It contended there were three ways of solving the language problem in Canada. 'We can try to make this an English-speaking country – the way of conquest. Or we can allow it to be made French-speaking – equally impossible. The third is to take the *via media* – usually the *via senta* – and make Canada bi-lingual; to teach French and English throughout the Dominion; to concentrate on them and to teach them *well*. While it is as unlikely that every one will properly speak the two languages as that all our citizens can be made ambi-dextrous, that is no argument against the idea. To be able to under-stand one another, to remove prejudice, to find common grounds of intent we can use the time that in the curricula of our primary schools we waste on hygenics, or fool away at carpentry, or devote to doyleys.'[24]

The attitudes and ideas expressed in *The Arbor* were far removed from the world of business and piety in which Vincent had been reared. Yet the assumption of these attitudes and ideas did not create any devastating personal crisis for him; he was simply adopting the repertoire of the young intellectual, who might startle his family at the dinner table by the virulent unorthodoxy of his views, without any intention of cutting family ties. In one area, however, he had made a sharp break. He had repudiated the narrow, restrictive code of behaviour that was the chief outward sign of Methodism – a repudiation facilitated by the weakening of family bonds following the death of his mother and his father's remarriage. As a young boy at the Central Methodist Sabbath School on Bloor Street, he had signed the total abstinence pledge and had solemnly sworn to 'abstain from the use of all intoxicating liquors as a beverage, and from the use of tobacco in any form, also from the use of profane language and the reading of bad books.' The college undergraduate must have viewed this document (it survived to find a place in the Massey papers) with a mixed feeling of merciful release and ironic superiority. On 13 August 1911, a year after his graduation, he noted in his diary that he 'had sipped gin till an ungodly hour' – and this on a Sunday too; 'an un-sabbatarian debauch,' he added with obvious relish.

During his college years he became increasingly critical of the Methodist manner and approach. The diary, for long stretches a blandly factual document, takes on a sharply satirical tone when the subject is Methodist shortcomings. One of the earliest entries was a contemptuous dismissal of a Methodist sermon. It 'was a monotone of high pitched platitudes – a wordy effusion of attempted (and missed) oratory.'[25] In his final undergraduate year, his interest in education intensified by his father's recent announcement of a gift for a student union, he looked at Methodist educational ventures and decided that they were the 'apotheosis of mediocrity.'[26] Even Chautauqua, Methodism's most impressive bridgehead in the world of the arts and science, began to lose its appeal. He couldn't make up his mind about Chautauqua. 'In some ways,' he wrote, 'it incorporates all the faults of the usa: superficiality, puritanism, misguided zeal, and a general vulgarity.' He went on to deplore the kind of audience that Chautauqua attracted, 'twenty percent of it ... meek subdued males' and 'the remainder ... middle-aged women whose faces do not betray the presence of a single idea nor the desire to receive one.'[27] His doubts about Chautauqua were temporarily stilled by the active participation in its work of George Vincent, Bishop Vincent's son, at that time dean of the faculties of arts, literature, and science at the University of Chicago. (George Vincent became president of the University of

Minnesota, 1911–17, and president of the Rockefeller Foundation, 1917–29. In this latter capacity he saw a good deal of Mackenzie King, who valued his association with the Rockefeller Foundation and with the members of the Rockefeller family. This may have aroused King's interests in Massey: as a Vincent, Massey was close to one of King's patrons.)

The revolt against Methodism never took a dramatic, ultimate turn. Vincent did not drift into secularism and agnosticism. The extent of the revolt is revealed in his comments on a popular American play of the time, *The Servant in the House*, which derived much of its popularity from what was thought to be its iconoclastic approach to formal religion. Through the principal character of the play, a mysterious butler with a vague eastern past, the author expounded a gospel compounded in equal parts of cheerful humanitarianism and eastern mysticism. The butler, who is, of course, really the vicar's long-absent brother transformed into a mighty spiritual leader during his stay in India, declares that his church is 'no dead pile of stones and unmeaning timber'; it is made up 'of the beating of human hearts, of the nameless music of men's souls.' The enraptured butler goes on: 'The pillars of it go up like the brawny trunks of heroes; the sweet human flesh of men and women is moulded about its bulwarks, strong, impregnable; the faces of little children laugh out from every cornerstone; the terrible spans and arches of it are the joined hands of comrades; and up in the heights and spaces there are inscribed the numberless musings of all the dreamers of the world.'[28] The play opened in New York on 23 March 1908, with the role of the butler played by Walter Hampden. Vincent saw it in Toronto a year later. To the young Vincent these were fresh, bold words. In his diary he recorded the holy silence with which the audience greeted the conclusion of the play, and then observed boldly that to him the sentiments were not sacrilegious.[29]

Vincent's college years were a time of religious doubt and of a cautious, gradual repudiation of the mores of his family. But he never in this period severed his association with the Methodist Church. Indeed, to the public eye, unaware of his personal reservations, he was a conspicuously active member of the church. He continued to teach Sunday School, although he found the activity less and less rewarding; at Owen Sound he laid the cornerstone of a Methodist Church, although at the subsequent dinner he was amused by the way in which the celebrities 'vied with one another in extolling Canada and the Methodist Church.'[30] He wrote an article for the official Methodist periodical the *Christian Guardian*, although it was an attack on the Methodist system of itinerancy on the ground that it viewed ministers and congregations as mechanical, exchangeable posts. As he assumed a more central place in the Massey family, he worked with the formidable group of Toronto Methodist businessmen on special church projects.[31]

Yet Vincent's Methodism was not all formal show, an unenthusiastic concession to family tradition. At University College religious work among students was the peculiar responsibility of the YMCA, and at that time the YMCA in the college was profoundly influenced by the national secretary, an American, John Mott, a man of deep Methodist conviction and strong, resolute character.

Mott never abandoned the fundamentals of his Methodist faith, but he sought to cleanse it of parochial elements and to make it into a world movement. His constant theme was the necessity for world evangelization; he was an internationalist for whom the world triumph of Christianity alone held out the hope of a genuine league of nations. Christianity was not simply one of several religions that offered salvation to man. It was an absolute religion, the only one that by emphasizing the sense of sin drove men to repentance and to a new life. The non-Christian world, he argued, had no true concept of sin. 'The prevailing belief that they are in the hands of fate tends to deaden the feeling of personal responsibility. Their moral sense is dull.'[32]

For Mott, the great event towards which his whole career had been leading was the World Missionary Conference in Edinburgh in June 1910. He was convinced that Christianity was making progress throughout the world, and that the missionary message was being heard and noted in the home churches. He singled out the city of Toronto as a golden example, and, in particular, two churches that had distinguished themselves by their generosity to missionary work, the Methodists, who had gone from a contribution of $62,000 in 1907 to $103,000 in 1909, and the Presbyterians, from a contribution of $46,000 in 1907 to $112,000 in 1909.[33]

A Canadian delegate at the Edinburgh Conference was Vincent

Massey, recent graduate of the University of Toronto and prospective Oxonian. He had been elected a delegate, presumably by a national church body, and he was, as he reported in his diary, 'very glad to be able to go.'[34] No doubt his delight arose in part from the chance to return to a country to which he was becoming deeply attached. (For him, Old Country meant England primarily, although Edinburgh could be considered as a northern extension of England.) He was also genuinely interested in missions, particularly in their educational thrust, and, on his return, he spoke and wrote on the subject. But the great pull was Mott's presence. In the description of Mott's speech to the conference, he wrote with unusual fervour.

... and then the meeting was put in John Mott's hands. Silent prayer, invocation, and stern admonitions from the speaker gave the meeting the atmosphere of a gathering of Covenanters. The Assembly Hall was packed with people, and was absolutely silent and Mott's words sounding like a battery of artillery before a storm. He is a wonderful man – intensely spiritual, unquenchingly enthusiastic, and unswerving in his direction. He is like the reincarnation of a Hebrew prophet – with one idea in his mind and all his tremendous dynamic force behind that one idea. His speeches have no eloquence, no poetry, no charm. They have but one quality – conviction. Last night when he was handling the most vital facts of religion and speaking in such steel-like piercing sentences it was almost revolting. Religion really needs warmth and poetry. But such a modern Cromwell as Mott does great good. His austerity and zeal and horror of compromise constitute a sort of far-off ideal – and one which would not be well for all men to attain to. I confess I am almost afraid of him.[35]

The young man was of two minds with respect to Mott the pulpit orator, although admiration was predominant. In reply to a letter from Murray Wrong that was critical of Mott's public performances, Vincent agreed with much that was said.[36] Then he went on to observe 'that a humbler man does not exist.'[37] He was not to be shaken in his admiration. John Mott always stayed with him in his frequent visits to Toronto after the war. He was a strong, unblemished link with the past.

The picture that emerges of Vincent Massey, BA, aged 23, is that of a serious young intellectual, critical of society, but not rebellious, gradually abandoning the church that has for generations shaped the lives of the Massey family, but maintaining an outward show of devotion and still responding emotionally to the spirituality that sustains the work of devout Methodists. Still, his Methodist earnestness has been secularized. His new prophets are the Victorian seers – Ruskin, Carlyle, and Arnold, whom he has read and studied in an undergraduate literary club; and his immediate mentors are not clergymen but the university spokesmen, Maurice Hutton, George Wrong, Goldwin Smith, and others under whom he has sat in the classroom. Yet his world is not greyly intellectual. Sportiveness and light irony keep breaking through. He believes that the cultivated young man should not take life too seriously; life is not a moral allegory, but a pageant full of the unexpected and the absurd.

Two of his earliest compositions are European travelogues, a persistent *genre* in undergraduate publications until air travel and a casual *wanderlust* eliminated it. Vincent had been a European traveller since childhood – first with his family, then in college days with fellow students. He had long since passed beyond the stage of breathless platitudes, and now could select his details with cool detachment. The first piece had the unpromising title of 'Spain – very Random Impressions' – the expectation is of a Baedeker with coy footnotes. It does indeed follow the prescribed ritual, a sweeping itinerary, with a romantic fade-out to the accompaniment of a familiar tag, 'Nobly, nobly, Cape Saint Vincent to the North-West died away.' But in the body of the article its author fastens upon particular places or events, punctuating the sober descriptions with humorous asides. He describes a bullfight in some detail and then adds, 'It is one "sight" which can arouse interest in the most jaded tourist. The Blue Grotto at Capri may appear green, St Peter's may look insignificant, but a bullfight lives up to its worst reputation in the penny dreadful or travel novel.'[38]

The second travel piece had an even more ominous title, 'Stag-hunting on Exmoor.' The expectation now is for a glorifying of quaint old English customs. But although the tone is generally warm and enthusiastic, as befits a young colonial permitted to take part in the ancient sport, it is suffused with an ironic sense of incongruity. Over such esoteric aristocratic sport hovers the shadow of Lloyd George's radical budget and the harsh egalitarianism of Keir Hardie. The defence of stag-hunting is conducted with tongue-in-cheek sobriety.

For retired majors 'a knowledge of the sport is necessary to existence in this world and essential to happiness in the world to come.' For the aristocracy, stag-hunting generates a peculiar language that helps to insulate them from the common man. 'The English aristocracy really stands upon a much securer foundation than land – the exclusive knowledge of what is meant by "burning scent" and "a good crash." Of this no Welsh ogre can deprive them. The conversation in a neighbouring hotel in the hunting season is as intelligible to the innocent layman as a spirited debate in Chaldie.'[39]

Vincent's most impressive piece was written after graduation and appeared in *The Arbor* of November 1912, while he was at Balliol. The subject was Edward Lear, with much of the material coming from the recently published letters. It is doubtful whether Lear was widely known in Canada – Vincent speculates that he was even frequently confused with 'the legendary monarch of the same name, whose character and career were, of course, not at all similar.' Lear, he assumes, was a great writer, and he sets out to explain the nature of that genius. He disdains psychological speculation, although Lear's life provided tempting material. That life he summarizes briefly, permitting himself only a few reflections – on the drawing lessons Lear gave to Queen Victoria, 'perhaps the greatest strain imposed on his fortitude'; on his loneliness; on the 'half-sad, half-jocular tone of his affection for a hypothetical career.' The article – by far the longest and most finished Vincent wrote at this time – is largely a celebration of the writer. Lear, he states, created a world of absolute nonsense that has its own subtle autonomy. Without actually saying so, he argues that Lear wrote 'pure' poetry that depended on sound, chance association, and a reality that transcends logic and consistency. He gave us a world of absurdities and incongruities, and this, Vincent concludes 'is very good for a world that takes itself too seriously.'

Vincent attempted a few light verses himself, although not in the high Lear vein. They aspired to be crisp and witty, and to delight by ironical reversal. The final stanza of *Vox Deae* illustrates, not unskilfully, the mode. He has been praising the girl who seemed to him gloriously fair:

> *But when she spoke, I thought I heard*
> *A buzz-saw in the treble clef,*

> *Files on a slate, a bronchial bird.*
> *My flame was cooled, my hope deferred;*
> *Blind Love may be the truest word,*
> *But Love's not deaf!*

This was the beginning of a life-long devotion to the writing of light verse, a subterranean act, but, I suspect, closer than much of his serious prose to his instinctive way of looking at things.

When Vincent undertook editorial responsibilities, he wrote about little absurdities with comic gusto. When a news release from Pennsylvania revealed that a classical statue for the main entrance of the state capital was to be draped, he commented, in the spirit of Samuel Butler's famous lines, 'O God, O Montreal,' 'soon we hope to see the Venus of Milo comfortably attired in a neat gingham wrapper' and 'the Apollo Belvedere ... becomingly garbed in blue pyjamas.' Even the rituals of Empire, of which he warmly approved, could slide into the ridiculous. 'We have all been unfortunate enough,' he wrote, 'to hear our school-children wail "the Maple Leaf" into the ears of a distinguished visitor and shake their little Union Jacks until the hapless man was both deaf and dizzy.'[40]

The tone of amused, at times flippant, withdrawal only occasionally breaks down. He deplores the habit of Torontonians of identifying high culture with appreciation of music while, at the same time, they delight 'in the veriest rubbish on the stage.' He sets out to write an amusing account of student fashions in pictures and furnishings, and ends up with an aesthetic homily in the manner of William Morris. 'If one enshrines in his aesthetic heart the essential principles of harmony, and economy, it will relieve one's guests from the sight of colour combinations that look like a sunset with the rabies. Until we look on a clash in colour with the same highly cultivated horror with which most of us regard a bad discord in the piano, we are not educated.'[41] Edward Lear fades away suddenly and John Wesley looms up shadowily – a young and dapper John Wesley with a revised version of sin and salvation.

CHAPTER THREE

Hart House

When in 1922 Neville Chamberlain, making the grand tour of the Empire, visited Toronto, he 'commended the city equally for its Mendelssohn Choir and its pure supply of milk.'[1] Chamberlain, whose family had a relationship to Birmingham similar to that of the Masseys to Toronto, was, without knowing it, exalting two of the Massey contributions to the city. The Mendelssohn Choir was one of Hart's enthusiasms, and Massey Hall gave it a superb home; and Walter, through his dairy operations at Dentonia Park and in the city, had, more than anybody else, ensured the supply of pure milk.

The Massey legacy that Chamberlain perceived came from the nineteenth century. When Vincent began to look beyond his student preoccupations, he was conscious that the initiative had left the generation preceding him. Of that generation only his father, Chester, and his Aunt Lillian remained. Chester was responsible for the management of the funds that Hart had left for public purposes: he was thoroughly in sympathy with his father's goals, but was not capable of any bold or imaginative interpretation of them. Lillian, a fellow executor, had her special interests in the elevation of the domestic arts, and directed her support towards a household science building for the University of Toronto. It was clear that any broader initiative must come from the younger generation, and that of this generation Vincent alone could be the spokesman. Chester's older brother, Charles Albert, had died in 1884, and his children had drifted away from the family centre on Jarvis Street; his two sons were fated to have brief careers that both ended tragically. Walter had left a family of four, all gifted, but the only son, Denton, was thirteen years Vincent's junior. Vincent's brother, Raymond, aged fourteen in 1910, was beginning to emerge from the shadow of a prolonged and mysterious illness, but the indications were that he was not temperamentally inclined to assume the larger family responsibilities. In 1910 Vincent joined his father and aunt as a trustee of the Hart Massey estate, and almost immediately took command.

Eight years later, Vincent was responsible for an act that changed the estate into a foundation, thereby extending its life and making it a far more powerful instrument for good. Hart had wanted the estate to distribute its resources within twenty years of his death. But this was an imprudent and short-sighted provision for the patriarch to have made. The estate was made up chiefly of Massey-Harris shares: their dispersal would have had a downward effect on the market, and would have forced the immediate selection by the executors of a few big capital projects. By the establishment of a foundation the capital was preserved, and the income could be carefully controlled and devoted to many specific purposes. In forming the foundation, Vincent had the advice and support of his favourite cousin, George Vincent, who had by this time become president of the Rockefeller Foundation and was, therefore, versed in the politics and economics of public benevolence.

In answer to an enquiry Vincent succinctly set forth the rationale of the Massey Foundation. '... we felt that the Estate could be made to some extent a Bureau of Research in matters which came within its scope, and through a strict discrimination, in the disposal of its funds, could do something to create a new and valuable institution, or to improve the standards of existing institutions ... We try to make the Foundation a thinking as well as a giving body, on the assumption that a great deal of the giving of private individuals, generous as it is, lacks sufficient thought to give it direct constructive value.'[2]

In 1910, before the settting up of the foundation, the estate was prepared to make a major contribution to capital purposes. It was to be the most important decision made by either the estate or the foundation, and the building that resulted was to be a major concern of Vincent throughout his life – for a decade, indeed, the visible mark of his public spirit, and a means for turning his personal enthusiasms into public benefits.

Chester Massey was the actual benefactor. In February 1910, he wrote a brief, drily factual letter to the chairman of the board of governors of the University of Toronto, Mr B.E. (soon after Sir Edmund) Walker:

On behalf of the Executors of the Estate of H.A. Massey I write to say that, if the project be considered favourably by the Board of Governors, they will be pleased to erect and equip a building for the University Young Men's Christian Association, also for the Students' Union, the two buildings to be connected by an Assembly Hall, and to occupy the ground suggested in our conversation. The cost would be say three hundred thousand dollars.

It is the desire of the Executors to make this gift a memorial to my Father, the late Hart A. Massey.[3]

Chester Massey's letter was a simple résumé of university needs of which, as a member of the board, he was aware. To the three needs he mentioned was subsequently added a fourth – a new gymnasium and facilities for physical exercise. It is characteristic of Chester that the religious needs came first in his mind, and the union and the assembly hall were simply addenda. It was left to Vincent, who had first proposed the general idea to his father, to give the building shape and form.

Even before his graduation, Vincent was involved in its planning. On 16 February 1910 he recorded attending the first meeting on Hart House, and by the spring he was conferring with the architect, Henry Sproatt, on the general design. This was no casual association. 'Spent the morning,' he writes, 'with Sproatt at his office working over plans of new students' union at Varsity. They are coming together.'[4] He decided to postpone going to Balliol, to which he had been admitted, until the following year, and persuaded Dr MacDonald, the headmaster of St Andrew's, to take him on as a master for a year. He could thus remain close to Hart House planning. In actual fact, he spent only half the year in Toronto. The summer was taken up with attendance at the Edinburgh Missionary Conference and a lengthy visit to Oxford. After a brief return to Toronto, he decided to go back to England with his regiment, the Queen's Own Rifles, which was being sent, by the munificence of its colonel-in-chief, Sir Henry Pellatt, to take part in manoeuvres at Aldershot. During the exercises in September, he, along with others, fell victim to an epidemic of enteric or typhoid fever. It was a dangerous illness – the same disease, he must have reflected, had carried off two of his uncles, Charles and Walter, early in their careers. A fellow officer, Roy Gzowski, stricken at the same time as Vincent, died of it. Vincent recovered slowly, and he spent the remaining part of the year – ten weeks – in hospital and convalescent home. Not until early January 1911 did he get back to Canada, where he 'was soon in the bosom of my enthusiastic and really not half-bad family.'[5] It was too late to take up the St Andrew's appointment and, at any rate, the doctors forbade any demanding routine. Now, providentially, there was plenty of time for the important things like editing *The Arbor* and working on Hart House. 'Since coming home,' he wrote, 'my energies have been largely taken up with the new Union building at the University which the Estate is putting up ... It is a magnificent problem – from an administrative and structural point of view.'[6]

The administrative and structural problems were all related to the idea behind the building. Vincent had no doubts about the idea. Eight years later, he expressed it tersely in the address he gave at the opening of Hart House: 'the discipline of the class-room should be generously supplemented by the enjoyment, in the fullest measure, of a common life. A common life, of course, presupposes common ground.' Hart House would supply that common ground, or, in more positive terms, the unifying force. The idea arose out of his own experience. The University College he knew as an undergraduate had lost both its residence and its students' union, and was incapable of generating any sense of community. His graduating dinner there had been 'flat and spiritless' and the students 'a disunited, unharmonious lot.'[7] Vincent had found his greatest stimulus outside the classroom, in student clubs and journalism, and in informal associations with his contemporaries – those who read adventurously, wrote for student publications, and held strong political views. His academic standing at Toronto had gradually improved, and when he went to Balliol his scholarly reputation was high enough to evoke genuine commiseration when, in the final schools, he was put in the second class; but he was never enchanted by pure scholarship. This attitude was strengthened by what he had already seen of British education, and it did not need the later Balliol immersion to turn predilection into dogma. In his trip to the United Kingdom in the summer of 1910 he had looked at universities as possible models for the Toronto students' union. He had started in Edinburgh, and pronounced a harsh judgment on the spirit of Scottish higher education. 'Edinburgh strikes me as being rather an inferior place in the arts at any rate. Man there is taught through books and books alone and living in a solitary boarding-house room and grinding at lectures and writing exams and doing nothing else is *not* an education. The Arts man in both places [he visited Glasgow as well as Edinburgh] is a pitiful grubbing creature.' Oxford and Cambridge rose above such grubby literalness. 'At Oxford and Cambridge they have got far enough to realize that second class honours often indicate a more symmetrical and more able man than do first. May Canada reach this goal rather than that of Scotland.'[8] A particular incident further illuminated this contrast in approaches to higher education, and pointed forward to the emphasis on the educational value of 'the casual book' that was to become part of the creed of Hart House:

I was amused at an incident which illustrated the difference between England and Scotland. The other day when I was going through the Oxford Union with George Smith he proudly showed me a library of novels of the lightest sort which occupied one of the rooms and was available for any member. Yesterday in the Edinburgh Union the treasurer showed me the library and in explaining its contents, said 'of course, there is nothing light, nothing light.'[9]

The Scottish-English antithesis was to become a favourite theme for disputation during his Balliol days. He recorded, for instance, a heated argument on the subject with a contemporary from New College notable for 'narrow-minded Scotch ideas'[10]

Vincent conceived of Hart House as another college, to which members of the four teaching colleges and of the professional faculties would belong, and in which education would be carried on by the interchange of ideas and the practice of the arts. Despite its origin in a number of loosely associated needs that happened to converge at one time, Hart House would generate its own commanding unity. In the early stages of discussion, Vincent, with some allies, withstood two assaults on that unity. There was, first, some likelihood that the YMCA, at that time the strongest non-collegiate force on the campus, would demand a separate identity; but it finally agreed to accept the status of a tenant. Then the administration was dubious about using the great hall as a dining room for students: student dining halls, it was argued, were notoriously bad financial risks. But to Vincent communal dining was both a pleasure and an essential ritual, and his idea triumphed. Other unifying ideas evolved with experience after the opening of the building in November 1919, but they were present in outline in Vincent's early speculation. Hart House was to have as much autonomy as possible within the university, and that autonomy was to be exercised through a body representative of all the university estates, in which students would play a principal role. It was a bold concept of democracy; it would be fifty years before the university itself would warily approach a similar concept.

But these administrative measures were less important for unity than two concepts of a more organic nature. The first was the building itself. A writer in *The Arbor* of March 1910, just when Hart House was taking shape in the minds of Massey and Sproatt, had harshly reviewed the university's building record. The walls of the main building – University College – were, he declared, 'a veritable museum of decorative detail, from every type of Romanesque, Lombard, Norman, English, and German,'[1] and buildings of a later date in the nineteenth century – the library and the biology building – were unfortunate attempts to imitate the main building. Now, however, in the first decade of the new century, the university had shaken off subservience to the past. Convocation Hall, the medical building, and the physics building represented 'a forward movement.' The signs of this were, it may be assumed, the plain, unlovely brick, nondescript style, and general atmosphere of brisk utilitarianism. Hart House belonged to neither phase; it was not a tapestry of the past nor a part of the 'forward movement.' It was a revival of a specific style – the Gothic – but in an austere, early form that did not deny a modern function. No doubt Massey and Sproatt both had Oxbridge generally in mind, but there was no question of imitating a particular building, certainly not Vincent's second alma mater, Balliol, which, among Oxford colleges, was not known for its architectural splendour.

Throughout all the changes of the next fifty years, culminating in the great expansion of the 1960s, which added a whole new layer of buildings in a variety of contemporary styles, Hart House continued to exert a quiet dominance. The building of an adjacent memorial tower to graduates of the university who had been killed in the first world war, and its integration with Hart House, gracefully emphasized the latter's centrality. The building proved to be infinitely adaptable: it responded to the small, intimate group, to the packed audience listening to a music recital or debate, to restless boisterous streams of party-goers; and after the second world war it incorporated a pub as easily as it had earlier embraced a chapel.

Almost as important to the young aesthete, Vincent Massey, was the décor and furnishing of Hart House; and, after peace returned in 1918, and construction – halted during the war – resumed so that the building could realize its original purpose, Vincent had a partner as enthusiastic and as competent as himself. This was Alice Parkin, who, in June 1915, had become his wife.

Alice was the daughter of Sir George Parkin, a Canadian, the secretary of the Rhodes Trust. She and Vincent had met in England; when Alice came to the University of Toronto in 1914 as head of the women's residence, Queen's Hall, they saw each other frequently. Vincent's diary records during the year 1914 two visits with Alice (no doubt properly chaperoned) to New York, where they went to galleries and theatres, and, in a more relaxed mood, ascended the Woolworth building and visited the aquarium in Battery Park, there, in a festive mood, achieving the distinction of eating a banana *en plein air*.[12] They were married in Kingston, where Alice's sister Maude and her husband, William Grant, Vincent's old mentor, then a professor at Queen's, had their home. George Wrong assumed his ecclesiastical robes, long since discarded for the professorial gown, and assisted at the ceremony. Befitting the time, the ceremony in St George's Cathedral, Kingston, was sternly informal. A picture of the wedding party taken in front of the Grant house shows Alice smiling a little self-consciously, and Vincent, relaxed and urbane, with one hand in his pocket, and the other holding the bowl of his pipe. Two of the men, Raymond, tall and boyishly handsome, and William Grant, holding his infant daughter Charity, are in uniform.

Alice was a strikingly handsome woman with fine, classical features.

She had had a good many romantic attachments, and Maude was rumoured to keep a card index in which she recorded Alice's early affairs. After the wedding Maude and her husband conspired to send a telegram to Alice, ostensibly from a heart-broken admirer, ending plaintively, 'Must I then abandon all hope?' She and Vincent were deeply devoted to each other, and their marriage was to become an extraordinary partnership. To Alice's family and friends, however, and indeed to Alice herself, the decision to marry had not come as the natural conclusion of a passionate attachment. Alice thus revealed to Maude her innermost feelings:

And now I must tell you what has come to me last Sunday week between 12 and 1 a.m. V. and I decided that life wasn't worth much without each other. Really Maude it's no violent reaction, but oh such a contented peaceful absolutely happy feeling I have about it all. I know he's younger and that you don't like that but Maude he is so much older really. Anyhow I don't believe it will ever matter and oh – I am so thankful and happy. V. with all the precariousness of life at present won't wait until next year ... I knew I liked V. but I haven't all along really cared and then it just came over me all of a sudden and I just feel as if nothing else could ever have been and I am so happy.[13]

The difference in age was of real concern. Alice, or Lal, as her husband usually called her, was eight or nine years Vincent's senior (Alice kept her birth day a secret). At the time of her marriage, she was thirty-six or thirty-seven to his twenty-eight. But she had great vivacity and vigour; and Vincent, despite his youthful appearance, was accustomed to moving with his seniors on a basis of equality. Their interests and talents quickly cohered, no more completely than in the development of Hart House.

Alice thought of herself unashamedly as a housewife. As a young girl she had taken courses in cooking in France, and she was proud of her accomplishments in the art, whether she was supervising others or working in her own kitchen. She had strong views about colour and design in house decoration and furnishing; a house, she felt, must have an atmosphere of simplicity, comfort, and informality, with strong colours used as vivid and sparing contrast. Hart House became the first of many houses – both her own and those in which she and her husband had an interest – that she fashioned and presided over.

Alice also had strong views about people and about their qualifications for special jobs. The selection of the warden of Hart House was always to be one of her great interests. Hart House was, of all university enterprises, the one most dependent on the man who headed it – the warden, as he was called. It was a few years before the most influential warden emerged. The first in that office was Walter Bowles, a recent graduate of the university, an active member of the first dramatic group that appeared in Hart House Theatre. His appointment, however, had a tentative quality about it. Vincent was looking for a man who could hold his own with his academic associates, a scholar and a teacher, who would divide his time between scholarly work and Hart House. In a letter he wrote early in March 1921 to a prospective warden, who held a senior position in an American university, Vincent assured him that 'if you become warden of Hart House the work would be so arranged as to make it possible for you to do steady research work.' Eventually, the emphasis on academic qualifications largely disappeared. The warden who succeeded Bowles, Burgon Bickersteth, who was to serve for twenty-six years and to give substance to the concept of Hart House, was at ease in the academic world, but he was a man of action rather than contemplation, an indefatigable generalist rather than a specialist, an expert in human nature rather than in printed texts.

Bickersteth had not been a visible candidate for the wardenship. In the summer of 1921 he was on his way back to England after two years in Edmonton as a lecturer in history. He stopped off in Toronto to spend a weekend with George Wrong, whom he knew both as an historian and as a fellow lay worker in the Anglican Church. Wrong was aware of the vacancy in the wardenship, and he arranged for his colleague in the history department, George Smith, who was a member of the Hart House board of stewards and a close friend of Vincent Massey, to show the visitor through the building. Vincent had already met Bickersteth a year before at the Wrongs, but at that time the question of the wardenship had not come up. Now, however, the situation had changed: Vincent had not yet secured a successor to Bowles; Bickersteth had severed his connections with Edmonton. Moreover, Alice was enthusiastic about Bickersteth. Her family had numerous ties with prominent English figures in public life and in the Anglican Church, and her father and Bickersteth's father, vicar of Leeds and later canon residentiary of Canterbury Cathedral, were friends. This powerful network of associations, combined with Bickersteth's impeccable background, his knowledge of Canadian life, and his intense and eager interest in youth, made him an ideal candidate for the wardenship. Bickersteth was not initially interested in the job: he was determined to return to England. But at Ottawa, where he stayed with the governor-general, the Duke of Devonshire, he had some after-thoughts. The duke had officiated at the opening of Hart House, knew and understood the work it was doing, and thought Bickersteth ideally suited to undertake its guidance. After returning to England Bickersteth cabled his acceptance. He was then thirty-three, one year younger than Vincent Massey.

If Vincent envisaged Hart House as a means of realizing educational ideals that were peculiarly English, he could not have chanced upon a person more completely suited for the task of leadership. Bickersteth's career up until then was a paradigm of the English intellectual establishment – a major English public school, Charterhouse; a famous Oxford college, Christ Church; further work at the University of Paris. He was a survivor of a generation of Oxbridge graduates who had been decimated in the first world war, and he had done so the hard way – through service from the very outset in a front-line regiment, the Royal Dragoons, the nature of that service proclaimed by his receipt of the Military Cross and bar, decorations awarded only to those who show bravery in action.

The appearance, the voice, the very name declared his background. He looked like a serious young guardsman; his movements were quick and energetic, the reflex of a thin, wiry body; the voice was a little high-pitched, the words coming in cascades, elliptic and padded with the ritual English phrases that had a comic ring to Canadian ears. Twenty-six years in Canada brought no modification. But there was no resentment among the students; rather, a delight in the warden's distinctive style. In the days of the light-hearted, satiric revues during the twenties and thirties, one number would inevitably feature the warden, and he would join in the laughter at his own eccentricities. The students knew that the style and mannerisms were authentic – the natural expression of upbringing and education – and did not clash at all with more robust qualities. For two years prior to the first world war, he had been a lay member of the Archbishops' Western Canada Mission in the Athabasca-McLeod Territory northwest of Edmonton; and when at Toronto students commiserated with him on the vigour of winter, he would smile and recall camping out in Alberta in forty-below-zero weather.

The wardenship of Hart House did not mean for Bickersteth the abandonment of his English associations, which, by reason of family, army service, and church connections, were wide and diverse, with a strong concentration on those who were near the centres of power. Whenever he returned to England, he became part of the intimate network of gossip that depended on special associations and friendships. Here is a typical letter reporting on the English scene:

I had a long talk with Gregg who is very keen about his job in Kenya though he realizes it is a hard nut to crack. I dined with Euan Wallace one night and also went to the House. The Conservative party is a regular Family Compact again – it is Charlie this and George that and Archie something else – at least 20 ex cavalry and guards officers – very pleasant, but surprisingly strenuous ... Duff Cooper made a brilliant start but the general feeling is that Harold Macmillan will leave them all behind.

Humanly speaking, I find I could have got an absolutely safe seat at the last general election. Derby was shouting for young conservative candidates with only a modicum of brains for some of his Lancashire constituencies. Waterloo, a very safe seat, is held by a man who I am told has not even a modicum! They say I could get a tolerably safe seat almost any time. England is still a country I am thankful to say where the 'people' like a 'gentleman' – or at any rate it goes a long way!

'Fruity' Metcalfe leaves HRH *in a blaze of glory. He marries Alexandra Curzon shortly. She is really in love with him, as is shown by her intentions to accompany him to some outlandish station in India where his regiment is at present posted.*[14]

This background, far from being a disadvantage, was part of his strength as warden. It enabled him to keep Hart House sharply visible to visitors from the United Kingdom, and helped him to ease the way for students and friends with missions abroad. Yet there was never any doubt about his primary loyalty: he was first of all warden of Hart House, and, in spirit at least, a Canadian.

Bickersteth's wide range of associations and friendships was not simply the result of birth and upbringing. He was, in his way, a gregarious man, and, provided he could be assured of some privacy, he was happy mingling with the thousands of students who came to Hart House. Despite an initial impression of austerity, and a habit of launching a conversation in a bewildering whirl of words, he made friends easily. The austerity could dissolve in an engaging smile, and the words could sharpen into informed, concerned directness. The network of English friends was soon paralleled by a network of Canadian friends, ranging from naive freshmen getting their first taste of the arts or of politics to business leaders and leading politicans.

Bickersteth's closest political association was with Mackenzie King, not, on the surface, a likely association since King was not well disposed to Englishmen who carried their upper class manner across the Atlantic. But King was impressed by Bickersteth, and in May 1927 invited him to assume a proposed new position of deputy minister in the prime minister's office. Bickersteth, after a flurry of discussions with his powerful friends, declined the offer. He doubted whether King had made any distinction between a civil servant above party and an executive assistant who would be drawn inevitably into party affairs; and he had heard disturbing reports about King's callousness to his colleagues. At the time, King was also intent upon enlisting Massey in the Liberal cause. Massey, more politically ambitious than Bickersteth, less realistic in his assessment of King, had no initial doubts about the benign intentions of the prime minister.

The final factor in Bickersteth's decision not to accept the prime minister's invitation was his belief that his work in Hart House was of great national importance, and should not be abandoned. Ironically, King agreed with him. Bickersteth reported that, at a final discussion, King said that 'as I drove up to Hart House a few minutes ago and saw the beauty of the place in the moonlight and realized afresh what it must stand for in the lives of the students, I said to myself that if the care and direction of such a great foundation had been entrusted to me I doubted whether I would easily give up my work for any Prime Minister.'[15]

The assocation with Mackenzie King was important for Bickersteth and for Hart House. It gave him a sense of being close to the centre of power and influence in Canada, and it enabled him to strengthen his political associations in England. Henceforth he would be a sort of superior courier between England and Canada. No doubt it also brought him closer to Vincent Massey. They became close friends, and Bickersteth was a constant member of the group that assembled at Vincent's country home. Vincent was impressed by Bickersteth's closeness to King, especially since he had become increasingly dependent on King for the advancement of his own political career. Bickersteth was thus in a good position to keep Hart House needs to the fore, which he did with an aggressive bluntness that even Vincent found, from time to time, irritating.

In the twenties and thirties Hart House was not only a student centre; it was a cultural centre for the community, what Vincent must have thought of as a revitalized and secular Chautauqua. By the time Hart House was opened in 1919, Vincent had emerged as an important young man in the community – affluent, talented, with interests that embraced education, politics, and the arts. Hart House was an institution that embraced all three, and he could use it to advance the cause of each. It was during the early years, in part, a personal extension of Vincent Massey. The personal emphasis expressed itself with special clarity in the arts, particularly in theatre and music.

If Vincent – especially during his pre-diplomatic days – had one obsessive interest, it was the theatre, an interest that Alice, although less obsessively, shared. His diary, from its beginning in 1908 through the next two decades, is a record of theatre activity in the English-speaking world. Toronto provided only a minor entrée, and in Ottawa, where he spent much of 1918 and 1919, he was forced to substitute the cinema – for instance, he never missed a Charlie Chaplin film – for play-going. During his regular visits to London and New York, he spent most of his evenings – and many of his afternoons – in the theatre. His range of interest was wide, from popular musical comedy to Greek tragedy. A long succession of the great names of the theatre unrolls in his diary: Nazimova in Ibsen's *The Doll's House*, Maude Adams in Barrie's *A Kiss for Cinderella*, Margaret Anglin in Wilde's *A Woman of No Importance*, Gladys Cooper in Dunsany's *If*, Sir John Martin-Harvey in *Oedipus*, John Barrymore in Tolstoi's *Redemption*, Louis Calvert in Shaw's *You Never Can Tell*, Mrs Fiske in St John Irvine's *Mary, Mary, Quite Contrary*, Sybil Thorndike in Shaw's *Saint Joan*, Ethel Barrymore and Elinor Ulric and George Arliss in long-forgotten plays, Eva LaGalliene in Ibsen's *John Gabriel Borkman*, Ruth Draper, a great favourite and future friend, first seen at a London soirée in 1920. Vincent had an omnivorous appetite for the theatre, and many of the plays he saw, popular in their time, were slight confections, dismissed contemptuously in the diary with a withering adjective. If he had a favourite dramatist, it was Shaw. The first Shaw he saw was *Fanny's First Play*, performed in 1911 at Oxford; from then on Shaw appeared regularly, and became a staple at Hart House during the period when Vincent kept a watching brief on the selection of plays.

As he began to think of a theatre for Hart House, his playgoing became more specialized, concentrating on little theatres in New York outside the Broadway circuit – the Washington Square Players, the Greenwich Village Theatre, the Neighborhood Playhouse – and he consulted Livingston Platt, a New York theatre director, and Margaret Anglin about the running of a little theatre. He and Alice hit upon a natural place for the theatre in the sub-basement underneath the quadrangle which, as a little brochure published in 1928 puts it, 'is supported by a series of concrete arches of unusual size and great beauty of form.' No doubt the idea had occurred early in the war to Lieutenant-Colonel Massey, in charge of the school of musketry, when he had the sub-basement converted into a rifle range. Already, as Ian Montagnes picturesquely put it, 'the future theatre housed a macabre puppet show. At one end, a ruined Belgian village rose in miniature: from behind its wrecked buildings and in its shattered windows, marionettes in German field grey popped suddenly into view – life-like targets for student riflemen posted at the far end of the room in a sand-bagged imitation trench.'[16] The officer who had built the site, Lieutenant Lawren Harris, might well have had the same ideas as Vincent about the eventual use of the space; for he and Vincent were bound together not only by the accident of a business merger, but by common artistic interests; and Harris was to design sets of a less literal nature for the future theatre.[17]

The theatre, thus conceived and shaped by the Masseys, remained for many years their peculiar and treasured responsibility. Up until 1926, it had the first claim on Vincent's time – a claim that he accepted with delight. He loved to attend rehearsals, and a favourite way of entertaining guests was to take them with him. In a slightly atypical week, early in 1926, he went to Hart House Theatre three nights to see Stephen Phillip's poetic tragedy, *Paolo and Francesca*, twice for a performance, and once for a rehearsal. All of the directors were the Masseys' personal choice, and the organization and administration were developed by them and were constantly under their scrutiny. For a short time, the theatre was used primarily by the Players' Club, an organization that predated the theatre, formed by students and staff at the University of Toronto, but including members from the community. In 1921 a governing body known as the board of syndics was set up with representatives from the Players' Club. But when the club began to interfere directly in the affairs of the theatre, and, in particular, to take sides as between the director and the art director, Vincent called a halt to further participation. In a statement that he carefully revised, the syndics declared that 'the only proper status for a Director of a theatre is that of an autocrat responsible to a small sympathetic Board.' The board of syndics was reduced to four, with Vincent as chairman, Alice as a member Dr George Locke, the city's chief librarian, as a second member, and G.F. McFarland, as secretary and effective financial officer. Through McFarland Vincent exercised very careful financial control, and no detail escaped his scrutiny. The theatre had to pay for itself, and the occasional contributions from the Massey Foundation were given charily and with frequent admonitions about the necessity of economy. McFarland was a lawyer, eventually elevated to the Supreme Court of Ontario. Later on he assumed the further responsibility for the finances of the Hart House String Quartet, an organization even less amenable than the theatre to financial control. McFarland was, for Massey's purpose, an ideal officer: a tough administrator, with a good humoured contempt for an actor's or a musician's grasp of a budget, but, with it all, sympathetic to the arts, and quick to recognize artistic excellence.

The Massey benevolent dictatorship extended occasionally to the choice of plays, despite the theoretical belief in the absoluteness of the director's sway. When a new director took over in 1927, Vincent was conscious of a declining public interest in the theatre, and he was deeply concerned about how the new director's proposed season would appeal to the Hart House audience.

We have some doubt about your proposed bill
The Sea Gull I would think a very doubtful bet. Tchekov I am pretty sure would not go down with our audience.

Hassan is less doubtful. Alice and I saw the London production which was a failure. I think, however, it was smothered by too much elaboration, but isn't Hassan a dramatic poem rather than a play?

We think better of the Antony and Cleopatra. This would be a fine thing to do.

On the constructive side I would make two suggestions. One is that we should do a Shaw play. There may be some difficulty about the rights in view of Maurice Colborne's tour, but I would strongly urge a Shaw production as one of the three, because GBS has never yet been a failure in Hart House Theatre.

I think we must be careful not to have too sombre a bill. Can you think of something on the jolly side for Christmas? Is Peter Pan too hackneyed? Is not there a stage version of Treasure Island?[18]

Today we may be amused at this cautious, unexperimental approach, especially by the doubts about Tchekov, who has become as solid and as popular as Shakespeare. But the observations, given the period and the stage in the development of Hart House Theatre, are shrewd and professional, and the comment on Flecker's *Hassan* critically sound. Vincent was far more than patron and administrator, far more than a literary gentleman with a fondness for the theatre. Something of Vincent's and Alice's passionate involvement comes out in this letter to Walter Sinclair, director of Hart House Theatre from 1925 to 1927, written from Washington, when Vincent was beginning his diplomatic career: 'My wife and I long to get into Hart House Theatre for a quiet evening, in fact we are quite homesick for the fun of watching a rehearsal and talking over a production with the Director.'[19]

During the early years of Hart House Theatre, Vincent was a complete theatre man. He played every role except stage manager and artistic director. (Alice, too, made her contribution; she, for instance, designed the costumes for *Outward Bound*, which Vincent directed.) Although he did not lack strong views on technical and visual matters, he was chiefly interested in the dramatic text and its interpretation. He was the unofficial but authoritative reader of prospective Canadian plays for Hart House production, and his correspondence contains many letters in which he gave polite, judicious, but firmly critical views on manuscripts. The 'Canadian Bill' – usually two short plays – became a feature of the season (although usually a hazardous financial adventure) and was initiated and sustained largely on his insistence.[20]

He was also producer and director. In the early days of the Players' Club he had produced two plays that made up a double bill, Shaw's *Dark Lady of the Sonnets* and Galsworthy's *The Pigeon*, which were performed in the dining hall of Victoria College. He was active too in the theatrical activities of the Arts and Letters Club, of which he had become a member in 1911. This club was the centre of experimental theatre in Toronto prior to the establishment of Hart House Theatre, and the first director of Hart House, Roy Mitchell, had been in charge of Arts and Letters productions. Vincent played a directorial role in at least one production there: in October 1917, he recorded that he 'came to rehearse *The Man of Destiny* for the Arts and Letters Players performance.' His final direct involvement in the Hart House program was as director of *Outward Bound*, Sutton Vane's religious melodrama. The play was first performed on 4 May 1925, and had been preceded for several weeks by almost daily rehearsals. At the time Vincent was president of the Massey-Harris company, and deeply involved in political discussions; but there was never any doubt of slighting his work in the theatre. It came first, and was crowned with great success. *Outward Bound* was the hit of the year, played to packed houses, and was repeated the following year. The reviews were exuberantly complimentary.

But it was as actor that Vincent demonstrated his deepest devotion to the theatre. There is a traditional story about his quality. It takes this form. Somebody inquires about Raymond Massey's achievement on the stage. An elderly expert replies that it was very great, indeed, and then, after a significant pause, adds: 'But Vincent was the better actor.' The story has the quality of pleasant shock that characterizes anecdotes of the great and near-great, and is presumably to be taken as genial exaggeration. Still, in this instance there is an element of realistic comment. The comparison of acting ability between the two brothers is pointless because one was a single-minded professional and the other a casual amateur, but there is no doubt that Vincent had qualities as an actor that could have given him a career on the stage. He had inherited his father's gift for mimicry, and had, according to contemporary accounts, refined it into an art. George Glazebrook recalls as a young boy watching Vincent perform in a charade: the subject was Bruce's ordeal in the cave, and he looked on in fascination as Vincent transformed himself into a hideously realistic spider.

Vincent appeared on the stage in each of the first five seasons of Hart House Theatre. He played 'character' roles – usually an elderly man of unconventional behaviour: the gentleman's gentleman in *The New Sin*, a drawing room comedy by Basil Macdonald Hastings that had been a West End success when it was first performed eleven years earlier; a Chaplinesque clown in Barrie's *Pantaloon*; a cockney burglar with clear Shavian antecedents in a one-act play by a Canadian, Marion Osborn, *A Point of View*; the bored enchanter in a Christmas play by Bertram Forsyth, the second director of the theatre; and the Pope, the stubborn proponent of ecclesiastical power, in Paul Claudel's *The Hostage*. He is best remembered for this last role, in part because it is preserved in a remarkable photograph that Vincent treasured. But I suspect he relished most the role of the servant in *The New Sin*, a minor character with one splendidly comic moment. The name of the servant is Pontius Pilate Peel, given to him by an irreligious father when, at his christening, the curate declined the father's choice of Machiavelli and urged a scriptural substitute. At one point, Peel delivers a long speech to his two young masters, one of whom is a novelist and playwright. Peel recalls a former employer, a brother of a duke, who wrote a book; then he says:

Beautifully bound it was too, but – sir! Well, we all know what a humbug Ruskin was ... it simply sickened me to read what that man recommended as a rule of life. Art may be the end-all and be-all of our earthly existence, but I couldn't bear reading homilies to that effect from a man who always helped himself to butter with his egg-spoon.[21]

In the perspective of history the high point in Hart House Theatre was the opening night of the fourteenth production, 1 November 1921.

The new director, Bertram Forsyth, had arranged a bill of three one-act plays: Lord Dunsany's *A Night at an Inn*, Barrie's *Pantaloon*, and *White Magic*, a play that Forsyth himself had adapted. Vincent took the leading role in *Pantaloon* and Raymond, who had just returned from England with his English bride, took the leading role in *A Night at an Inn*. The setting for *A Night at an Inn* was by Lawren Harris, for *Pantaloon*, by Arthur Lismer, and for *White Magic*, by J.E.H. MacDonald; and the music for *Pantaloon* was composed and played by Healey Willan. Forty years later, when the Canada Council inaugurated a special award for contributions of a high order to the cultural life of Canada, the council found nine whose careers were worthy of the award. Three of the nine – Lawren Harris, Vincent Massey, and Healey Willan – had worked together on the fourteenth Hart House production.

Hart House Theatre was the creation of Vincent and Alice Massey, and a remarkable achievement. If the physical structure emerged almost fortuitously, the concept was clear in Vincent's mind. In the early twenties he talked informally to various groups about the theatre, and, in particular, about what was needed for a Canadian drama, and he brought these ideas together in an article for the *Queen's Quarterly* entitled 'Prospects of a Canadian Drama.'[22] He wrote about what he called the 'free theatre,' the theatre rooted in the community and independent of the commercial theatrical networks originating in New York and London. The theatre he envisaged would be a community of artists and craftsmen, of actors, artists, musicians, technicians, and writers. It would be a repertory theatre, presenting a representative group of plays from the entire range of dramatic literature, and it would rigorously eschew the star system. Above all, it would work closely with writers, who, in their turn, would learn about the mechanics of the theatre, and how best to fuse the imagination with the demands of the stage. Vincent placed great emphasis on the development of the playwright. He was contemptuous of the popular emphasis on Canadianism. 'It is the struggle to discover a Canadian point of view that creates the artificial Canadianism that is an offence against honest art.' He envisaged a drama that would be frankly regional and that would assert itself simply by a critical look at customs and manners. The fruit of the collaboration between Hart House and writers was the two volumes of *Canadian Plays from Hart House Theatre,* edited by Vincent Massey, and published by the Macmillan Company of Canada in 1926. It is difficult to think of any Canadian theatre since then that could claim the parentage of as various and as vigorous a progeny.

The high period of Hart House Theatre was between 1920 and 1926 – the years when Vincent Massey was most directly involved. Its influence, however, under various changes in direction has continued until the present day. It was the first of Vincent Massey's contributions to the cultural life of Canada – first in time, and, some would say, in importance.

In the early twenties the theatre was clearly Vincent Massey's principal interest, reinforced by the near-professional competence he possessed in this field. Other interests in the arts were developing, too – in painting and music particularly – but these were the interests of the amateur enthusiast, the collector, and the patron. The interest in painting was the stronger and more informed of the two, and over the years was to develop into a discriminating connoisseurship. In 1910 he records his first purchase of art: etchings by Whistler and Synge bought in England in July 1910. Two years later, now a student at Balliol, he has reached a point where he can speak with critical self-assurance of the popular and the famous. He visits Sir Lawrence Alma-Tadema and describes him as a 'nice old man who can't paint pictures.'[23] On his return to Canada, he rapidly develops an interest in the young men who are in the process of giving Canadian art a bold, distinctive stamp. He acquires some Tom Thomson sketches in March 1918, and, for a presentation portrait for Hart House, he chooses the young, unorthodox painter, Frederick Varley, who disdains flattering surfaces and probes the character of his subjects.

In the plans for Hart House, Vincent included a sketch room where undergraduates could receive informed instruction from artists; and he encouraged and supported the scheme whereby the House built up, by yearly additions, one of the strongest private collections of contemporary Canadian art. But it was in music, the least highly developed of Vincent's artistic interests, that he made a national contribution comparable to that he made in the theatre, and through the same agency, Hart House.

The family tradition had given Vincent a general interest in music.

Methodism was a sect devoted to song and praise, and it could, in an urban setting, broaden its scope to include such unmethodical celebrants as Handel and Mendelssohn. Hart was devoted to religious choral music, and Vincent's mother introduced her husband and family to opera. Vincent's interest certainly was never a question, as it was in theatre and, in a modest way, in painting, of practical skill. At Oxford he recorded, over a brief period, taking singing lessons, with no audible results; the references in the diary to music are few, and these, tentative or negative. In the summer of 1910, he heard Elgar's 'Dream of Gerontius' and observed lamely, 'Though I don't know much about music, I enjoyed this very much.'[24] Some years later, he found a performance of *Parsifal* at the Metropolitan in New York 'boring' and gave it as his opinion that 'opera is an impossible artistic conception.'[25]

In Toronto, however, he was not likely to be disturbed by appeals on behalf of opera. The staging of an opera was beyond the resources of Toronto or of any other Canadian centre. But orchestral music was beginning to challenge choral music for attention. In the arts, Canada was reaping the cultural benefits of European immigration, especially from Jews who were fleeing persecution in Russia and eastern Europe; and in the post-war world of the twenties, private music conservatories found it possible to exist. Assistance came from businessmen, some of whom, like Sir Edmund Walker, had wide cultural interests. The most sympathetic and best informed supporter of them all was the young Vincent Massey, who was prepared to act as well as to listen.

Vincent's interest in orchestral and then in chamber music developed after the war. The small musical soirée was becoming a mark of cultivated society. In November 1920, Vincent and Alice attended a 'Nine o'clock recital in Jenkins Galleries when the singer Campbell McInnes and the Hambourg brothers, Boris, cellist, and Jan, violinist, were the artists.'[26] The following year he was elected president of the Chamber Music Society, an organization that does not seem to have flourished. Activity in chamber music had to await his own initiative and the dreams of a small group of artists.

On 10 March 1924, Vincent recorded: 'Boris Hambourg to see me at 4.20 about the formation of a H.H. String Quartette.' Boris was a member of a famous Russian musical family that had sought sanctuary in London. In 1911 he and his brother came to Toronto and established the Hambourg Conservatory of Music. He and three of his musical associates had been playing quartet music together: these were Geza de Kresz, a violinist, a Hungarian, formerly concertmaster of the Berlin Philharmonic, who had just come to the Hambourg Conservatory to head the violin department; Milton Blackstone, violist, a Russian Jew, who had come to Toronto from New York twelve years previously at the age of sixteen to play in the first Toronto Symphony Orchestra; Harry Adaskin, violinist, also a Russian Jew, who was a small child when his family came to Toronto in 1902. Events moved rapidly. At the next interview five days later Hambourg brought along de Kresz, who, at forty-nine, was the oldest and most distinguished member of the proposed quartet, and Vincent called in Frank McFarland, who, as a lawyer and as secretary and financial officer of the Hart House board of syndics, could give advice about incorporation and administration. Vincent proposed that the quartet give a concert in his house before a small group of prominent Torontonians who were known to have an interest in music. The concert, Vincent reported, was 'most promising,' and justified the announcement of an official launching. The inaugural concert, held in Hart House Theatre before an invited audience of five hundred people on the night of 27 April 1920, was a great success. Vincent wrote laconically in his diary, 'I made a short speech introducing the new adventure.' Harry Adaskin has given a more enthusiastic account: 'Vincent Massey got up from his seat and began walking towards the stage ... what he said was astounding. He referred to the problem of keeping the quartet together, since all the members had to rely on a number of sources for their income. "These gentlemen must not be allowed to disband," and he concluded with an appeal for financial support.'[27]

The response was generous – some $4,000 was raised – but it was inadequate for any long-term program. Vincent realized that a quartet could not hope to reach high professional standards unless its members were able to concentrate exclusively on their work. The solution was an absolute guarantee of yearly salaries, irrespective of deficits. This the Massey Foundation agreed to give. Initially the total salary bill was $10,000, divided equally among the four members; the sum increased with each new contract. If by any chance the revenue from concerts yielded more than was needed to cover expenses and the minimum salaries, the surplus was to go to the musicians. The Massey Foundation's decision was not a bold philanthropic act, but it did, nevertheless, bring a great quartet into existence. Adaskin comments: 'Rarely since the time of Haydn had this happened anywhere, and certainly never before in Canada. And, may I add, never since either!'[28]

Once he had made his decision, Vincent was deeply involved. He made it possible for the Hart House String Quartet to work and live together during two summers in the old Massey home in Newcastle. And throughout the quartet's first years, from 1924 to 1935, he and Alice, despite their absence from Toronto for much of the time, followed every move and lived through every crisis. Tensions began to emerge at an early stage: de Kresz's leadership abilities (and, on occasion, his musical abilities) were called into question by the other three members; they suspected him of having less than complete loyalty to the quartet, and of still retaining his European bias. Vincent was called upon to use diplomatic talents of a far more exquisite quality than those then required in the Washington legation.

The quartet survived in its original membership until 1935. It rapidly achieved international recognition. Indeed, de Kresz made that his overmastering goal. The programs were designed for New York and London, not for provincial Canada. Blackstone, who looked after the bookings, complained about the stony ground close to home. 'Ontario,' he wrote to Vincent, 'that is between Kingston and Windsor, is very hard territory. They are very unmusical and not the least bit cultured, nor have they any desire to be so.'[29]

Vincent sympathized with the high international goals. When the quartet decided on an English tour in the fall of 1929, he prepared its way by writing to his friends in London and Oxford who were in a position to influence opinion and by persuading the English conductor Adrian Boult to give a welcoming musical party. The public relations program was, no doubt, helpful, but the quartet proved that it could flourish on its own merits. The reviews of the concert given in Wigmore Hall on 8 October – an exacting program of Bartok, Beethoven, and Debussy – were uniformly laudatory with a suggestion of a wide-eyed astonishment that such excellence should emerge from such an unlikely place. But the supreme critical endorsement came when the quartet, on its way home, stopped off in Brussels to play Debussy and Beethoven for the great violinist Ysaye, under whom de Kresz had studied. Ysaye wrote that 'it became an evening of enchantment for me, and I will never forget the profound sensation I experienced in listening to these works played with an incomparable mastery, an ensemble of almost unique perfection. One would have to go back to the time of Joachim's original quartet to equal it.'[30]

The quartet was, of course, far less a part of Hart House than the theatre. Most undergraduates would not even have been aware of its existence. But it bore the Hart House name, it came under the direction of the Hart House board of syndics, and, in the terms of the agreement, it was to give 'one or more series of recitals in Hart House Theatre.' In England, thanks to Vincent Massey's network of friends, its assocation with Hart House was well known. Indeed, to one London critic Hart House was not so much a student union as Toronto's cultural centre. 'Toronto,' he wrote, 'is one of the most artistic cities in the world, and it owes its musical and dramatic reputation to Hart House. This institution is unique, certainly as far as the British Empire is concerned. It not only attracts cosmopolitan musicians, but it runs a theatre, presenting Shakespeare, modern comedies, musical comedies, and pantomime, all of which are produced within its walls and are, so to speak, home-made.'[31]

After Vincent left Canada in 1935 for ten years in London, the role of Hart House as cultural centre for the community declined in importance. The city was developing a series of centres, and Hart House no longer enjoyed primacy. But that in no way disturbed what had always been its final goal – the creation of a society that did not depend on traditional loyalties, that was bound together by an interest in the arts and in public life. Hart House grew out of Vincent's admiration of the English concept of collegiate education; but by its inclusiveness (albeit only for males) and its espousal of radically democratic ideas, it proclaimed itself an institution of the new world.

CHAPTER FOUR

The Emergence of the Public Man

In the early twenties Vincent Massey had become a principal figure in the artistic and cultural life of Canada. His role was not so much that of philanthropist as of entrepreneur; he used his position, his control of resources, and, above all, his own enthusiasm and knowledge to support individual artists and to bring vital institutions into existence. His greatest achievements, as we have seen, were in music and the theatre. In literature he was active too, but with less success.

During his student days, literature had been Vincent's principal interest and the area in which he had shown the greatest promise. History, however, was his official subject, both at Toronto and at Oxford; in Vincent's undergraduate days at Oxford, before the establishment of a strong English school, history was a favourite subject for those with a literary bent. He thought of himself as a student with broad literary interests. When, for instance, for a brief period following his return to Toronto in 1913, he was a lecturer in history, he also undertook, at the request of Pelham Edgar, the professor of English literature at Victoria, a course of lectures on Tennyson's *In Memoriam*. His chief extra-curricular preoccupation at Toronto and Oxford had been in editing and in writing for literary magazines; and the relish with which he performed the first and the competence the second pointed to a possible career in literary journalism. As an undergraduate his literary tastes were personal, unconventional, and discriminating. Edward Lear and George Gissing, his two most pronounced favourites, were not popular Edwardian choices.

After his return from Oxford, and the rapid increase of his

commitments, he ceased to write regularly for formal publication. The article on 'The Prospects of a Canadian Drama' was the exception; it was a perceptive analysis of the issues, and the most sustained piece of literary analysis that Vincent ever wrote. The edition of Canadian plays from Hart House was an important document, but Vincent's contribution was confined to a brief, graceful introduction. Otherwise, his literary activity was confined to informal presentations to various groups, and to the writing of light verse to mark special occasions. The last became an activity pursued throughout his life, although the occasions that prompted the compositions were more and more widely spaced as formal public life crowded in. The form for these occasional verses was usually the four-beat rhyming couplet, which he used as an instrument for good-humoured characterization. Thus his presidential address at the Arts and Letters Club dinner in 1922 was done in rhyming couplets – some 160 lines all told, subsequently printed in pamphlet form by the club – in which he sketched a gallery of leading members. Some members like Ivor Lewis, who bestrode the Hart House stage by night and an executive office in a large department store by day, merited a single couplet:

> *There's Ivor Lewis – art and business blent –*
> *Sweet are the uses of advertisement.*

Others were swept into a group, which was then boldly characterized. The academic membership of the club, then as now inclined to make only fugitive and apologetic appearances, was thus despatched:

> *There are some people up at Varsity*
> *Who're members of this club – apparently –*
> *Needler and Wallace, Sissons, Edgar, Fairley,*
> *Mavor and Dale and Hooke: we see them rarely;*
> *Is living here too plain with shepherd's pie?*
> *Or is the thinking just a thought too high?*

Vincent used a similar technique in proposing a toast to the staff at the dinner of the Canadian Bank of Commerce in January 1923. The form now was the limerick, the wit hobbled by the dignity of the occasion and the splendour of the surroundings, and the consequent necessity of forcing the verses into propriety.[1]

Only once did he abandon light banter, and that was in a long poem of some two hundred lines carefully preserved in several copies, but, as far as I know, never publicly delivered. The form is still the couplet, but the line is lengthened from four to five beats appropriate to a serious, satiric interest. It is entitled 'The — — —ad,' recalling the mock satirical epics of the eighteenth century. In one copy Vincent has pencilled in over the blanks in the title the initials R.B., and the subject, as the opening makes clear, is Richard Bedford Bennett, leader of the Conservative party, 1927–38, and prime minister of Canada, 1930–5. The lines belong to a later period, to the early thirties, and the venomous gusto with which they were written had a specific context for Vincent Massey, both personal and public, that will be described later. The *R.B.ad* is good satire, not crippled by politeness and good taste, aiming straight for the jugular. Bennett, for all his virtues, was a good target for satire: he was a rhetorician, easily enslaved by his own eloquence, and an opportunist, not in any petty way but with a grand, breath-taking sweep. These are qualities upon which the satirist feeds.

The poem is divided into two cantos, the first describing the hero's rise to power, and the second, his vacillation, hypocrisy, and incompetence once power has been achieved. The first canto, indeed the opening twenty-five lines or so, are the best; the second canto tends to splutter into angry incoherency. Here is the opening – the birth and fantastic education of our epic hero:

> .... *bore him but impute no ill*
> *To that fair Province, she has virtues still,*
> *Despite the fact that in her virgin woods*
> *Our statesman early learned to 'get the goods.'*
> .... *they called him, but no lion-heart*
> *Helped* him *to play the foremost ....'s part*
> *The second .... yet, in words' excess*
> *He aped and showed a vanity no less;*
> *And mirrored too the third in ruthlessness.*
>
> *Westward he went, while still in early years,*
> *Ambition's call beat on his ready ears.*

'No harm,' you say, 'no reason for contrition.'
'Right!' but one asks, 'How served he this ambition?'
The great west suckled him and fast he grew a
Monstrous child, Alberta's gargantua.
And, as some lesser infants oft have sinned,
The pabulum he ate was chiefly – wind –
Wind from the foothills; wind from the Chinook.
The August wind which dries the standing stook,
Wind, North, East, South and West, blew all the while
And formed his mind and shaped his verbal style.
The West which brings to most an outlook spacious
Produced in him a nature simply gaseous.

And so he climbed, inflated like a bladder,
Rung after rung the politician's ladder.

I give one further passage in the first canto of felicitous and unbridled invective:

And yet he throve – this gutsy politician –
This windy-bellied diorrhetorician,
And if our statesman through his watery words
Should need some substance, just as whey and curds,
Pedantic legalism then he brought
To serve as easy substitute for thought.

As a literary entrepreneur, Vincent was neither as vigorous nor as successful as he was as a theatrical and musical entrepreneur. He maintained a cool and appraising interest in the literary periodical *The Rebel*, which was the direct successor to the undergraduate periodical *Arbor*, and at the demise of *The Rebel* in 1920 he wrote a mock heroic poem, describing the shock waves that ran through the campus at the news of its passing.[2] In April 1919, he was briefly excited by the prospect of a new weekly review which he was invited to support, but nothing came of it.

Vincent's interest in the arts – the theatre, literature, music, painting, architecture – was always to occupy an important place in his life. In the early twenties this interest was central, and was reflected in his preference for the Arts and Letters Club over more genteel and amply endowed clubs to which his financial position gave him an immediate entrée. The Arts and Letters Club had been founded in 1908 by Augustus Bridle, a newspaperman who wrote confidently about literature and all the arts. Vincent first mentions the club in January of 1911, during the year between graduation from Toronto and going to Oxford: he went to the club for tea and 'met many weird geniuses, but the place is refreshing after the complacent philistinism of most Toronto drawing rooms.'[3] A little later, after 'a gloriously bohemian evening' with Henry Sproatt, the architect of Hart House, W.A. Langton, the current president of the club, and Pelham Edgar, he became a member. During his Balliol days he visited the London equivalent, the Savage Club, but reported 'commonplace men and entertainment inferior to the Arts and Letters Club.'[4] In the fall of 1920 he was elected president of the club, and officiated at the opening of the new club house, making, he recorded modestly, 'Quite a good speech.'[5] During the early twenties the Arts and Letters Club served Vincent as a headquarters for a variety of cultural campaigns. At luncheons there he would meet with architects to discuss the plans for Hart House, or with musicians to discuss the formation of what became the Hart House Quartet. There was also a close relation between dramatic activity at the Arts and Letters Club and the early development of Hart House Theatre.

As patron and expositor of the arts, Vincent had his allies in the business community, chiefly older men who had developed specialized interests, like Sir Edmund Walker, who was an art connoisseur and a music lover, and Colonel Albert Gooderham, who, according to a newspaper account, 'spent a large fortune in music.' But a combination of business eminence and interest in and support of the arts did not give the basis for wide public recognition, and increasingly in the early twenties Vincent saw himself as playing a public role, as helping to set the course of the nation. For a new and firmer base he turned to education, where his interests had always been strong.

In the early twenties education emerged as a subject of national interest, almost a national obsession, just as it did in the early fifties. In each case it came as a response to the end of a prolonged and depleting war. For the veteran, whose life had been largely one of grubby and sordid detail, or the citizen, still aglow with patriotic idealism, education seemed to hold out answers, to be both relief and promise. Although schools and universities were provincial preserves, fiercely guarded by local watch dogs, they had much in common – much more, for instance, than organized religion, divided into the two opposed blocks of protestantism and catholicism, the former a patchwork of schismatic sects – and they seemed to provide a means by which the national unity that had emerged fitfully during the war could be preserved and strengthened.

In the post-war discussions on education Vincent was accorded a central role. Hart House was now fully in use by the university; its fame both as a building and as a concept had spread widely; and Vincent Massey was accurately portrayed as its spiritual father. Moreover, he had begun his career, following his return from Balliol in 1913, as an academic; he had held, in fact, a double appointment, dean of the men's residence at Victoria College and special lecturer in history in the university. In offering the appointment several months before Vincent took his final Oxford schools, the president, Robert Falconer, had observed 'that your prospects in the Oxford examinations are excellent, and I hope that we shall have good accounts of the outcome soon.'[6] Actually Vincent failed to get his anticipated first – he was ranked in the second class – but this did not deter the university. His was, after all, a minor appointment not likely to be of long duration, and the professor of modern history, George Wrong, Vincent's mentor and friend, was not unmindful of the resonance that a young man of wealth, wide cultural interests, and distinguished manners would bring to the department.

As a special lecturer with part-time responsibilities and a salary of $500, Vincent had, by modern standards, a bulging timetable. He wrote to Murray Wrong of 'two lectures a week on modern France – about which I know nothing – prepared on the hand-to-mouth plan, 2 or 3 hours on *In Memoriam* – a concession to Pelham Edgar and the Victoria English department, and four groups on constitutional history.'[7] His residence position was likewise demanding, but clearly one that the ardent young Oxonian revelled in. He wrote, again to Murray Wrong, that 'I think I have been able to convince people that the introduction of Gothic architecture and collegiate life is not a conspiracy to rob the Canadian of his birthright, nor is it an attempt to superimpose "Oxford customs" on the freedom-loving Toronto student. In fact the undergrad is beginning to talk of "founding traditions of the right sort" and of "giving college life more dignity" etc. I am working as far as possible through the House Committees and I find them understanding and sympathetic. Civilization is a slow process but I am satisfied that we are making some progress.'[8] In another letter, he pronounced this solemn decanal judgment: 'The introduction of residential life has apparently induced a different sort of undergrad to register at Victoria and his rather fearsome crudity is being softened.'[9]

Vincent's academic career was interrupted by war service, and he never resumed his academic duties. But education continued to be a central concern. He had a particular interest in the talented student of limited means. Such students, he believed, should be encouraged to continue their studies abroad. In the summer of 1916 he established a committee to raise money for a fellowship in honour of Edward Kylie, a brilliant graduate of Toronto and Balliol, a member of the Toronto history department, and a popular and beloved figure, who died suddenly that spring. Three years later he persuaded the American University in Washington, a Methodist foundation, to divert a Hart Massey bequest into graduate fellowships for Canadian students wishing to study abroad. These were known as the Massey Fellowships, and the list of recipients includes a prime minister of Canada, Lester Pearson, a justice of the Supreme Court of Ontario, S.H.S. Hughes, and an impressive list of senior civil servants, prominent industrialists, and leading scholars in the humanities, social sciences, and physical sciences.

In the early twenties, he acquired fresh credentials. He became a member of the selection committee for the Rhodes scholarship. In 1920 he was appointed to the board of governors of the University of Toronto. Above all, as vice-chairman of the newly established Massey Foundation (his father was the titular chairman) he was able to give his ideas a telling thrust.

A foundation's principal device for influencing education, as he doubtless learned from his cousin George Vincent, the president of the Rockefeller Foundation, was to sponsor a commission. The commission should be made up of experts, preferably those occupying high and visible positions, and it should create an impression of sober and informed objectivity. Its conclusions and recommendations should be strong and precisely formulated in the knowledge that most of them would subsequently be modified, distorted, or ignored. One of the first acts of the newly created Massey Foundation was the appointment of a commission on 'the Secondary Schools and Colleges of the Methodist Church of Canada.'[10] The commission had the official approval of the Methodist Church, which doubtless chose one of the members, the Rev. James Smyth, principal of Wesleyan Theological College, Montreal.

Most of the report is taken up with examining in detail the resources and the curricula of the eleven Methodist secondary schools and colleges spread across the dominion. An introductory chapter raises and discusses two general issues, and it is obvious that the chairman of the commission, Vincent Massey, had a strong hand in selecting those issues and in shaping the comments. The first issue was curricular: the undue emphasis on practical and fringe subjects – bookkeeping, art, music – which were often taught in isolation from the academic subjects. The justification for the practice was financial, since these subjects attracted students and were, thus, a source of income indispensable to institutions that had no regular support from the church. The commission urged that the church recognize its financial responsibility, and that the schools devise curricula in the practical subjects that were related to the future work of the students – most of whom would not go on to university, but would return to the farm or the home or enter on business careers. At the same time, 'the greatest care should be taken that, through literature, history, the study of social ethics and of the principles of citizenship, they become conscious of their duties and their privileges as members of the State and inspired to realize their high calling and destiny as human beings.'[11]

The curricular recommendations were sound and practical and demonstrated that the fervid young Oxonian had not lost touch with the realities of rural Canadian society. But the second general issue raised by the commission was, I suspect, of primary importance only in the mind of the chairman. The issue was 'co-education,' and Vincent had strong views on the subject. He had always delighted in the society of young women – the diary has frequent reference to girls who aroused his interest, although usually in a high Victorian manner. On his English trips in the summer of 1910 – aged twenty-three – he recorded two brief attachments. 'Miss Van der Smissen is one of the most charming girls I know. The only one – about the only one – with whom I can talk easily and to the best advantage';[12] 'met Ruth Hutton, spent a joyous evening in the company of this goddess.'[13] There is one reference in the next year to a susceptibility that is not so carefully hedged by the proprieties. During a trip to the west, he 'dictated my first two letters to a little French typist at the Massey-Harris Co., and was so unnerved by the novelty of the situation and the beauty of the stenographer that my letters read like the election-speech for a Scandinavian politician translated into the journalese of a Toronto daily.'[14] But by the time of the commission he had been happily married for five years; so his antipathy to co-education had no taint of misogyny. He was convinced, nevertheless, that education was best carried on in an atmosphere serenely free of the sudden gusts of sexual attraction. There can be no doubt of who was responsible for inserting the following quotation, an exotic outcropping in a sober Methodist landscape. The author is Bishop Weldon, a former headmaster of Harrow: 'It is in the boarding-schools that the ethos – the sense of honour, the feeling that *noblesse oblige*, the pride of ancestry, the consciousness of duty, and the spiritual communion between succeeding generations of school fellows – has attained its sovereign grace of elevating dignity.' The implication is that the highest morality develops only in a male society, and that the boy's boarding school is a forcing ground for all the principal virtues.

The section on co-education was, in context of the problems of the day, a harmless indulgence. The commission contented itself with some cautious negatives. Some of the commissioners, the report said, were stronger on the subject than others, but all were agreed that co-education was not the ideal system for secondary schools.

Before the commission on Methodist education had published its report, Vincent conceived of a much wider investigation that the Massey Foundation could undertake, nothing less than an inquiry into the entire Ontario educational system below university level. At a preliminary conference with the Ontario premier, E.C. Drury, he received so much encouragement that he proceeded with a proposal for the membership of the commission. A premature newspaper announcement appeared, and Drury found himself in an embarrassing position with respect to his minister of education, who had not been consulted. There were governmental denials on all sides: of course the Ontario government would not abdicate its responsibility to a private foundation. The proposal died, and Vincent absorbed the lesson that, without political power, private resources and superior ideas must accept a limited role.

Vincent achieved his greatest popular distinction as an educator in an organization that originally had no relationship to the Massey Foundation and that had, indeed, origins that he must have looked upon as mildly suspect. The National Council of Education originated in Winnipeg under business auspices. A.L.F. Chaiton, the historian of the movement, traced its origins to the Canadian Industrial Reconstruction Association (later the Reconstruction Association), which had two objects – first, to maintain industrial stability, and second, to secure wise consideration and prudent treatment of problems of post-war reconstruction.[15] The Reconstruction Association was clearly apprehensive, as well it might be, of the growing militancy of the labour movement in the west and the rise in popularity of revolutionary ideas. What it thought the country needed was a revival of traditional values of character, a fusing of the ideals of church and school. There finally emerged the concept of a National Conference which would concern itself with 'Character Education in Relation to Canadian Citizenship.' It took place in Winnipeg on 20–2 October 1919, under the patronage of the Duke of Devonshire, governor-general of Canada, with an opening address by Sir James Aikins, the lieutenant-governor of Manitoba, who had taken a prominent part in early discussions.

The tone of the conference was set by Major the Rev. C.W. Gordon (Ralph Connor) in the opening address on 'Moral and Spiritual Lessons of the War for Canadian Education.' It was a fervidly emotional exhortation by Canada's most famous 'sky pilot,' in which he maintained that the war had brought great spiritual gains – 'the re-affirmation of conscience as supreme in human conduct,' 'the re-assertion of the supreme worth of humanity,' 'the discovery of the supreme value of comradeship in the making of a nation,' and 'the supreme place of religion in character-making and nation-building.'

The remaining addresses were in a more sober and academic mode (the president of the University of Toronto, Sir Robert Falconer, gave the weightiest address on 'The Education of National Character'); but the emphasis was consistently on the formation of character, a word used to indicate self-discipline and an awareness of spiritual values. The industrial origins of the conference, especially against the immediate background of the Winnipeg strike, were discreetly hidden, although they emerged by implication in the session on 'The School and Industrial Relationships.' Peter Wright, a strong British trade union leader of non-revolutionary views, drew applause as he moved to his peroration, a celebration of the peace-making power of the 'English-speaking race': 'Karl Marx's doctrine is not suitable for our race. It is acceptable to people who, prior to coming over here, were subject to a tyrannical monarchy and did not understand democratic government like we have here today ... we should give liberty to a foreigner. I have love for the whole of mankind. But when they come here they must submit to our democratic government or else get the hell out of it.'[16]

Vincent was not one of the shapers of the Winnipeg meeting and he took no part in the program. But at an organizational meeting following the conference, he became one of the three vice-presidents of the new National Council on Education and rapidly assumed a position of leadership. The council decided to hold triennial conferences; the next would take place in Toronto in 1923, and Vincent Massey and a Toronto committee were made responsible for its preparation.

Under Vincent's guidance the council substituted some specific goals for the vague uplift of its founding statement. It would attempt to establish a national bureau, where provincial educational authorities would meet regularly to discuss common problems and to draw upon information assembled and co-ordinated by the bureau. It would publish a children's magazine that, by emphasizing moral values and heroic Canadian achievements, would provide an antidote for un-healthy literary seepage from south of the border. And it would foster a national lectureship scheme, by which men and women distinguished in the arts, literature, and education would move across the country addressing clubs, organizations, and specially convened assemblies.

Of these three goals, the first – the establishment of a national bureau – foundered on the rocks of provincial suspicion, as ventures of these kinds always do, starting on a note of euphoric optimism and swiftly breaking up into discordant protests. The children's magazine, fortunately perhaps, never appeared, but the council hit upon a better scheme – the publication of a series of introductory books on Canadian subjects. The most successful was entitled *This Canada of Ours*, subtitled 'An Introduction to Canadian Civics.' It was written by Charles Norris Cochrane and William Stewart Wallace, two University of Toronto men who, like Vincent, had gone to Balliol and had then returned to academic posts at their alma mater.[17] The book is written simply and directly, with a refreshing absence of patriotic unction and moral uplift. Other books of value were Ernest MacMillan's *A Canadian Song Book*, a compilation of songs of Canadian origin or association;[18] and *The School Theatre*, by Roy Mitchell, who was the first director of Hart House Theatre, and a thoughtful and innovative writer on drama and the theatre.

The council's most ambitious program was the bringing of special lecturers to Canada. This scheme bore upon it the imprint of Major Fred Ney, the secretary of the council and a man of boundless energy, resolute optimism, and strong, inflexible views. He was born and educated in England, spent some time as a young man as headmaster of the English College in Cyprus, came out to Canada in 1910 as the principal of a high school in Manitoba, served with great distinction in the war, and then returned to Canada. When he became secretary of the council he retained his interest in the Overseas Education League, which he had founded to organize teachers' trips to the United Kingdom. Ney's idea of a distinguished speaker was an Englishman who had one, or preferably several, of the following characteristics: a title, distinguished service in the world war, high office in an exemplary organization like the boy scouts, a senior educational appointment, especially in a university or a public school, and a reputation for what could be classified as inspirational writing. A lecturer who qualified on most of these criteria was Sir Henry Newbolt, who, in addition to lecturing throughout Canada, was a key man for the Toronto conference, where the major theme, 'Literature and Life,' was based upon his 1921 report on 'The Teaching of English in England.' The council's brochure about Sir Henry breathes hushed adulation; his ancestry is an epic poem in itself:

He divides with Kipling the poet's greatest popularity with the masses of England, and while Kipling has been a laureate for the army, Newbolt has warmed and kept glowing the glorious traditions of the Navy. He is of the very soil and atmosphere of England itself. One of his sires was the Mayor of Winchester who donned his armour to face the Spanish Armada. He is a descendant of one of these noble families that have lived in their old manor home for over 500 years, true to ideals of humble service to the State and countryside ... it is said that his inspiring poem 'Vita Lampada' (The Torch of Life), with its stirring appeal to 'Play up, and play the game,' was responsible in no small measure for the splendid response of the young men of the Empire in the Great War.

Some of the lecturers were chosen because, in Ney's phrase, they were 'great lights' who were widely known – Sir Robert Baden-Powell and Field Marshal Viscount Allenby are the best examples – but most of them did speak with authority in some branch of education. Newbolt may have been a minor representative of the English muse, but his report on the teaching of English was full of sound ideas and observations. Others were even more impressive. J.L. Paton, who had been headmaster of Manchester Grammar School, spent three months looking at schools all across the dominion, and wrote a report that managed to be both polite and scathingly critical. Sir Michael Sadler, the vice-chancellor of Leeds University (shortly to become master of University College, Oxford), another lecturer, was perhaps the dominating figure in English education at the time. The lecturers were overwhelmed with engagements and enthusiastic audiences. Michael Sadleir's memoir of his father mentions the Canadian tour only in terms of its excessive demands: 'for six exhausting weeks he was billed to appear at meetings and, the object of overwhelming hospitality, fêted to the point of collapse. Excitement and pleasure at his generous welcome kept him going while the tour lasted (often he made as many as three speeches a day); but he fell sick as the homebound liner started down the St Lawrence and was laid up during the whole voyage.'[19]

The council was not entirely committed to titles, and did not always insist on an overt connection with the establishment. Mrs Philip Snowden, the wife of the chancellor of the exchequer in the first Labour government, and herself a veteran of the suffragette movement and noted socialist orator, was a lecturer in January and February 1925. The Toronto *Telegram* expressed characteristic displeasure at her acceptance by sound Torontonians. Vincent was contemptuous of such narrow Toryism, and expressed great enthusiasm for her performance: 'Mrs Snowden's visit to Toronto was a tremendous success. The Canadian Club-Empire Club lunch, subject First Labour Government of Great Britain, with about 750 present was, I think, the finest address I ever heard before either body, and her address in the evening, subject Russia, to a crowded Convocation Hall, a superb performance. She was badly heckled all evening, but more than held her own and captivated the audience in general.'[20]

Vincent Massey was chairman of the committee responsible for the Toronto conference. It was a great advance on the Winnipeg conference, which had been a summons to dissolve social discontent in a vague idealism. The greater part of the Toronto conference was devoted to a consideration of the nature and influence of three subjects: history, geography, and literature. At the end there was a return to the subject of education in relation to personality and character, and the conference ended on a high inspirational note. Sir Michael Sadler, in his concluding speech, speculated as to why 'the world felt education to be a new religion.'[21] On the Sunday following the final Saturday session, the conference spilled over into the churches, and the lecturers took to the pulpit.

At the concluding session, Vincent was elected president of the National Council. The conference, which he had shaped and over which he had presided, had been a great success. He was an active and diligent president, but gradually over the next three years the council ceased to be a dominating concern, and following the third conference, three years later in Montreal, he rapidly obtained his release from any direct responsibility. He left the Montreal arrangements to a local committee, with Edward Beatty, chancellor of McGill University and president of the Canadian Pacific Railway, as chairman and J.M.

Macdonnell, an executive with the National Trust Company, as secretary and the active organizer.[22]

The Toronto conference had had some parallel sessions for French-speaking delegates; the Montreal conference adopted a formal bilingual structure. In preliminary correspondence Vincent expressed concern about the bilingual issue, which was bound to arise in the consideration of 'The National Importance of Language in Education.' He was referring to the broad political question, and had in mind recent Ontario legislation that had restricted the teaching of French in the schools. His concern, however, was only about the divisive nature of the question at a conference that sought to emphasize the national character of education. He had no qualms about the need in Canada for a systematic program in bilingualism. In his presidential speech to the conference, he made statements about French Canada and the French language that were forthright and generous, and that were widely quoted. The Toronto *Star* subsequently cited the passage: 'Let us thank heaven for the diversities of races, religions and social cultures which save the country from a devastating uniformity, and in welcoming diversity, let us remember that after all a nation is civilized in proportion to the sympathetic understanding with which it welcomes just such distinctions in languages, customs, manners, frames of mind, that make French- and English-speaking Canada different one from the other in one sense, as I believe they are united in fundamental things.'[23] *The Times* of London quoted approvingly an even more sharply phrased passage: 'The time is not far distant when an English-speaking Canadian, who desires to be really Canadian, will consider it an imperfection for which he will blame himself if he is unable to express himself in the French language with as much ease as in his own.'[24] (Vincent had taken firm steps to eliminate this 'imperfection' in himself. He was taking regular lessons in conversational French.)

After the Montreal conference, Vincent's connection with the council was purely nominal. For four years, from 1929 to 1932, the Massey Foundation assisted the council – to the extent of $5,000 in the first two years, and $3,000 in the last two – but after that its support dwindled and disappeared. Vincent was becoming apprehensive about the direction the council was taking. Ney was leading it into broad questions – censorship of literature and national fitness were two of his obsessive interests – and in the fevered atmosphere of the thirties these questions could develop unpleasant political overtones. During an Italian week in Toronto in January 1933, the council sponsored speakers sympathetic to the Mussolini regime, and there was later a proposal to provide a similar program on Germany. Carl Goldenberg, a prominent Montreal lawyer, wrote a letter of protest to Vincent, whose name still appeared as a member of the executive. Five days later, on 21 April 1934, Vincent wrote to the president of the council, James Richardson, asking that his resignation from the executive be accepted, expressing polite sentiments about the work of the council, but adding in a postscript 'that of late I have been increasingly disturbed over some aspects of Ney's programmes and the way in which they are carried out.'

On balance, the council had been a healthy force: it had aroused support for education, drawn attention to defects in the schools, and stimulated interest in the humanities; and on particular questions – on public broadcasting, and bilingualism, for instance – it had fostered a liberal and articulate public opinion. Its period of greatest influence and highest visibility coincided with the years of Vincent's presidency, and it was then that he began to emerge as a national spokesman, an attractive figure on a stage largely dominated by sombre, self-indulgent politicians – young, wealthy, idealistic, untrammeled by political obligations. The Toronto *Star* was particularly enthusiastic about young Mr Massey. The writer of a column entitled 'The Spotlight,' possibly Augustus Bridle, the *Star*'s authority on all the arts, described Vincent as 'born for idealism as the sparks are for upward flight. He has the thin, drawn face of the ascetic, but without the occasional ascetic look of unconquerable asceticism.'[25]

Vincent remained a private citizen, but he had almost an official position in society, as if already he occupied a vice-regal post. He moved from one interest to another with easy authority. The last weekend in January 1924 illustrates the kind of program he followed. It is, perhaps, atypical in its breathlessness, but it is representative in that he touched upon all his main interests. On Thursday evening he went to see Sir John Martin Harvey in *Oedipus Rex*. On Friday morning he left for Kingston, where he addressed a Massey-Harris agents' conference. At Kingston he also visited the Royal Military College, where he was received by the commandant and invited to speak to the cadets. On Saturday he went on to Ottawa where he spoke to the Canadian Club. This he regarded as a major engagement. He was constantly deluged with invitations to speak, chiefly from service and business clubs throughout Ontario, with an occasional invitation from another province or from the United States, but he almost invariably refused. At this time, as later, he was happy as a public speaker only when he had a carefully prepared text and an occasion that he considered of suitable importance, like a seasoned actor who would appear only in a play that he knew well and before an audience capable of savouring his subtleties. The Ottawa Canadian Club provided such an audience, with the added likelihood that it would include a representative group of those who made and unmade national careers. (The audience included the prime minister, Mackenzie King, the leader of the opposition, Arthur Meighen, and assorted dignitaries.) Vincent had worked zealously on the speech, and he recorded in his diary that he 'made the best speech I've yet made, thank heaven!' In the afternoon, he went to Government House to have tea with the governor-general and Lady Byng, and later with Sir Robert Borden and two senior civil servants. He dined at the home of Duncan Campbell Scott, and after music and drinks boarded the train for Toronto.

There is no record of Sunday's activities, but they no doubt included attendance at church, and a variety of social calls. On Monday, the day was crammed with meetings. It began with a meeting at the university of a committee of the board of governors, in all likelihood the property committee of which he was chairman. He lunched with Frank McFarland, the secretary of the board of syndics of Hart House Theatre, and discussed with him the delicate relationship between the director, Bertram Forsyth, and the art director, Arthur Lismer. In the early afternoon he went to see Dr A.S. Vogt, the conductor of the Toronto Symphony Orchestra, about a director of music for the university. The evening was devoted to a conference at the home of Sir Robert Falconer on the subject of 'religious activity amongst students.' In three days he had touched on his principal interests, shifting quickly from business executive, to patron of the arts, to educational theorist, to public spokesman on the general state of the nation.

Vincent's satisfaction in his Canadian Club speech was shared, although less rapturously, by the most influential member of his audience, Mackenzie King. In his diary for 26 January 1924, King wrote: 'At noon went to Canadian Club at which Vincent Massey of Toronto gave a very good address on Canadian spirit. It was most carefully prepared, a fine literary flavour about it, a little too much of the "lamp" for an oration, but revealing a fine discernment of underlying influences and factors in our national life. It was splendidly liberal and tolerant.' King remembered the speech, and in the debate on the speech from the throne, 3 March 1924, used it in his peroration. After deploring the pessimism and the appeal to sectional interest that, he said, characterized the remarks of the leader of the opposition, he went on to observe: 'My right hon. friend and I had the privilege of hearing the other day an address, delivered by Mr Vincent Massey – one of the young men of this country accustomed to observe matters carefully and in an impartial way. He was speaking to the citizens of Ottawa, and equally to the people of Canada. He said "It is not Downing Street but Main Street which is the foe of true Canadianism."' King then referred to a passage in the speech in which Vincent deplored emphasis on problems of sectionalism, and quoted this newspaper account of Massey's words: 'But he had not much sympathy with those who saw blue ruin, red revolution, and a yellow peril, a sort of Joseph's coat of misery, which he thought was hardly the best kind of flag under which to move towards better things.' Here, proclaimed King, was 'the voice of the younger generation of Canada today' as opposed to 'the continual note of detraction, of pessimism, and of sectionalism which has been sounded so much of late by my right hon. friend and his friends.'[26]

King had his eye on the young Toronto business executive who spoke with such studied eloquence about Canadian affairs, and he set out to cultivate him. On 12 January 1925, Vincent lunched with King at Hart House. Afterwards King announced to the students that Massey was to be made a trustee of the National Gallery. The appointment was officially made on 23 January, and King sent a telegram to Vincent in which he expressed hope 'that you may find much enjoyment in the opportunity of increased public service thereby afforded.'

CHAPTER FIVE

The Lure of Politics

Mackenzie King's reference to 'increased public service' raised questions in Vincent's mind about his future. Since graduating from the University of Toronto he had had a varied formal career: from 1910 to 1911, a year during which he was free to pursue his own interests; from 1911 to 1913, attendance at Balliol; from 1913 to 1915, an academic appointment; from 1915 to 1918, military service followed by a year in Ottawa in a government post; then from 1919 to 1925, an executive in the family firm. But amid the multiplicity there were two constants: a devotion to education and the arts, and an interest in politics. The latter was more general in nature, but increasingly attractive. The intervention of Mackenzie King forced Vincent to bring his political interests into sharp focus. As he looked back over his career from 1910 to 1925, he could see a consistency in the growth of his political ideas; and he also realized that, important as education and the arts were, they relied, as almost everything else ultimately did, on political decisions.

Vincent Massey in his youth had not shown any special bias towards politics. Nor had the Massey family taken any great interest in matters that lay outside the orbit of the family business. The general tradition was, however, in the early part of the nineteenth century, anti-Tory with some populist tinges. This persisted into the later decades of the century, although the populist tinge faded gradually. The firm enjoyed an unchallenged pre-eminence in the field of agricultural implements, with domination of the Canadian market and increasingly successful access to overseas markets; it did not seem to need special tariff concessions. By the eighties, however, as we have seen, Hart became apprehensive of American competition, and supported the Macdonald National Policy of protection. His early liberalism had never gone as far as to accept the trade union movement; but this unsympathetic attitude towards organized labour was modified by his sons who, without abandoning rigid control, introduced concepts of co-operation and cultivated a benign paternalism. In his own home, Vincent was largely insulated from business concerns, since his father gradually withdrew from active participation in the firm and concentrated on his charities. As he grew to adulthood Vincent could thus assume a general liberal stance, without any sense of conflict with activities that gave him affluence and a secure social status.

Later on, when he was accused of being a renegade Conservative, Vincent could reply that he had always held Liberal views. 'My views on such matters [he was referring to the tariff question] were much the same as those of my grandfather when he lived in Newcastle and was a supporter of Edward Blake.'[1] He could have summoned the witness of his early diaries, where his liberalism was expressed with uncompromising fervour.

Vincent's first extended political comments were about British politics. He spent the autumn months of 1910 in hospitals and nursing homes recovering from an attack of typhoid fever incurred during manoeuvres at Aldershot with his militia regiment, and during this time he had plenty of opportunities for reading and reflection. It was a period of great political tension in England. The election of 1906 had resulted in a strong Liberal majority, which, first under Campbell-Bannerman, and from 1908 on under Asquith, addressed itself to reform legislation. The House of Lords vetoed much of the legislation, including Lloyd George's budget of 1909 – the budget that was, through increased taxes on the affluent, to finance a 'war against poverty.' Asquith introduced the Parliament Act, designed to assure the ultimate power of the House of Commons, and after two elections in 1910, in each of which his majority, although reduced, was maintained, he secured the reluctant assent of the House of Lords. Vincent's comments on that bitter conflict show him to have embraced the complete panoply of progressive liberalism, with a friendly hand extended to the emerging Labour party.

I am extremely glad that the Liberals were returned even if their majority comes entirely from labourites and nationalists [Irish home rule supporters] ... The Unionist [essentially the Conservative party, although the term 'unionist' was widely used so as to include Liberals opposed to Irish Home rule] tariff reform policy is absolutely fallacious and the German war scare is positively sinful. On the other hand the Liberal policy of Home Rule for Ireland at last does justice to a harassed and misunderstood country. Their programme of social reform is distinctly more commendable than that of nine dreadnoughts and the effort to annul the Lords' veto. This issue on which the campaign has been fought is, in my uninstructed opinion, eminently just.'[2]

During his Oxford days he continued to refer contemptuously to spokesmen for the British right wing. F.E. Smith was 'brilliantly clever' but a 'bounder'[3] and Sir Edward Carson, who spoke at an Oxford Union debate on the question of Irish Home Rule, was 'a genial ruffian.'[4] By contrast to them, Ramsay MacDonald, the Labour leader, 'struck me as fair-minded and tremendously sincere and in solemn earnest.'[5]

Along with the stock liberal ideas went an enthusiasm for the Empire. His views in this connection had been formed as a student of the Oxonian history department at Toronto and nurtured by many happy holidays in Britain. They owed a good deal, too, to the influence of two men outside the university, both many years his senior, but close associates and friends.

The first was Arthur J. Glazebrook, the youngest of five children in an English family that made its mark in the church, education, and the arts. Arthur followed a business career that brought him to Canada in 1883 and to Toronto in 1900 as an exchange broker. But business, by which he earned a modest but comfortable living, was subsidiary to an interest in ideas. He was a generous host, a witty talker with a Johnsonian gift for the pregnant phrase, and he had a special influence on young men. One of his favourites was Vincent Massey, whose interests in new ideas could not be satisfied by the slightly liberated Methodism of his family. The Glazebrook home, like the Wrong home, became a place of happy refuge for the young student.

Arthur Glazebrook had retained his association with people and causes in England. A close friend was Sir Alfred Milner, governor of

Cape Colony and high commissioner of South Africa during the crucial years from 1897 to 1905, who, at the end of the Boer war, devoted his energies to the restoration of a civil administration in the Boer republics. He gathered about him a group of able and devoted young men, most of them fresh from Oxford, who became known as 'Milner's kindergarten.' Milner was a devotee of Empire, with simple racist views of the god-given role of the Anglo-Saxon people in the evolution of civilization.

When Vincent left for Oxford in the autumn of 1911, Glazebrook wrote to Milner about his young friend.

I have given a letter of introduction to you to a young man called Vincent Massey. He is about 23 or 24 years of age, very well off, and full of enthusiasm for the higher things in politics, a very rare combination. He has been giving me the most invaluable assistance in the Round Table and in connection with the junior groups ... He is going home to England to Balliol, for a two years course in history, having already taken his degree at the Toronto University. At the end of his two years he expects to return to Canada and take up some kind of serious work, either as a professor at the University or at some other non-money making pursuit. I have become really very much attached to him, and I hope you will give him an occasional talk. I think it so important to get hold of these first-rate young Canadians, and I know what a power you have over young men. I should like to feel that he could become definitely by knowledge a Milnerite.[6]

But Vincent did not become a 'Milnerite.' When he finally met the great man he recorded these impressions, with the fine assurance of the young intellectual, and also with some shrewdness: 'Struck me being a man of splendidly high ideals and absolute sincerity but rather an administrator than a man of judgment or acute critical ability. He has I should think very deep prejudices.'[7] More attractive to Vincent than Milner was Lionel Curtis. He was the second major influence at this time in the shaping of Vincent's political outlook.

Lionel Curtis was one of Milner's 'kindergarten.' He had read classics at New College, Oxford, and after leaving the university in 1895 was active in mission and settlement work among the poor in London. In January 1910, he was one of a group that launched what was to be known as the Round Table, whose aim was, by wide publicity and discussion, to bring about 'an organic union ... by the establishment of an Imperial Government, constitutionally responsible to all the electors of the Empire and with power to act directly on the individual citizen.'[8]

Curtis was assigned the task of going to Canada and forming little groups of influential people who would accept the goals of the Round Table and discuss methods of implementing it. Toronto, with its nest of Oxford historians at the university, and with Milner's close friend, Arthur Glazebrook, active in the intellectual life of the city, was the key centre. Vincent was rapidly swept into the Round Table discussions, and became an enthusiastic and central figure in a group that eventually contained many of the leading men in education and business – Joseph Flavelle, a millionaire with a Methodist conscience and a sharp mind, who, as chairman of the Imperial Munitions Board in Canada from 1914 to 1920, was the most powerful civil servant in the country; Edward Peacock, a former teacher at Upper Canada College, who launched a business career as private secretary to the head of a Toronto securities corporation and became, in a later English career, Sir Edward and a governor of the Bank of England; J.M. Macdonnell, an executive of the National Trust Company of Canada, and eventually its president; Sir Edmund Walker, president of the Canadian Bank of Commerce, a noted philanthropist and collector and patron of the arts; two Canadian correspondents of *The Times* of London, Sir John Willison and J.A. Stevenson; Sir Robert Falconer, the president of the University of Toronto; and a solid group of academics, including George Wrong, Edward Kylie, and Kenneth Bell of the history department, James Mavor, professor of political economy, and W.L. Grant, lecturer in colonial history at Oxford, 1906–10, professor of colonial history at Queen's, 1910–15, and principal of Upper Canada College from 1917 until his death in 1935.

Curtis was a great proselytizer, who aroused men by his own intense sense of conviction, his messianic ardour for a new age, and his gift both for lucid exposition and seductive rhetoric. In his exposition of Round Table ideas he was constantly idealistic, stressing a unified empire as a fulfilment of national aspirations and as a means by which individuals could assume their responsibilities. At the conclusion of the first part of his book, *The Problem of the Commonwealth*, he suddenly ceases to be a patient expositor and becomes an inspired preacher, the sentences taking on new and august rhythms, the language acquiring a scriptural resonance with echoes of seventeenth century religious poetry.

As sure as day follows the night, the time will come when they will have to assume the burden of the whole of their affairs. For men who are fit for it, self-government is a question not of privilege but rather of obligation. It is duty, not interest, which impels men to freedom, and duty, not interest, is the factor which turns the scale in human affairs. In peaceful and prosperous times it is all too easy for nations intent on 'the conquest of nature' to forget the task of controlling themselves, and to treat what is tasted, handled, or seen as the end and object of national endeavour. 'But when the whole world turns to coal' they see these things as the dust they are. They realize the nature of the quest upon which they are bent. They find that the one prize to which they are called is not the ease, nor wealth, but still, as of old, the arduous grail and the ensanguined crown. For material interests are matters of change – to-day one thing, to-morrow another. They are vapours of earth, clouds that blot the eternal sky, which shift with every shifting breeze, and bring to nought those who are minded to follow their track. Above and beyond them abides the unchangeable duty of each to his kind, primal, boundless, and sure as the firmament itself. Clouds will pass but the stars remain; and whenever the heavens are swept by some mighty wind, the nations will lift their eyes to those ancient lamps and reset their course to what was, is, and shall ever be, the end towards which the whole creation moves – the government of each by each, and of all by all.[9]

Vincent responded warmly to Curtis's message and approach. In many ways, Curtis was reminiscent of John Mott, like Mott an evangelist with an austere, intellectual side. Mott had seen the spread of Christianity as a forerunner of world government, and Curtis saw a similar role for British parliamentary government and a united Empire. The merging of religion and politics becomes explicit in this passage from Curtis's magnum opus, *Civitas Dei*. 'I see in these threadbare details [of the British parliamentary system] the first beginnings in the Christian era of the process whereby that creative and political idea, the Kingdom of God, as viewed and expounded by Jesus of Nazareth, is destined to be released. I believe that the process here begun will be continued, till the role of law produced from the mind and conscience of those who obey it will not be confined to natural frontiers.'[10]

The message of Curtis enabled Vincent to reconcile his liberalism with imperialism. He expounded his ideas in a remarkable article he wrote for the Oxford publication *The Blue Book*, entitled 'The Wrong Imperialism.' He argued that imperialism should not be associated with stock Tory ideas: 'loyalty to the past, to an immutable establishment, an unchanging constitution, the House of Lords, the Welsh Church, Imperial protection and the navy.' In a fine satirical passage, he ridiculed the emotional symbolism of Tory imperialism.

Theirs is an Imperialism strongly reminiscent of Mafeking Night, ringing with ill-considered oratory, and lavishly embellished with red bunting. It rejoices in insular arrogance and frank vulgarity. It looks longingly to that happy millennium when all the world will speak English and eat honest beef. In the music-halls it is interpreted by the stirring melodies of Boer War days; in the class-room it is graphically expressed by a much-ensanguined map of the world. Both are misrepresentations, if you will, but for cultivated audiences the same bristling lion and the same red paint are officially translated into dignified prose – and then the music-hall Imperialism loses all its picturesqueness and none of its vulgarity.[11]

He then shifted to the Canadian scene, and deplored the eagerness with which Conservatives saw in the defeat of reciprocity with the United States the triumph of crude economic imperialism.[12] Protectionism, he argued, would not work within the Empire – the Empire contained too many people who would not accept it – and far from providing a 'bond of Empire' would only make a wedge driving 'through the very heart of Imperial unity.'

At Balliol Vincent found a society highly receptive to political discussion. The great Jowett days were past when the master of the college set out 'to inoculate the world with Balliol' and largely succeeded.[13] But in Vincent's time there were men like Walter Monckton and Harold Macmillan who would play prominent roles in British politics; and the prime minister of the day, Herbert Asquith, was a quintessential Balliol man, whose language of public discourse hovered between legal precision and subtle eloquence. It was a society immensely attractive to Vincent: within its limited social range tolerant of eccentricity, not given to the idolizing of athletes in the manner of many Oxford colleges, revelling in dining clubs and societies where high thinking joined easily with high living. It was also a society darkened by the barbarism that Matthew Arnold saw as an essential characteristic of the English aristocracy. Vincent thus coolly recorded an example of aristocratic play: 'In evening several members of the Annandale Society – suspecting some hostility towards them in the College selected B.W. [Robin Barrington-Ward] Henry Boulby and me as their representative of the opposition. Grenfell [Hon. William] Grove came into my room assailed me personally, broke my windows to atoms and threw my bed into the "jungle." They did the same to Boulby and B.W.'s rooms.'[14] No wonder Evelyn Waugh characterized the Annandale society as 'arrogant, rowdy, and exclusive.'[15] This incident must have aroused doubts in Vincent about the nobility of the English aristocracy, but he managed in later life to conceal most of them.

Vincent looked upon his two years in Balliol as a brief golden age. It lived in his memory as an example of a vital community, and the friendships made there were more enduring than those he made in Toronto. But the actual Balliol years were not as important to him as he thought. To begin with, his stay at the college was short. He moved out of college rooms for the second year, and shared quarters in the town with Murray Wrong; and he returned to Toronto for the long summer of 1913, and there followed the conventional Toronto routine of holidays in Muskoka and, later on, attendance at the Canadian National Exhibition, with work on Hart House between periods of relaxation. At Balliol he was not a callow colonial waiting to receive the impression of a rich and ancient culture. He already knew England, and even Oxford, well, and he arrived in Oxford as already a man of affairs – a leader in a new political movement, the exponent of fresh educational ideas, and an editor and writer of self-assurance. In some respects, he brought more to Balliol than Balliol gave to him. *The Blue Book*, in which his article on imperialism appeared, was inaugurated and edited by him. It was in the general tradition of *The Arbor*, although the range of subjects was greater and the writing more accomplished. From within Balliol there were articles by L.B. Napier, R.A. Knox,

Walter Monckton, A.L. Smith, R.M. Barrington-Ward, and Murray Wrong; from outside, articles by Michael Sadler, G.D.H. Cole, and Denis Mackail. *The Blue Book* had a strong Canadian bias. Besides Vincent's article, Murray Wrong contributed a poem and a critical article on Francis Thompson, which demonstrated a wide familiarity with contemporary poetry. Margaret Wrong, Murray's sister, also at Oxford during these years, contributed a short story in which she drew upon her knowledge of French and Indian life along the St Lawrence; and, from Toronto, Pelham Edgar reviewed in a magisterial way *The Letters of George Meredith*. One of the best book reviews, possibly by Vincent, was of Stephen Leacock's *Sunshine Sketches*. 'The sentiment of Dr Leacock,' wrote the reviewer, 'is the healthy sentiment of the humorist, just as his humor is the humor of the man who sees a little deeper into things than the commonplace "literary gent." None of your roaring, bouncing transatlantic guffaws here – nor yet the jesting of the Common-Room, very precious, thin-blooded, with a long tail of allusion – just *Sunshine Sketches*.'

The diary for the Balliol days dwindles into a record of meetings and social engagements. He is an active member of two debating and discussion societies, the Arnold and the Brackenbury; he reads a paper on Edward Lear before a small literary group called the Mendicants; he appears as a 'super' in a production of *Julius Caesar* by the Oxford Dramatic Society; and he is active in the Ralegh Club, which, along with Lionel Curtis, then a special lecturer at Oxford, he had founded. The Ralegh Club (the spelling had a deliberately antique flavour) was really a branch of the Round Table with Oxonian trimmings. Besides Vincent, there were two other Canadians, Murray Wrong and Frank Underhill. Wrong was, of course, a close friend; Underhill, shy and introspective, was at that time an acquaintance, for whom Vincent developed a high regard that outlasted Underhill's repudiation of the Ralegh Club and all it stood for.

At Balliol Vincent had been more activist than student. Balliol was, for him, more a political than a scholarly community: a place where he made friends, worked with particular groups, and began to think of the role that he would play in society.

Vincent's subsequent brief and happy academic career at Victoria College and the University of Toronto was brought to an end by the war. He had been an enthusiastic officer in the Queen's Own Rifles during his undergraduate days; from 1915 to 1917 he was on active duty, achieving the rank of lieutenant-colonel in 1917 and the status of chief musketry officer for the large central Military District No. 2. All his service was in Canada, indeed largely confined to a small triangle of Toronto, Camp Borden, and Niagara. The speculation arises why he did not succeed in being posted overseas, given his intense love for Britain and the perfervid atmosphere, particularly in loyalist Toronto, as the war turned from colourful outing into a nightmare of slaughter. Jim Macdonnell and William Grant, close friends and brothers-in-law of Vincent, served overseas in front line units, and two of George Wrong's sons, Harold and Hume, did likewise. (Harold was killed on the Somme. The third son, Murray, tried to enlist but was turned down because of a weak heart.) Raymond, Vincent's brother of eighteen, promptly enlisted and, in a short time, had a brief terrifying experience of front line duty. In his memoirs, Vincent said: 'My war service in the Canadian Army was, perforce, in Canada (I was no happier about this than others who were unable to go overseas) and consisted of staff duties.' The 'perforce' may have several explanations. The family obligations were heavy. In a letter to her brother Murray, Margaret Wrong wrote sympathetically of Vincent's dilemma 'There is not a soul to take his place here. His father leaves everything to him now.'[16] In many respects, she speculated, Vincent would have preferred to resolve the dilemma by going to the front. Reasons of health may have been a factor also; no doubt there were still after-effects of the long bout with typhoid fever in the autumn of 1910. Certainly, the diary betrays no sense of guilt beyond a wry cynicism about his rapid rise in rank. He wrote to Murray Wrong: 'To make the position of a soldier permanently employed 2,000 miles behind the front-line trenches all the more anomalous they have made me a lieutenant-colonel. My resemblance to the Kentucky variety of officer is now complete save for one important respect – prohibition – which was put in force on Sept. 16 and has already proved to be a good thing.'[17]

His military activities had a pronounced political flavour. He had occasion to encounter at various times Canada's minister of militia and defence, Sam Hughes, and his diary becomes a minor document in the copious literature of abuse that minister inspired. He takes part in solemn conferences about the defence of the frontier and power plants, and records increased activity in training 'in view of possible trouble in Quebec.'[18] He has 'many talks ... with officers in training staffs who are victimized by the cessation of training on this side and the failure to recognize work done here as a consideration in appointments in England and France.'[19]

In early January 1918, Vincent was asked by Newton Rowell, former leader of the Liberal party in Ontario and a member of Borden's Union Government, to become associate secretary of the war committee of the cabinet. Despite the publicity given to the appointment, it turned out to be of minor importance. The war committee did not meet often, and Vincent's work consisted of liaison with various government agencies and the preparation of pamphlets describing Canada's war effort. Following the armistice he was appointed secretary of the repatriation and employment committee of the cabinet. When he left Ottawa in April 1919, he noted that the cabinet had 'decided contrary to my recommendations to scrap most of our machinery.' He added, 'Short is the vision and limited the courage of the statesman!'[20]

The Ottawa year had been more an exposure to the fumbling intricacy of government than a period of positive service. But he had left a good impression and had formed some helpful associations. One of these was with Joseph Flavelle, the chairman of the Imperial Munitions Board, and still a powerful force in governmental business despite accusations, passionate and exaggerated, of war profiteering.[21]

From the autumn of 1919 to the spring of 1925, Vincent was a businessman. He was secretary-treasurer of the Massey-Harris company until late in 1921, and then for over three years the president of the company. At the same time, he maintained his position as a patron of the arts and as a national expositor of cultural values. The diary gives the impression that business made only modest demands on his attention and his time. But any diary, especially a selective and fragmentary one like Vincent Massey's, tells us more about personal interests than about the current problems faced by the writer. Vincent's years as president were hard and disturbing ones for the company – for the first time in its history there were over-all losses recorded in the yearly reports, with the suspension of dividends. But they were also, according to Merrill Denison, the official historian of

Massey-Harris, crucial years during which policies of retrenchment and preparation were skilfully blended so that in 1925 the company was prepared to take full advantage of improved conditions. Denison said the period 1921–5 'witnessed greater changes in farm machinery and agricultural techniques than had the four previous decades,' and he praised the Massey regime for preparing for 'the swift changes in the economic climate' and for estimating accurately 'the needs and nature of the times.'[22]

The major credit for these wise policies should probably go to the general manager, Thomas Bradshaw. When Vincent became president, he insisted that Bradshaw should become the chief executive officer, reporting directly to the board of directors, and that the president should confine himself to broad matters of policy – internally to the relations between workers and management, externally to the relations with the government and to the expansion of overseas trade, in short, to the politics of business. Vincent addressed himself to three major questions: the further development of workers' councils, informal organizations in which workers and management discussed company policy, particularly with respect to wages and working conditions; the tariff, which was becoming a crucial issue; and world trade. The Liberal government of Mackenzie King was obviously intent on lowering tariffs on agricultural implements, its theoretical tenderness for low tariffs transformed into official policy by pressure from western farmers. The speech in which King praised Vincent Massey and hailed him as a cherished seer was also the speech in which Vincent Massey, listening in the galleries, detected a 'sinister reference to the tariff.'[23] At the time Massey-Harris was leading a consortium of agricultural implement manufacturers in an attack on government policy. When substantial tariff reductions were announced in the budget, Vincent proclaimed his firm opposition. When the leader of the opposition, Arthur Meighen, detected some wavering in the official Massey-Harris position, Vincent wrote to him saying that he regarded the new duties 'as having done grave injury to the industry of which we form a part,' and concluded, in a mood of righteous indignation: 'It is difficult to avoid a feeling of deep resentment at the action of the Government. We were assured by responsible Ministers, up to the very last moment, that nothing would be done to injure the farm implement industry. The whole attitude of the Cabinet, in this matter, seems to reveal an even mixture of cynicism and hypocrisy.'[24] Shortly after, however, Massey-Harris issued a statement, widely printed in newspapers, breathing a generous spirit of reconciliation, and indicating that the company could live with the new policy. The principal author of the statement was Vincent Massey, and there were suggestions that he had in private discussions worked out an arrangement for cushioning the blow through related economic concessions. Whether or not Massey had worked them out, concessions were indeed made of such a nature that the Massey-Harris Company could comfortably live with the reduced tariff. The two concessions were the remission of the sales tax on agricultural implements and the placing of raw materials, such as steel, pig iron, and paint, entering into the manufacturing of farm implements either on the free list or in a reduced scale of duties.

Massey-Harris had become an international company, and during the depressed years 1921–5 its overseas sales had compensated for the collapse of the Canadian market. In the summer of 1924, following the resolution of the tariff crisis, Vincent set out on an extended trip during which he visited the various European offices. As far as Vincent's recorded impressions are concerned, however, the trip turned into an exploration of Communist Russia. To most Canadians, the Soviet Union was either a bright Utopia or a sinister threat. Vincent maintained a cool objectivity. Initially, 'all classes looked reasonably well fed and happy.'[25] He was pleased to find that some criticism of the state was tolerated. At the theatre that he inevitably attended, he saw a play that satirized in broad terms 'the mechanical quality of the communist state.'[26] He listened sympathetically to Walter Duranty, the American journalist and Russian expert, who explained the uglier aspects of Communism in terms of the slave mentality developed under oppression and the fanaticism of a new religion; and argued that the doctrine of the domination of the proletariat could be understood as a justification for giving power to the only class not tainted with its abuse. But Vincent's over-all impression became steadily gloomier. Russia was a depressed, melancholy, humourless, cruel society. He found a little relief in attending a splendid service at an Orthodox church, which was 'full of interesting people chiefly of the aristocratic and educated classes – mostly poorly dressed and with faces that bore the mark of suffering.'[27]

The Russian experience seems to have had a democratizing influence on the young executive. On the final stage of the return trip to
England, he reported the following incident: 'Been rather disgusted
on the train at group of English men who were in the restaurant car,
were not pleasant. Discovered they were members of the Exec. of the
Transport Workers' Union of G.B. Met several of them, got to like
them and finished up the voyage by drinking whiskies and soda with
Ben Tillett MP and his pals. Most men are not too bad when you see
them "close up".'[28]

By 1924, then, Vincent Massey had developed both a theoretical and
a practical interest in politics, but a political career was still only one of
several choices offered to him. He could follow the life of a gentleman
patron of the arts and exercise more systematically his skills as a literary
journalist and public speaker. His interest in education gave these
activities the serious, public-spirited tone that he found necessary, but
interest in education waxed and waned unpredictably and he had now
cut himself off from his base in the academic world. He could continue
his business career now with confidence. But he was impatient of its
grubby details, and fellow businessmen were suspicious of one who
played comic roles on the stage and listened to Beethoven quartets.
Politics, he reflected, could give him a chance to develop his large views
about foreign trade, the Empire, and industrial peace; and the
politician, who used words cunningly, could exercise great power.
Moreover, if he chose politics, he could rely on strong domestic
support.

Alice Massey, as we have seen, rejoiced in her skills as a housewife.
But she was no recluse: she had grown up in a home in which public life
was a natural extension of domesticity. Both her parents came from
families deeply rooted in the Canadian Maritimes, with Loyalist and
Anglican traditions. In his rapid rise from humble beginnings, Sir
George Parkin had paralleled the career of Hart Massey, although
Parkin's success was measured in influence and not in wealth. After
graduating from the University of New Brunswick in 1867, he had
been a schoolmaster for twenty years in his native province. He had
spent one year, 1873–4, at Oxford, had spoken about the Empire at the
Union, and had made an enduring impression on his contemporaries,
some of whom, like Milner and Asquith, were to become dominating
figures in Britain before the first world war. Later he was persuaded to

become a spokesman for the Imperial Federation League, and for six years he carried his message throughout the Empire, 'the bag man of the Empire' in Lord Roseberry's words, or, in the more flattering designation of *The Times*, the man who 'shifted the mind of England.' Then followed seven years as principal of Upper Canada College, and in 1902 a final appointment as secretary of the Rhodes Trust.

The Parkin house, both in Toronto and England, was a meeting place for influential spokesmen in education, in religion, and, above all, in the higher politics of the Empire. The four Parkin daughters married men who, like their father, were concerned about public questions and had positions from which they could exert considerable influence. Maude married William Grant, who became principal of Upper Canada College; Grace married an Englishman, Harry Wimperis, who in 1925 became director of scientific research in the air ministry, and played a leading role in the introduction of radar; and Marjorie married J.M. Macdonnell, who became president of the National Trust, and later served in the Diefenbaker cabinet. Alice did not have high academic credentials. Her education was sketchy – a year or so at a school in Switzerland when she was a young girl, and later, in Toronto, secondary education at Bishop Strachan School, from which she never graduated. There was no likelihood of her being called a bluestocking. She had managed, however, to give herself a general education: she had acquired some fluency in French and German; she was fond of the theatre, music, and painting, and in the last of these demonstrated practical skills.

The Parkin drive and self-assurance triumphed over her erratic and restricted education. In talks to the girls at Queen's Hall and to womens' clubs, she enunciated her ideas on university education, which, not surprisingly, resembled those of her father and Vincent. She became a spokesman for more and better job opportunities for women. She published a little book, largely statistical and analytical, about eighteen possible areas in which women could find interesting and important employment. 'American women,' she wrote, 'are moulding business, industrial, and social work. British women are counting in every sphere of activity. But to the average Canadian girl nursing, teaching, and stenography cover the range of her choice.'[29]

She became Vincent's confidante and adviser. A contemporary observation that 'without the driving force of a wonderfully able and ambitious wife behind him Vincent Massey would still be dabbling in amateur theatricals' contained an element of truth within the gross exaggeration.[30] Undoubtedly Alice helped Vincent to make up his mind about entering politics. Patron of the arts and national education was all very well, but it could not match a public position of power and influence. Vincent, it no doubt crossed her mind, might become prime minister.

If Vincent resolved on a political career, would he ally himself with the Liberal party, specifically with the Liberal party as it was being shaped by Mackenzie King? His early undiluted liberalism had been clouded by events. He had supported Union Government and had parted with the Laurier Liberals who had opposed conscription. In a letter to his father-in-law of 28 September 1917, he speaks slightingly of the Liberal party: it 'has a French-Canadian core. This element together with those voters of alien origin which the war time Election Act still leaves on the register must needs give it a colour which will lead many loyal Liberals to disregard the counsels of their traditional leaders.' In subsequent comments on the Liberal party after the war he is no less disparaging. He refers to 'the watery sentimentality' of King, and goes on, 'I am sure there could be nothing more damnable in political life than sentiment completely detached from reality.'[31] In another letter at the same time he writes 'Mackenzie King commands but little respect, and has few friends even in his own party.'[32]

But despite these damning comments, he still supports the Liberal party *faut de mieux*, and even extends a faded bouquet to its leader. 'King,' he adds, 'is very wisely playing for as much support from the Progressives as he can get, and this, I feel, is really in the national interest.'[33] What Vincent wants is a clear cut ideological split between the two major parties, with the Liberals absorbing the farmer's Progressive movement in the west. He enunciates this in a letter to his old Balliol friend, Robin Barrington-Ward. Although he does not say so directly, he would clearly find it easy to support a Liberal party of uncompromising liberal views. He has not yet permitted his business interests to deflect his theoretical ideas.

If Mackenzie King's flirtation with the West is successful, and his party, in its policies, swings to the left, Liberalism in Canada stands some chance of meaning something again. If it becomes the low tariff radical party it will throw the type of

Liberal, who is an ultra-Conservative under another name, into the Conservative camp where he belongs, and we may have some chance of having two great parties, representative of the Dominion as a whole and sincerely divided on the ancient lines. If this happens and a revived Conservative party, with protection and the greater emphasis on the Imperial tie, emerges on the one hand, confronted, on the other, by a new Liberal party adhering to low tariff, or free trade, and with its emphasis on Canadian nationalism, then I think the political air will be very much clearer, and the utterances of politicians inevitably more sincere.[34]

When in the summer of 1925 Vincent began his serious political conversations with Mackenzie King, he was not talking to a political leader he admired, much less to a friend. King's initial enthusiasm for Massey may have been based largely on political expediency – here was a leading businessman who was prepared to support him and his party, living in a city that had abandoned the Liberal party in the elections of 1911 and 1917. At first King asked him to stand for election with no commitment that he would have a cabinet post; but when Vincent indicated that he would not take such a step without the assurance of a position of responsibility, King invited him to enter the cabinet immediately as a minister without portfolio, a specific cabinet post to come as soon as he had been elected.

In a lacklustre political scene, the announcement in early September 1925 of Vincent's joining the Liberal cabinet was received by the press as a major event and another witness to the political cunning of the prime minister. The appointment seemed to proclaim that the Liberal tariff policy was not harmful to eastern industry, since the president of one of the largest manufacturing firms had joined the enemy. Even the violently partisan opposition newspapers agreed that getting Vincent Massey was a great political coup, since he was widely and favourably known as a man of wealth who had devoted himself to sound public causes. The Toronto *Star* was loud in praise; it was Vincent's principal supporter, its regular and lengthy reports on his career and present activities achieving a consistently dithyrambic tone.

Vincent was offered several ridings, including Stormont and N.E. Toronto, but chose Durham. He was now a resident in the constituency, his family associations with the area had been close, and he could invoke the memory of the great Liberal, Edward Blake, who had been a member for West Durham. Durham had been held by a Conservative since 1914. But the present member, F.W. Bowen, had had the advantage in the last election of a split vote between Liberals and Progressives. Vincent was now assured the Progressive vote, and this gave him a lively hope of success.

In his memoirs, he observed that the Liberal party went to the country with a particularly dreary set of policies. Massey, the campaigner, thought otherwise. From the beginning he sought to put the campaign on a high plane. The Conservative policy of protection was, he maintained, a sectional policy that would destroy Canadian unity, setting east against west. In his opening speech he proclaimed his belief in a moderate tariff, and his tenderness for the welfare of western farmers.

I have never been a believer in high protection. My lack of belief in that doctrine is not due to any sudden conversion, but due to my approaching the problem many years ago as a student, and also my relations today, as a man of business.

I believe that those who deliberately attempt to impose upon this country a measure in face of determined and solid and unyielding opposition of 2,000,000 people in three great provinces are assuming a very great responsibility which makes one tremble for the consequences. We businessmen in the central provinces find it difficult to get it out of our heads that the west is not simply a market for eastern goods, but a community with ideas of its own ... Canada is suffering primarily because hundreds of thousands of farmers have been for four years out of the buying market.[35]

'The Observer,' writing a special column in the Toronto *Globe* about this speech, outdid the *Star* in rhapsodic approval:

I find it difficult to imagine any single speech that could conceivably have been made in Canada at this hour which would have counted for more in the present election campaign or in the future political development of the dominion. The only recent political utterance I can compare it with was Mr Bryan's famous 'cross of gold' speech.

That the head of a great manufacturing concern, brought up and living in Toronto, and with his social and business connections, should say such things is one of the most inspiring exhibitions of Canada's disinterestedness and courage that our public life has known at least in our generation. It touches the heroic.[36]

Vincent was not successful in keeping the Durham campaign on a high theoretical plane. The Conservatives concentrated on him with a venomous intensity, and they had some telling points. His continuing association with the Massey-Harris Company made him vulnerable. Was he not as president proclaiming that Massey-Harris supported his moderate tariff views when it was well known that many prominent shareholders strongly disapproved of his stand? The question of conflict of interest had not yet achieved its present prominence, and was not actively raised in the campaign. It had been raised privately, however, by some of his private advisers, in particular by Sir Joseph Flavelle, who had asked him the following questions: '(1) Can you discharge your honest obligations to the shareholders of your company if you continue as President, while you spend practically the whole of your term in Ottawa? (2) Can you, with propriety, continue to be identified with large Corporations in senior position, while a Minister of the Crown?'[37] Vincent finally saw the force of these questions and on 5 October – three weeks before the election – announced his resignation as president and director of the Massey-Harris Company, and as a member of the boards of the Canadian Bank of Commerce and the Mutual Life Assurance Company. The announcement began with a solemn, self-denying statement. 'During the very short time I have been in public life I have come to believe that, even at some personal sacrifice, I should resign from all directorships in corporations, so as to leave myself perfectly free to discuss and deal with public issues without having my actions or my motives subject to question.'[38] He was much commended for his action, but cynical observers pointed out (with some cause) that he had been forced into it by the increasingly vocal protests of Massey-Harris shareholders.

Another and more serious issue was Massey's tergiversation on the tariff issue, highlighted by Meighen's intervention in the campaign late in October and his insistence that Vincent permit him to publish the April correspondence. Massey reiterated in a telegram that the letters had been written 'officially on behalf of company representing its point of view and cannot be released.'[39] Publicly he admitted his inconsistency, but argued that he had been guilty of a temporary aberration from a basic Liberal point of view.

Other issues were of a personal, petty nature. It was contended, for instance, that the Massey-Harris Company employed, proportionately, far more workers in its American plant at Batavia than at its Canadian headquarters, and that, presumably, Vincent was responsible for this. On an even less elevated plane, it was asserted that he had left the Methodist Church for the Anglican, an action that presumably betokened religious skittishness and a drift towards establishment conservatism. Vincent had indeed discussed confirmation in the Anglican Church during a visit to England in 1924, but he was still a member of the Methodist Church. He refused to make any response to the criticism, contenting himself with a statement that his church affiliations had nothing to do with his politics.

Vincent conducted a vigorous campaign. He held nightly meetings and gave numerous speeches. Alice was always present on the platform, and when her husband was subjected to heckling, suffered visibly. But Vincent's platform manner, fashioned on debating societies at Balliol, in the university classroom, and on the Canadian Club speaking circuit, could not easily be adapted to the rough and tumble of politics. His speeches were unpunctuated by the ritual slogans for which political audiences expectantly wait and to which they joyfully respond. In addition Vincent didn't devote enough time to canvassing the individual voters, perhaps sensing the distance that separated the sophisticated Toronto industrialist from his constituents. Liberal city newspapers were not always happy in their supporting stories. The characterization of Alice as the Lady Astor of Canadian politics was not, for instance, an effective way to win the endorsement of rural voters.

In the election Massey received 6074 votes and his opponent 7020. The Conservative victor, F.W. Bowen again, was a Durham worthy, whose family had deep roots in the country. He was an honourable man who refrained from personal abuse of his opponent; he was also an unpretentious man who would continue his parliamentary record of the last four years and serve his party in untroubled silence.

CHAPTER SIX

The American
Years

The defeat in Durham had not quenched Massey's political ambitions. Indeed, he could argue that he had reason to take heart, for he had faced formidable handicaps and had fallen short of victory by only a small margin. Moreover, he was one of many Liberal casualties, of which the prime minister himself was the chief. In the year between his defeat in Durham and his appointment to Washington – during which the Liberals clung to power with only a minority in Parliament, lost it, and then triumphantly regained it – Massey pursued a vigorous political course, confident that a cabinet post – in all likelihood trade and commerce, frequently mentioned by King – would be offered him. King still thought of him as a close political associate who shared his own high-minded attitude towards public life. 'It is a blessing to me,' he wrote, 'to have someone who shows the spiritual side of public endeavour. Massey will be a great help, a tower of strength, of that I am sure. Our aims and ideals are the same.'[1] Massey was despatched to confer with Charles Dunning, the Liberal premier of Saskatchewan whom King wanted for his cabinet, and he was a principal adviser in the preparation of the speech from the throne. He became the liaison man between the Liberals and the Progressives, who held the balance of power; he conducted behind-the-scene discussions with the Progressive leaders that swung their support to the minority Liberal government and enabled it to survive a crucial vote. In his memoirs, Massey recalled that his conversations played a 'decisive part in the course of events.' In his diary he was more positive: his conversations, he asserted, 'saved the government from defeat.'

King appeared to be eager to have Massey in the cabinet, and explored the possibility of finding a safe riding – first, in Saskatchewan, where, however, it was feared that the Massey-Harris company associations would be a fatal obstacle; then in Quebec, where, unfortunately, King reported 'our Quebec friends hesitate on finding him a seat.'[2] Massey still remained a key adviser after the dissolution of Parliament and the calling of an election. King was elevating a constitutional question – the governor-general, Lord Byng, had refused him dissolution but granted it shortly afterwards to the new Conservative government of Meighen – into a major issue, and Massey was concerned lest the Liberals should arouse loyalist sentiment against themselves. He insisted on maintaining a high constitutional stand, and, at the same time, avoiding any suggestion of an attack on the royal representative. In this attitude Mackenzie King may well have sensed a moderation inappropriate for the anointed Liberal; but he still professed full support for Massey's political ambitions. He proposed that Vincent should run in North Temiskaming, which was looked upon as a safe Liberal riding. Massey's nomination was contingent upon his receiving a unanimous call from the riding, but the call never came. On 27 August 1926, King wrote in his diary, in the tone of a sympathetic but uninvolved observer, 'I am sorry Vincent Massey will not get N. Temiskaming.'

Despite King's repeated declarations, both to Massey directly and to his daily confessional, the diary, that he was anxious to have Vincent as a colleague, the thought is inescapable that his unconscious warred with his conscious wishes. His doubts must have been actively aroused when, at the first cabinet meeting following the disastrous 1925 election, Vincent was the only member to support Byng in his preference for inviting Meighen to form a government.[3] King's doubts were no doubt sharpened by unfavourable reports from influential Liberals. Sir Clifford Sifton 'did not favour Vincent Massey': 'he was a "cobdenite Liberal" waiting to reduce duties,' and, less enigmatically, he 'lacked experience.'[4] Joseph Atkinson, the increasingly powerful owner of the Toronto *Star* that was the rallying point for Liberal interests in Ontario, was strongly opposed to Massey, who was 'too aloof, not in touch with people.'[5] He preferred Percy Parker, an old-time politician. King was not convinced: if Massey lacked the common touch, he was, unlike Parker, a man of sober habits. Even Newton Rowell, a leading Liberal, retired from active politics but still greatly influential, who had been Vincent Massey's political patron, was lukewarm in his endorsation; he said that Massey was 'able, had limitations, not likely to have many enthuse, but a good man and right stamp for public life.'[6]

Early in 1926 King began to mention a Washington appointment as appropriate for Massey. Vincent was not enthusiastic; no doubt he sensed that such a move was King's way of politely closing the door to a political career. The prime minister made the formal proposal in a letter of 25 April 1926, in which he strongly urged acceptance 'despite my own personal preference and desire to have you at my side in the House of Commons to which I have looked forward more than words can express.'[7] Two months later, Massey was still wavering in his reply. He inquired about London, presumably thinking that the current high commissioner, Peter Larkin, who was advanced in years, might wish to retire.[8] King brushed the idea aside. Washington was a certainty, but London was not yet a counter in the game of political bargaining. There may have been, one suspects, a gentleman's agreement, however, that if the Liberals won the election and Larkin, for any reason, left his post, Massey would succeed. Washington, under these conditions, would be palatable. It would be a pleasant prologue, a first act in the swelling imperial theme.

The official announcement was made shortly after the election of 14 September 1926, which gave the Liberals a comfortable majority. Massey was not to take up his appointment in Washington until the new year, and King proposed that he should first go to the Imperial Conference that was to meet in London in mid-October. Vincent could not have been more subtly flattered. He was thereby elevated to a position of authority in the party; the other senior delegate besides the prime minister was Ernest Lapointe, minister of justice, King's lieutenant in Quebec, and a man whom Massey looked upon as the chief spokesman of enlightened French Canadian liberalism. The appointment seemed to carry a hint of what lay ahead for Massey once he had served his apprenticeship in the United States. He would go to England now as a man about to assume a new and interesting position, and his English connections, carefully nurtured since Balliol days, could be greatly extended.

Massey played little role in the actual discussions. The Canadian delegation and, to a great degree, the conference were dominated by Mackenzie King, acting with a new self-assurance bred by his victory in the election, and with a conciliatory magnanimity now that he had won his self-proclaimed battle with old Tory imperialism. In his diary Massey demonstrated a greater interest in informal discussions outside the conference. At social gatherings and at weekends in country houses, he had an exhilarating sense of being close to the centre of British political life. He delighted in the intellectual boldness that enlivened upper class English society. John Strachey, for instance, was beginning to emerge as the ideologist of the left; Massey described him as 'a really good example of the intellectual and aristocratic recruit in the ranks of labour'; and noted with satisfaction that he was 'a fully accredited member of the Labour Party, and a publisher of a Miner's Strike Journal.'9 He was less impressed by another aristocratic convert to socialism. At a lunch with Sir Oswald and Lady Mosley he 'told them I thought they had laid the local colour on too thick as members of the Labour Party. Not impressed with Mosley's sincerity, a touch of the charlatan about him, brilliant as he is.'10 Even within the Conservative party, Massey discovered signs of restiveness. He found his old Balliol classmate Harold Macmillan 'a young and somewhat insurgent MP distressed by the apparent lack of guts in Stanley Baldwin which prevents his fine qualities from being made effective.'11 Macmillan's strictures were repeated more sharply by Tom Jones, a permanent civil servant closely associated with the prime minister's office. Baldwin, he said, had 'good will,' but was hobbled by 'indecision and mental indolence. He accepts on any given policy the strategy worked out for him ...'12 Massey himself took up the critical theme. Austen Chamberlain, the British foreign minister, he observed patronizingly, was 'a man of second-rate mind, but high character.'13

If Massey responded with considerable satisfaction to sharp comments on the establishment, he did so in an impeccably establishment environment. Tom Jones, for instance, delivered his confidences about Stanley Baldwin during a visit to Cliveden, Lady Astor's country house. Massey was on easy terms, too, with the hierarchy of the Anglican Church, and this gave him a chance to pursue a personal mission. He had come to the conclusion that he should put an end to his formal association with Methodism – the faith that for over a hundred years had sustained and inspired his family. The process of withdrawal had been going on for some time; he had already talked to the Canadian Archbishop Mathison about the possibility of confirmation.[14] During one of the dinner parties he attended in England, he quoted with relish a remark by the Bishop of Durham in explanation of why many Presbyterians remained outside the United Church of Canada: the bishop thought that the Presbyterians had a 'superior commercial morality'; a Nova Scotia friend of his maintained that 'he never gave credit to Methodists.'[15] Methodism abandoned, the easiest transition was to Anglicanism, the church that had contained the original Methodist movement. The motives for change were not doctrinal; they were largely aesthetic and social. And if he did not enter the Anglican Church with the zeal of the convert, he did so under the highest auspices. His memoirs relate that during this visit to England 'in a conversation with the Archbishop of Canterbury, Dr Randall Davidson, I mentioned that, although I had attended the Anglican Church ever since my university days, I had never been confirmed, and I thought I would like to be. The Archbishop said he would be delighted to officiate if I would come to Lambeth Palace Chapel one day. This I did. There were four people present: the Archbishop, Mrs Davidson, Alice, and I.'[16]

If the archbishop presided over Vincent's entrance into the Anglican Church, King George gave royal blessing to his admission to the diplomatic world. The diary has a good many references to royalty during the fall of 1926 – at the Elysée Palace in Paris, where he represented Canada at the opening of the Maison des Étudiants Canadien and listened rapturously to a speech by the Prince of Wales; at a reception at Buckingham Palace, where Alice and he were presented to the king and queen, and he reported that the king was 'deliciously indiscreet' in his conversation;[17] and at an evening party given by the Duke and Duchess of York, where, on being summoned to meet their host and hostess, they had apologetically to break off from a lively engagement with the Prince of Wales. The climax of this royal progress came shortly before the Masseys' departure for Canada. Vincent had an official audience with the king. The description in the journal has an agreeably light touch. The 'jaunty, frock-coated' young man acting as lord-in-waiting carried off each of 'the little group waiting their turn in a manner faintly resembling the selection of patients in a dentist's waiting room.' 'The King was interested in the fact that my appointment as a representative of a government other than of Great Britain was still his appointment. "I appoint you, don't I?" he asked with real appreciation of the constitutional significance of this new departure.'[18]

Vincent Massey thus entered upon his American appointment with imperial assurance – a sense of easy access to the upper reaches of English society, the blessing of the head of the state church, the endorsement of the royal head of the Commonwealth. Yet all this, he realized, was not an essential preparation for his new role. The Empire had evolved. The Round Table dream of an imperial parliament had long since faded; he now accepted emotional and cultural ties in the place of constitutional legislation, and complete freedom of action in the place of selected subservience. At the conference that he had just attended, the new relationship had been officially endorsed and embodied in words. The declaration had all the resonant eloquence and captivating vagueness of Pauline theology. 'They [the Dominions] are autonomous communities within the British Empire, equal in status, in no way subordinate one to another in any aspect of their domestic or external affairs, though united by a common allegiance to the Crown, and freely associated as members of the British Commonwealth of Nations.'[19] Mackenzie King had been responsible for some specific refinements of the grand theory. Henceforth, the governor-general would be a representative of the king and not of the British government; Great Britain would appoint high commissioners to the dominions who would be the direct representatives of the British government. These were measures that further illuminated the independence of Canada within the Commonwealth. But the appointment by Canada of a full fledged representative to a foreign state was, certainly to the outside world, the most conspicuous badge of sovereignty. The Washington appointment thus had a symbolic significance perhaps more important initially than its actual political and diplomatic substance. In addition, it carried with it echoes of an old and passionate debate.

The proposal to appoint a special Canadian representative to the United States had been raised in the latter part of the nineteenth century. The argument for it was not so much a natural extension of autonomy as the pressure of necessity. Canada's international relations, outside of Britain and the Empire, were largely American; the core of these relations was trade and commerce, and their satisfactory treatment demanded expert information, prolonged discussion, and a sympathetic understanding of each country's position. Entrusting these negotiations to the British embassy in Washington became increasingly unsatisfactory. Canada's colonial status in foreign affairs demanded an awkward and time-consuming procedure – first, between the British embassy and the governor-general, who was the representative of the British government in Canada; then to the British foreign or colonial office; then back to the government of either Canada or the United States – what an American secretary of state referred to as 'this wordy triangular ordeal.'[20] Moreover, this procedure was necessary for a very large share of the business that came to the British embassy. Estimates by British ambassadors of the proportion of purely Canadian work varied from the substantial to the dominant; and such work had to be undertaken by officials who had little knowledge of Canada, or by ambassadors, many of whom never visited Canada, and all of whom were obligated to address themselves primarily to Anglo-American relations.

The first world war sharply dramatized the Canadian need for a separate relation with the United States and generated arrangements that gave a firm basis for the appointment of a Canadian minister. After the United States entered the war in 1917, Canada found it essential to appoint a war mission, which had, in practice, a diplomatic role. It 'took over the control of commercial and financial matters arising out of the war and established direct contacts with the relevant US government departments.'[21] In the peace-making discussions following the war, the prime minister, Sir Robert Borden, insisted on a specific Canadian role, and secured at least symbolic recognition by winning the right for Canada to sign the peace treaty and to have separate membership in the League of Nations. The time was now ripe for legislation establishing a Canadian representative in Washington. This legislation was introduced in May 1920, and passed. It provided for a representative to be known as 'His Majesty's Envoy Extraordinary and Minister Plenipotentiary for Canada,' responsible to the Canadian government. He was, however, to be part of the establishment of the British embassy; indeed, he was to be a second-in-command, who, in the absence of the British ambassador, would take charge of the whole embassy and represent imperial as well as Canadian interests. This was a concession to British opinion, especially to the foreign office, which feared a completely separate Canadian representative would shatter the unity of imperial policy, confuse foreign powers not versed in the metaphysics of the Commonwealth, and make any orderly control of foreign policy difficult. Borden's legislation would preserve at least the façade of imperial unity.

Although provision was made each year for the expenses of the Canadian representation, nothing happened until 1926 when Mackenzie King finally took action. He dramatically altered the Borden legislation. King's idea of Canadian autonomy was not to expand responsibility in the Commonwealth but to consolidate it in the nation. The Canadian legation would be completely independent of the British embassy; informal consultation would take the place of formal obligation, and instead of having any responsibility for co-ordinating imperial policy, the Canadian minister would simply make his decisions in a Commonwealth context.

The sharper edge that King had given to the concept of the appointment – the emphasis upon the minister's independence and complete responsibility to the Canadian government – aroused some initial doubts both in Canada and in the United Kingdom. The imperialist wing of the Conservative party prophesied the demise of the Empire and the reduction of Canada's position in the world. Tommy Church, Toronto's ex-perpetual mayor, and MP-elect for Toronto N.W., declared that 'the appointment of Vincent Massey would lower Canadian status to that of the 26 Latin Republics represented in Washington.'[22] British newspaper comment was conspicuously cool, whether it came from the right or the left. The *Daily Telegraph* thought that the appointment was premature, the action of 'status worshippers,'[23] and the *New Statesman* argued that the appointment would confuse the US Senate with 'its old conception of the British Empire as a single power with an undivided aim.'[24] There were suggestions that the United States was unhappy about the Canadian move. The *New York Times* reported that Calvin Coolidge was not prepared to reciprocate with the appointment of an American minister to Canada. But if Coolidge had doubts, he did not express them publicly, and by his action he swiftly disposed of them. A few weeks after Vincent Massey presented his credentials, Coolidge appointed William Phillips as the American minister to Canada. Phillips was a senior official who was, at the time, ambassador to Belgium, and there could then be no doubt about the acceptance of the Canadian move and the seriousness of the American response.

Certainly the American press gave a great deal of attention to the appointment. Some of this was the attention that newspapers always pay as a matter of course to the first in any category, but the appointee himself aroused some modest flights of journalistic prose. Not only did Mr Massey possess the usual appurtenances of the senior diplomat – wealth, social status, and business experience – but he added others, less common, but no less desirable, namely a genuine interest in the arts and a cultivated and urbane manner. The Boston *Globe* printed a story from Toronto that did not treat these qualities with proper respect: 'his main contributions to life in Washington will most probably be the importation of a most beautifully cultivated Oxford accent.'[25] But the stories originating in the United States varied from the respectful to the reverential, sometimes with an imaginative flourish that was never demeaning. The Boston *Transcript* declared 'that his home in Toronto has taken the place of the late Professor Goldwin Smith whose hearthstone was the Mecca of European and American statesmen and scholars and artists.'[26] A good deal of attention was given to personal appearance. Massey gave the impression of youthfulness; and, at the same time, he communicated a gentle sense of melancholy that aroused associations of a religious or scholarly nature. A verbal portrait that appeared in several papers, both Canadian and American, touched upon all these qualities; beneath the elaborate search for associations and analogies, it is a good picture of Vincent Massey, aged 40, launched firmly on his public career, secure and happy in his marriage and children, his mannerisms and eccentricities now moulded into a distinctive style:

Vincent Massey, in the flesh, is essentially boyish. Tall, spare, clean shaven, a trifle ascetic of countenance, his black eyes deep set and luminous, bespeak that

vigor of mind and body inevitably associated with youth. Were it not for a
soldierly snappiness in turn and bearing he might be mistaken for a budding
poet or a clerical brother of some monastic fraternity 'let loose upon earth a
while.' For the Massey countenance, despite its suggestion of youth, is somewhat
gloomy; there is about it – except when its owner is mentally and physically on the
qui vive *– something of Hamlet's melancholy; one's eyes instinctively drop from*
its contemplation in search of that which it seems to suggest – a coarse cassock, a
knotted girdle and sandals.[27]

In Toronto, Massey was given a series of farewell dinners that
celebrated the man and the peculiar distinction of his appointment. On
24 January 1927, representatives of the University of Toronto
community assembled in the great hall of Hart House to do him
honour – governors, stewards of Hart House, deans of faculties, and
heads of colleges. The chairman of the board, Dr H.J. Cody, the
president, Sir Robert Falconer, the chancellor, Sir William Mulock, the
warden of Hart House, Burgon Bickersteth, rendered their tribute.
Vincent must have meditated on how his youthful concept of a great
and splendid meeting place in the university had now become the
setting for his triumphal graduation to a life of public service. Two days
later representatives of the political, legal, and commercial establishment assembled to do him honour in the dark-panelled main room of
the York Club, where traditionally affluence and higher education had
formed a polite alliance. A week later the climactic celebration took
place at the Arts and Letters Club. In his diary Vincent noted the first
two events with a few factual details. This event he described with
bubbling delight. The program consisted of a series of lantern slides
illustrating his personal history, an imaginary monologue by a middle-
western American farmer about the advent of the Canadian minister, a
short play in which Calvin Coolidge and the British ambassador
figured prominently, music by the Hart House Quartet, and finally the
presentation of a book beautifully bound in leather, with illuminated
cartoons, the work of J.E.H. MacDonald, a prominent member of the
Group of Seven. It was, Vincent wrote, a 'wonderful evening – with a
characteristic programme true to the best traditions of the Club.'[28]

Canadian newspaper comment on the appointment did not have the
ecumenical flavour of the official farewells. Massey had been an active

Liberal partisan, and he was fair game in the opposition press. The Toronto *Telegram*, the shrillest Tory voice, did its best to keep the appointment alive as a political issue. It was, acording to the *Telegram*, a betrayal of the Empire, and an absurdly wasteful expenditure. The *Telegram* despatched a veteran staff writer, Lucy Doyle, to follow Massey during his first days in Washington. She pursued him with unflagging animosity. He managed to avoid an initial confrontation by entering one door of the Mayflower Hotel, where he was staying, while his secretary, Tommy Stone, took the car to another.[29] Miss Doyle resorted to the technique of ridicule by irrelevant contrast. In an article headlined 'Washington not stirred,' she pointed out that the arrival of the new Canadian minister had been put in the shade by the arrival of another Canadian, the flamboyant evangelist Aimee Semple McPherson. The minister's 'installation,' she added, had been a 'dull affair.'[30]

Massey's fame as a Toronto host to the visiting great, his easy association with the English aristocracy, and his ready entrée to Rideau Hall as far back as his undergraduate days inspired speculation that he would use the Washington appointment for social display. Even the title he was given, 'Envoy Extraordinary and Minister Plenipotentiary,' was assumed to be a reflection of his preference for the pompous and high-sounding. Actually, the designation had been used in the original Borden legislation; it was, perhaps, thought of as a compensation for the modest status of minister. But speculation about Massey's love of display was given a factual base when he insisted upon the purchase of a handsome house for the new legation. The cost was $500,000 for building and furnishings – a very large sum at that time – and the outcry in the parliamentary opposition, the popular press, and even among government supporters was shrill and prolonged. But Mackenzie King, against all his canny Presbyterian instincts, stuck by his appointee and pushed the appropriation through a parliament that was either unenthusiastic or strongly opposed.

Massey devoted a good deal of space in his memoirs to the account of the purchase of the house, and clearly looked upon his action as justified by immediate needs and twice justified by subsequent developments. There is much to be said for his opinion. The house at 1746 Massachusetts Avenue was in an excellent location, and has become even more strategically situated with the movement into the area of government, university, and research organizations. It was, however, more suited for a residence than for an office; and contemporary critics sensed that he and his wife were swayed in their choice by the setting it provided for grand occasions – a noble staircase rising to a *piano nobile*, with large rooms ideal for dinners or receptions. The house, with its extensive dark panelling and general atmosphere of heavy opulence, did not lend itself to office use; and its subsequent conversion for that exclusive purpose (a house in another part of Washington was found for the ambassador) is reminiscent of the cruel transformation during the second world war of English country homes into army barracks.

A severe critic of the purchase was the permanent head of the department of external affairs, O.D. Skelton. Even after the purchase had been approved, he continued his dogged attack. In his memoirs Massey printed in its entirety Skelton's long letter to him on the subject – more, I think, to illustrate Skelton's intransigence than to present his argument. The incident did not point towards a happy relation between the new minister and the man in Ottawa who was to preside over Canada's external affairs during the years when they were emerging from obscurity. Although an embryonic department had existed since 1909, a definite structure had emerged only in 1925 with Skelton's appointment. Massey had for several years now enjoyed an easy relationship with the prime minister, who also held the external affairs portfolio in the cabinet: he may well have found irritating the insertion of a powerful intermediary. Temperamentally, the two men were not congenial. Both had come from the academic world; but for Massey the academic was only one – and a minor one at that – of the many worlds in which he moved comfortably. Skelton was the quintessential academic; he had been chairman of the department of political science and dean of arts at Queen's University, and he had written important, scholarly books. He had an incisive style, precise and exact, but tinged with irony, and carrying a lingering suggestion of his own superior wisdom. In manner he was mild and self-effacing, and he was quick to scent pretentiousness in others. Despite an early attempt to win a place in the British foreign service – modestly successful but never pursued – he now employed his formidable talents in the defence of his concept of Canada as a virtuous and stoutly independent country of predominantly British descent, set down, however, in an environment profoundly different from that of its parent. In basic concepts he and Massey were not far apart. The difference was more in style and emphasis. Massey believed that the offspring could emulate the manners and attitudes of the parent without bringing into question its own sturdy independence.

A month or so after the incident of the purchase of the house, Skelton and Massey clashed briefly on another matter. The matter was of minor importance, and the clash was contained within an icily polite exchange of letters. But the temperamental variations between the two men were sharply incised. In some comments on the official Canadian reception planned for the American minister, Skelton used the word 'informal.' Massey was immediately on the alert to a possible threat to the dignity and importance of the new diplomatic order. He pointed out in a letter to the prime minister that the American ceremony for him 'was carried out with great dignity according to a rigidly prescribed form' and the American minister should be received in a similar way.[31] He sent to Skelton a memorandum (three copies) on the ceremony at the White House. Skelton replied with thinly disguised irritation. 'The use in my telegram of May 19 of the words "quite informally" was unfortunate, though it has unduly alarmed the guardians of propriety in the State Department ... I am sorry I used these words, which out of their spoken context seem to have given a wrong impression, but I think I could have assumed that, even if the United States State Department might fear that the Viscount Willingdon, formerly Governor of Bombay and Governor of Madras, would fail to see that the ceremony was carried through with all due propriety and respect, at least the Canadian Legation would have taken it for granted.'[32]

During the Washington days, there were no further overt examples of strained relations between Massey and Skelton. A single phrase in the diary two years later gives us, however, a clear view of Massey's attitude. During a visit to Ottawa, he reported a 'talk with Herr Doktor Skelton.'[33] The dry manner, the precise diction, and the assumption of superior knowledge are thus succinctly recorded.

The staff in Washington was small, and, since the department of external affairs had as yet few permanent officers upon whom the legation could draw, Massey took the initiative on two appointments.

One was Tommy Stone, a graduate of the University of Toronto who had won a Massey Fellowship and had used it for studies in Paris. He served as third secretary and as the minister's private secretary; genial, socially adept, with a quick and vigorous mind, he was an admirable choice. He and Vincent had a warm and friendly relationship. One senior assistant was Laurent Beaudry, well known in Quebec journalistic circles, and recommended by the department of external affairs. For a parallel English appointment Massey turned to the staff of the University of Toronto, after first offering the appointment to James Duncan, the Massey-Harris officer in charge of French operations, and a close friend. He had discussions with Norman MacKenzie, then a professor of law at the university, later to be a fellow royal commissioner in Ottawa and to preside over the University of British Columbia during its emergence as a major Canadian university. Many years later MacKenzie recalled that nothing came of their discussions 'because Vincent and I were not too compatible and because I didn't want to leave the U. of T.'[34] Massey's choice next fell on Hume Wrong.

The choice was both logical and natural. Hume had followed his brother Murray, Vincent's closest university friend, and his sister Margaret from the University of Toronto (BA 1915) to Oxford, where he had received the BLITT and the Balliol imprint. Between Toronto and Oxford he had served in France as an infantry officer with an English regiment.[35] When Vincent approached him in January 1927 about going to Washington, he had been a member of the history department at the University of Toronto for five years, and was well established as a lecturer and scholar.

Hume was seven years Vincent's junior. When as an undergraduate Vincent had frequented the Wrong household, Hume was a precocious boy, the youngest of the children. When Hume entered university, Vincent was already installed as the dean at Victoria, and Hume reported to his mother that on one occasion he had dined with Vincent at the high table and had been greatly impressed by the beauty of the hall and the size and splendour of Vincent's private room. Although Hume, impatient of delay in Canada, had gone to England and secured a commission in an English regiment, he expressed satisfaction that Vincent's military career was not likely to take him outside Canada.[36]

At first Hume was happy to work with Vincent and took pride in the accomplishments of his chief. He wrote to his mother that there was great excitement about the purchase of the new legation and commented that 'it is an amazing mansion, and is generally admitted to be cheap at the price.'[37] He expressed his admiration for Vincent as a public speaker: 'We went to a Canadian Club dinner on Friday at which Vincent made an admirable speech and several other people made rotten ones.'[38] The tone of his letters home were unchanged for several years. Then the comments suddenly become violently critical. Hume was incensed by the Masseys' habit of spending a leisurely summer at Batterwood and then, on their return to Washington, announcing schemes that, it was implied, they had worked out in painstaking detail during the summer months; and he judged them severely. 'They are, I think, the most thoroughly insincere people whom I know.'[39] The 'amazing mansion' that was 'cheap at the price' became 'our empty and superfluous palace (a monument to the Masseys' ambitions).'[40]

There was no specific incident that brought about the remarkable cooling in relations. Vincent mentions only Hume's refusal to wear diplomatic uniforms at White House receptions, which he attributed to 'a characteristic perversity.'[41] This would not have been a small matter to Vincent, who insisted on a particular style of dress for each official occasion, like a theatre director prescribing costume changes in an elaborate historical drama. But the falling out went deeper than that. In a retrospective note added to an entry when Hume first came to Washington, Vincent poured out his accumulated irritations.

Hume Wrong's ability impressed me more and more as I worked with him just as the difficulties inherent to his temperament became more and more evident. ... We kept the peace however and in fact as far as the work itself was concerned collaborated very pleasantly, but the atmosphere which Hume created was very difficult indeed and at all times he imposed a very heavy burden on Lal and me. Jealousy of myself I believe was a key to his bearing in part. The irritation caused by his manner and now and then his actions led me to put down – perhaps a set of adjectives which at times accurately apply to Hume although I am bound to admit that when he wants to he can exhibit the opposite attributes. The adjectives are pompous, self important, arrogant, selfish, sycophantic, obstinate, vindictive, priggish, perverse, ungenerous, overbearing, incisive, dictatorial, officious, surly, inquisitive, calculating, disloyal!

After this self-indulgent outburst, Vincent added: 'Now I feel better.'[42]

These internal stresses did not endanger the work of the legation. Yearly reports listed an expanding number of issues that demanded the attention of the legation and a tremendous growth in communications to various departments both in Washington and Ottawa. It was not, however, a period favourable to the resolution of the great issues in Canadian-American affairs. Mackenzie King was committed on all the major questions to the politics of delay and indecision. The American government was pressing for a Canadian commitment on the construction of the St Lawrence Seaway, but King could sense no clear call to action from the electorate, and he was aware of deep regional and social conflicts that would arise from the new sources of water power that would be created. He preferred to use the seaway as a political bargaining point in a possible tariff war, and Massey was instructed to explain to the secretary of state that an American raising of tariffs against Canada would strengthen Canadian doubts about the seaway.[43]

King was even ambivalent about Canada's part in strengthening the American prohibition laws. There was no Canadian regulation against issuing a clearance to a cargo of liquor for inland commerce, and King maintained that it was not up to his government to enforce prohibition in the United States. Suddenly in 1929 he reversed himself, ostensibly for high moral reasons, although cynics remarked that the new policy helped Canada in her tariff negotiations with the United States. Canadians continued to be sympathetic to Canadian rum-runners who anchored beyond the twelve mile limit and arranged for the secret discharge of their cargo. The most famous case was that of the *I'm Alone*, which, although outside the twelve mile limit, was sunk by an American coast guard ship, on the principle of the sanctity of 'hot pursuit.' The Canadians inherited the case from the British. After arbitration, the United States paid a substantial sum in damages. Massey, in his memoirs, saw the captain of the *I'm Alone* in almost a heroic light. 'The skipper of the *I'm Alone*, Captain John T. Randell, was in spirit an Elizabethan – he belonged to the days of Drake. He was a man of great rectitude in other matters but disliked the principle of prohibition so much that he did everything he could to thwart it.'[44]

Another dominating question of the day, with, however, none of the immediate repercussions of prohibition, was the Pan American movement. American proponents saw in the arrival of a Canadian minister a declaration of independence that would enable Canada to take its place in the American community. Little support came from Canada herself; and Vincent Massey, in one of his final ministerial memorials, firmly dismissed the idea. His major argument was that Pan Americanism really meant American domination. The Pan American Union building in Washington, he said, proclaimed this in the very arrangement of its symbolism.[45]

In the great matters of peace and war the twenties were a period of confused idealism and fumbling suspicion, symbolized by the Kellogg-Briand pact of 1928. Vincent was impressed by Kellogg's search for peace, and was flattered when the secretary of state discussed with him his hopes for a new world order. There was no possibility of conflict with the Canadian government on this issue, for King looked upon the Kellogg-Briand pact for the outlawing of war as a harmless gesture that could not possibly lead to any Canadian involvement.[46]

The misunderstandings between Great Britain and the United States with respect to naval disarmament touched the Canadian legation only indirectly. Massey believed that the visit to Washington of Ramsay MacDonald, returned to power in the election of 1929, meant the coming of a new age of Anglo-American understanding. He joined the British ambassador in enthusiastic welcome to and support of MacDonald, whose large and liberal views on foreign affairs he found refreshingly superior to those of the former government spokesman, Austen Chamberlain.

Vincent Massey made his greatest contribution as a diplomat in the mounting and direction of ceremonial events that had a strong symbolic significance, and in explaining, on the public platform, Canada's position among nations. Of the ceremonial occasions the most important was the official visit to Washington of the governor-general and Lady Willingdon. In preliminary discussions in Ottawa, Massey insisted that the visit 'should be in all forms as a visit of the sovereign' and that the 'Governor-General will be given the honour of the sovereign by another state.'[47] In this way Canada, he believed, would be manifesting its independent status within the Commonwealth. During the visit, in December 1927, the American government punctiliously observed all the procedures appropriate to the reception of the head of a sovereign state. There was one departure, apparent neither to the public nor to the great majority of participants, but of vexatious concern to the Canadian minister. A month before the visit, Massey heard that the king had not been prepared to give a public expression to the new theory of the Commonwealth. 'Discovered to my horror that the King's objections to Willingdon's visit to USA as a chief of state had been communicated to Phillips and by him to State Department. Here's a how d'you do!'[48] The British ambassador had no doubt received a similar message: he was the king's representative in Washington and should not yield precedence to the governor-general of a dominion. At the dinner given by the British ambassador, the secretary of state and Mrs Kellogg were placed above the Willingdons, and Massey speculated that this was 'a quiet demonstration of conformity with H.M.'s views.'[49]

It is doubtful whether the state visit of the governor-general impressed the American people as a demonstration of Canadian independence. Indifferent to the niceties of symbolic protocol, they might well have concluded that Willingdon, who must have reminded them of seventeenth-century royal portraits they had seen in history books, was the Canadian equivalent of the American president. In his speeches across the country, Massey tried to make clear the nature of Canadian independence, and no doubt he succeeded with the informed. A simpler and less complicated gospel in his speeches was the vast potentialities of the Canadian north, a theme that became increasingly popular before and during the Diamond Jubilee celebrations of 1927 and has been periodically revived and refurbished since then. Massey's speaking tours aroused sharp criticism in Ottawa. The implication was that he had no right to expound the glories of Canada to the Americans. Even Mackenzie King had misgivings. But 'after an excellent talk as frank as it was friendly he told me to use my own judgement. He could not have been more appreciative of what Lal and I are trying to do in Washington. In conversations like this one can see what a wise person the P.M. is.'[50]

When Vincent Massey left the United States, he had, in a modest way, become an American public figure. The Columbia Broadcasting System invited him to speak to the American people, in a gesture to be reserved in the future for important presidential messages. Vincent thus recorded the event: 'Lal and I went to the Columbia Broadcasting Studio where I said goodbye to the people of the USA. Over the air in about 7 minutes. Preceded by "O Canada" and followed by the "Maple Leaf." A 45 station hook-up I was told.'

The little over three years that Vincent spent as minister established him – in the public eye, at least – as a successful diplomat. Although he realized that diplomacy was only an outpost of politics, it did provide opportunities for leisurely explorations of another culture, and for a process of self-education that was not so easily available in the hurly-burly of a political career. During his tour in Washington he made a serious attempt to study and to understand the United States.

After the announcement of his appointment to Washington, the American press noted with satisfaction his solid American credentials. The Salem *News* proudly announced that 'Mr Massey comes from an old family of Salem,'[51] and the Boston *Evening Transcript* pronounced him to be 'of early American stock.'[52] Farther west, the Watertown, New York, *Times* pointed out how one branch of the Massey family had left Watertown for Canada, and the other had remained. The newspapers were right to emphasize the American background of the Massey family. It was, indeed, more than a background: the United States for the Masseys had always been a continuous, friendly presence, and in both their personal and business lives they had gone back and forth across the border as if it were non-existent. When Vincent presented his credentials to President Coolidge he could point out that, for over two centuries, the Massey and the Coolidge families had followed parallel courses, moving westward gradually from the coast to Vermont and upstate New York; and he might have added that both families had stressed the Yankee virtues of frugality and self-reliance.

Nevertheless, Vincent himself had fought against the strong American tradition of the Masseys, in part because he associated it with a family to which he found himself increasingly unsympathetic. The diary for his undergraduate days at Toronto and Oxford contains frequent anti-American sallies. The United States is seen as inferior in every respect to England. But then, as he began his active life of teacher and patron, his anti-American bias was modified.

From his return from Oxford in 1913 until the early twenties – the war years slightly expanded – Vincent had the opportunity to explore the American cultural scene. Europe, except for a trip with Raymond in the summer of 1914, harshly aborted in France by the declaration of war, was closed, except to combatants. The eastern American seaboard, particularly New York, became the substitute. (When Vincent resumed his transatlantic trips on 23 April 1920, he observed that this was his twenty-first transatlantic voyage. This means that, since his last voyage had been in 1914, he had made twenty transatlantic trips by the time he was twenty-seven years old!) Although Vincent was in uniform during most of the war years, he appeared to have little trouble in crossing the border on leave. In their early married years, Alice and he made regular trips to New York, then the centre of the American renaissance in the arts.

New York was an obvious stimulant to a theatre lover restricted at home to the occasional road show featuring old and famous performers in stock classics, or to valiant amateur performances of new plays at the Arts and Letters Club. New York, and to an almost equal extent Boston and Washington, were also lively intellectual centres, where one could escape from the heavy haze of Canadian politics, which lifted only to reveal a patriotic fervour or a harsh contempt for American inaction. Vincent was wholeheartedly in favour of the Union Government; he had not the slightest doubt about the righteousness of the allied cause; but he was not disposed to berate the Americans for their indecision. At Oxford he had been a close friend of W.C. ('Whitney') Shepardson, an American Rhodes scholar with a lively mind, who was to become a senior official in the Carnegie Corporation; and, from discussions with him, he knew the problems facing those in the United States who were devoted to British civilization and supported the allied cause. But Vincent's main link with the intellectual life of an American came through an Englishman, Eustace Percy.

Eustace Percy and Vincent Massey were both born in the same year, 1887. Eustace was a son of the 7th Duke of Northumberland, and as he remarked in the first sentence of his book of memoirs, was born 'with the biggest of all possible silver spoons in my mouth.'[53] He went up to

Oxford precociously in 1904, leaving it in 1907, four years before Vincent arrived. Oxford left little impression on him; he was much too young to benefit from the life, complex and subtle, yet curiously informal. His real undergraduate school was the four years, 1910–14, he spent at Washington as a secretary in the British embassy. His tutor was the British ambassador, Lord Bryce, and his college was a house at 1727 Nineteenth Street which was owned by Robert G. Valentine, commissioner of Indian affairs. Valentine turned the house into a residence for a brilliant group of young men, among them Loring Christie, a Canadian who would shortly return to Canada as a special legal adviser in the department of external affairs and eventually reappeared in Washington many years later as the Canadian minister, and Felix Frankfurter, then a young lawyer working with Henry L. Stimson, secretary of war in the Taft administration, and later, as a professor in the Harvard Law School and a judge of the Supreme Court, to exert a dazzling influence on American jurisprudence. The house attracted others as visitors, two young journalists, for instance, who wrote with a philosophical amplitude, Walter Lippmann and Herbert Croly. The house at 1727 Nineteenth Street became known as 'The House of Truth,' where generous and informal hospitality was accompanied by lively and uninhibited search for sound philosophical and political principles.

Vincent had presumably met Eustace Percy during some of his trips to England. Their real friendship began in 1913, when Vincent, then a dean and lecturer at the University of Toronto, spent his Christmas vacation with Percy at 'The House of Truth.' From this dated his friendship with Frankfurter, Lippmann, and Croly, and his introduction to American critical and progressive thought. Percy was himself a spokesman for America. He admired American energy and receptivity to the new, and the capacity of the cumbrous American political system to generate swift and radical executive action. He believed devoutly that peace and justice depended on the preservation of understanding and friendship between the British Empire and the United States. The dark suspicions of British policy entertained by leading American politicians were, Percy maintained, based on a mythology of 'a hereditary class corporation' made up of the landowners, the universities of Oxford and Cambridge, the established church, and the civil service, with the monarchy at the centre, 'which somehow symbolized its essential reactionary character.'[54] Percy believed that English diplomats and politicians were largely responsible for American attitudes; often without intending it they gave offence by their public manners, which were too often akin to the manners of Mr Darcy, the aloof aristocrat of *Pride and Prejudice*. Percy was a refreshing variant of the Darcy pattern by temperament and by his sympathetic understanding of the American outlook; and he no doubt helped to prepare Vincent for his American years.

Eustace Percy returned to England on the outbreak of war, and Vincent ceased to see him for several years. But the association with Frankfurter, Croly, and Lippmann continued during the war and into the twenties, and was maintained during Vincent's tenure of office in Washington. During these years, their names occur with regularity in the diary.[55] All three of these American friends had been deeply involved in the founding of the *New Republic*, the first issue of which appeared on 7 November 1914. The *New Republic* was envisaged as an exponent of critical and progressive thought, in particular of the ideas already set forth by Herbert Croly in his book, *The Promise of American Life*.[56]

Frankfurter, Croly, and Lippmann were sympathetic to the British cause during the war, and the *New Republic* supported American participation on the allied side. No doubt this was a strong reason for Vincent's attraction to them. But he was also attracted to their general ideas about society and politics – radical, in the current American context, but with a conservative and intellectually aristocratic core. Croly was an apostle of 'The New Nationalism,' attacking Jeffersonian individualism as a dissolvent of national life. America needed a strong central government that would give it a sense of direction and purpose, that would elevate the public good above selfish interests. Democracy should not mean the enshrinement of mediocrity. 'The essential wholeness of the community depends absolutely on the ceaseless creation of a political, economic, and social aristocracy and their equally incessant replacement.'[57] Croly was not disposed to attack the twin evils that were singled out by more radical reformers for special denunciation – war and imperialism. 'War,' he wrote, 'may be and has been a useful and justifiable engine of national policy';[58] and 'the assumption by a European nation [of the responsibility for Asiatic and African communities] is a desirable phase of national discipline and a frequent source of genuine national advance.'[59]

The gravamen both of Croly's book and of the *New Republic* was the intellectual poverty of much of American life: its reliance on catch words and routine procedure; its belief that emotional outbursts or puritanical taboos provided a solution to social problems; its self-satisfied acceptance of regimentation as a recipe for the good life. In his unsparing criticism of America – far more sweeping than Vincent's had ever been – he was joined by Lippmann. Dull, mindless conformity was what both men most bitterly attacked. American businessmen, said Croly, 'are forced into a common mold, because the ultimate measure of the value of their work is the same, and is nothing but its results in cost.'[60] 'The American intellectual habit has on the whole been just about as vigorous and independent as that of the domestic animals. The freedom of opinion of which we boast has consisted for the most part in uttering acceptable commonplaces with as much defiant convictions as if it were uttering the most daring and sublimest heresies.'[61] Lippmann was even more iconoclastic in his observations on American society. An early book, *A Preface to Politics*, reads like a Shavian preface – and Shaw is, indeed, the writer to whom he referred most frequently – with American substituted for English institutions. 'The American college student has the gravity and mental habits of a Supreme Court judge; his "wild oats" are rarely spiritual; the critical, analytical habit of mind is distrusted. We say that "knocking" is a sign of the "sorehead" and we sublimate criticism by saying that "every knock is a boost." America does not play with ideas; generous speculation is regarded as insincere, and shunned as if it might endanger the optimism which underlies success. All this becomes such an insulation against new ideas that when the Yankee goes abroad he takes his environment with him.'[62]

The stinging generalizations of the critics were translated vividly into narrative and characterization by another critic whom Vincent knew and admired, although only through his published work – the novelist, Sinclair Lewis. Up until the publication of *Main Street* in 1921, Lewis had followed a wavering, uncertain course. Suddenly in this novel everything cohered, and Lewis wrote a book in which America found its own image. 'The sleeping beast,' wrote Mark Schorer, Lewis's biographer, 'howled in an ecstasy of self torture,' and for years bought and read the book until it was estimated that it reached two million readers.[63] Sinclair Lewis was the one American novelist that Vincent Massey read assiduously in the twenties and thirties – a hardy American plant in a genteel English garden. Lewis reinforced what Croly and Lippmann said, like them not out of hatred but out of love for his country. Calvin Coolidge's America was, in some respect, *Main Street* and *Babbitt* writ large, and at times even Washington seemed to Vincent Massey to be Gopher Prairie and Zenith in monumental marble, and the American president a slim Babbitt with a New England accent.

Calvin Coolidge's popularity was based on the belief that he not only proclaimed but exemplified the quintessential business virtues. In *The Man Who Knew Coolidge* (1928) Sinclair Lewis supplied this footnote to the title: 'Mr Calvin Coolidge was the President of the United States of North America from 1923 to 1929. He had filled many of the soundest American ideals, and he stands, along with the Ford Motorcar, the Rev. Dr William Sunday, and *The Saturday Evening Post*, as the symbol of his era.' Massey would have agreed with Lewis's ironical dismissal of the president. He delighted in anecdotes that illustrated Coolidge's self-satisfied provincialism. When Coolidge was asked by the British ambassador's wife whether he was going to visit Europe on his retirement, he replied, 'No. I guess we haven't got anything to learn from Europe.'[64] Occasionally, Vincent reported a bolder Babbitt-like oratorical flight by the president. On the occasion of a George Washington birthday celebration, before an audience made up of both Houses, the Supreme Court, and the diplomatic corps, Coolidge summoned all his rhetorical resources, muted by 'nasal tones and sub-arctic manner,' to present 'George Washington as the first American Rotarian – successful real estate dealer and forward-looking in transportation ventures.'[65]

His ministerial duties did not expose Massey to the raucous conventions at which George Babbitt and his fellow realtors exchanged reassuring statistics and listened to inspirational addresses by clergymen and local politicians. He addressed business groups on a higher and more austere plane: the Association of Life Insurance Presidents, the annual conventions of the American Institute of Steel Construction, the American Automobile Association, and the Chamber of Commerce of the State of New York. These were invariably speeches of factual sobriety, lightened a little by faint touches of humour, rising occasionally to a note of celebration, as when he declared that 'there is something of the poet in every great captain of industry, every great leader of finance and commerce.'[66] Some of these business gatherings did, however, open up suddenly into the Babbitt world. In Los Angeles, a city that he heartily disliked,[67] he spoke to a combined lunch of the Chamber of Commerce and Advertising Club. The text has not been preserved. The diary records the event in this chilly fashion: 'Tremendous aggregation of "pep, punch, push".'[68] At the Institute of Steel Construction, his own speech, a laboured attempt to find points at which the steel industry impinged on the world of international affairs, was preceded by a speech given by a woman from a business bureau representing 'Mrs Consumer.' Vincent reported with unusual acerbity that 'her speech was that of a high-priestess of waste and extravagance – a sycophantic eulogy of rapid turnover and large profits and a promise to contribute to these by the "education" of her sex as a purchasing agent.'[69]

Vincent's direct personal associations with businessmen tended to be with the great American potentates. These took place at dinner parties and at weekends at great houses. The reporter is generally gloomy. He found that the range of conversation among businessmen was narrow – a depressing contrast to the untrammelled wit and bold sweep of conversation at the English weekend party. A dinner given by John D. Rockefeller jr was an example *in extremis* of the heavy and joyless festivities of the great tycoons. 'The organ playing during dinner cast an ecclesiastical air over the occasion, and our host displays an earnestness which is not moderated by any *joie de vivre*.'[70] The only exception in Vincent's stern portrait gallery of American businessmen was Andrew Mellon, Coolidge's, and then Hoover's, secretary of the treasury – a curious choice for praise, since no businessman was more universally disliked by a wide range of social critics. Mellon was accused of introducing income tax measures that were no doubt inspired by orthodox conservative theory but had the effect of greatly increasing his own vast fortune. But Vincent was entranced by Mellon's 'love of beauty' and 'interest in the arts'; Mellon seemed to him to be 'more a poet than Finance Minister' (the Masseys met Mellon in June 1927; these comments were made retrospectively in a note added on 14 June 1930) – a judgment that to his friends of the *New Republic* would have seemed like a mixture of naiveté and ignorance.

Another concern of Lewis and the social critics was the American experiment in the prohibition of the drinking and manufacture of alcoholic beverages. It too, like the worship of the businessman, had reverberations in Washington beyond the legal and international problems that it raised and that absorbed a great deal of the time of the Canadian legation. For diplomats there were delicate problems of a personal nature – problems similar to those faced by law-abiding citizens in Zenith, and requiring the same concessions to human frailty. There were no problems within the embassy itself. The diplomatic corps was granted permission to import wines and spirituous liquors for its own consumption. But even this was challenged by the forces of righteousness. As 'the drys' became apprehensive of the triumph of 'the wets' they singled out the diplomatic corps for newspaper publicity and castigation. The diplomats were, 'the drys' declared, 'little better than a gang of bootleggers.' The British, with their reputation for loose and vinous ways, were given special attention. Sir Esme Howard, the British ambassador, having ascertained that there was enough wine in the cellar to suffice for his final embassy party before he left for another post, told the State Department that he would ask for no more licences to import wine and spirituous liquors.[71] When Massey was asked by the French ambassador what a self-governing dominion was going to do now that the British embassy was going dry, he replied: 'Remain self-governing.'[72]

As soon as the diplomat moved outside his own terrain, he found himself perforcedly a player in the great American farce. Should he abstain out of a scrupulous regard for the law, or bow to the current fashion of clandestine arrangements for the thirsty? At first Vincent inclined to the first solution, but finally accepted the official violation of the law. This, at least, provided some high comedy. At a government party attended by the attorney general, 'it was amusing as always to see the combination of a legislator producing cocktails made from illegal liquor and the symbol of law and observance looking on idly, although not participating.'[73] Canadian visitors added another comic depth. When the Pilgrims of the United States entertained a delegation of Canadian dignitaries, Massey arranged for the non-prohibitionist members, chiefly French Canadians, to have drinks in his room, while the teetotal president of the University of Toronto, Sir Robert Falconer, the prominent cleric and future successor to Falconer, Canon H.J. Cody, and N.W. Rowell, a leading Liberal and militant Methodist 'dry,' remained below with the main unserviced gathering. Just before he left his post Vincent Massey summarized his personal policy with respect to alcohol at public functions in Washington. It was an admirable embodiment of diplomatic sagacity, assuring his own security, but yet observing the legal niceties. '... it was not for me to run the risk of appearing "to set an example." The question of law was in my host's hands not mine. I was an innocent guest and my compliance with my host's invitation had no bearing whatsoever on the question of the 18th amendment whereas my abstention might be regarded as expressing an opinion.'[74]

The 'mindless associations' that Sinclair Lewis described with such relish made little impact on the Washington world. The chief of these – the most populous and the most sinister – was the Ku Klux Klan, which was at its height during the first five years of the decade. No doubt its indiscriminate attacks on Jews, Catholics, blacks, and radicals of any shade had a cumulative effect on federal politics, but the Klan was not in itself a federal presence. Yet in its use of crude rituals to arouse a sense of mass involvement, it provided a gross example of what was fairly common in American life. Vincent was constantly critical of the American failure to use ceremony honestly and effectively. American ceremonies were often stiff with protocol and bold in expression, but they lacked the British combination of dignity and informality. He commented with asperity on the presidential inaugural ceremonies for Herbert Hoover on 4 March 1929. The opening ceremony in the Senate was a 'curious mixture of business and ceremonial'; the procession, which lasted two hours, was 'well organized but more of a circus than a ceremonial parade.'[75]

As a diplomat, Vincent Massey was not in a position to comment publicly on the great divisive issues in the America of the twenties. Indeed, his natural curiosity about American affairs was discouraged by the Canadian government. When he proposed to attend both the Democratic and Republican conventions in 1928, his persistent vilifier, Tommy Church, argued in the House of Commons that it would be improper for a Canadian representative to attend a partisan political convention, even though Massey proposed to divide his time between the two parties and to attend, of course, only as an observer. Skelton informed Massey that the cabinet had discussed the matter and had decided unanimously that it would be improper for him to attend the conventions. The cabinet was nervous about fostering an indiscretion in these early stages of Canada's diplomatic independence, to which was added a desire, shared by both parties then as now, for a vacuous purity in international attitudes. Only in his diary, although, even there, circumspectly and obliquely, did Massey record his attitudes towards the big issues. The Sacco-Vanzetti case brutally dramatized the conflict between the progressives and the mass fear of radicalism in any form.[76] Vincent, no doubt influenced by his friend Felix Frankfurter, who published a detailed exposure of the improprieties committed during the trial, was not convinced of the guilt of Sacco and Vanzetti. During the visit of Ramsay MacDonald in April 1927, he was shocked at the conservatism of American labour leaders, and, in particular, at the speech of one leader 'denouncing the British Labour MPs for sending a message of sympathy to Sacco and Vanzetti.'[77] Elsewhere, he referred to Sacco and Vanzetti as 'the condemned alleged murderers.'

Racial segregation had not yet surfaced as an issue in the twenties. Massey accepted without demur the customs of the day. At Christmas time, he gave a party 'for all the official family ... except the coloured ones who according to local custom must be excluded.'[78] On a visit to the deep south, he talked with a cotton planter of liberal views who 'feels that the negro is capable of doing nearly everything which the white man does,' but yet believed that 'the Jim Crow deadline is necessary to white civilization.'[79] Vincent made no comment on the contradiction. On a visit to the Tuskegee Institute, the celebrated black university, he was deeply impressed by the 'charming manners' and scholarly achievements of those whom he met, but was puzzled about how to receive a coloured man in a white hotel in the south. 'Tommy [Stone] got the technique from the hotel manager. I received him of course cordially but I didn't ask him to sit down in the public lobby.'[80]

There is no anticipation in the diary of the economic depression, and no comment on its sensational beginnings. But in this he was not exceptional: the stock market collapse of 1929 had come without obvious forewarning, and when he left Washington in 1930 many trusted observers, including the president himself, maintained that the economy was fundamentally sound. Besides, he had little interest in economics, and no disposition to risk his own ample security by speculation. When his advisers at the National Trust, the guardians of his own resources as well as of the Massey Foundation, warned him solemnly about the dangers of playing the market, he no doubt smiled at the thought of his even entertaining such a possibility.

These critical passages on aspects of American life do not, however, determine the genuine tone of Vincent's comments. Basically his attitude was one of respect and affection. He never came near the virulence of a Croly or a Lippmann, let alone a Sinclair Lewis. He and Alice clearly enjoyed their stay, and responded warmly to the uniformly friendly reception they received. The enthusiasm comes out in the portraits of people he met. Even those with whom he had little sympathy politically or intellectually elicited a degree of commendation. Thus Senator William Borah, who personified American isolationist distrust of Europe, and of Great Britain in particular, received this moderate and good humoured appraisal: 'Borah is an extraordinary fellow – well informed, extremely able, high-minded and on the other hand essentially vain and non-constructive in his outlook. Perhaps it is a love of publicity and applause coupled with a capacity for self-deception that leads him into taking pretty sharp corners politically in the alleged interests of virtue.'[81] Even Dorothy Dix, the bathetic confidante in the twenties of middle-class America, is given a benedictory sentence. She is 'as distinguished an old fashioned southerner in person as her syndicated writings are fatuous.'[82]

His best portraits, sharply critical yet sympathetic, are of two Americans of genius who also had obvious weaknesses. Herbert Hoover, following his relief work in Belgium during the first world war, had aroused universal admiration. The young Felix Frankfurter hailed him as 'a truly great man ... intelligence supremely moved by the misery of the world.'[83] Yet as president of the United States he failed to give leadership under stress, and became more and more immersed in his own striving for self-justification. He was inaccessible to his critics, even to his colleagues, and he rarely saw the representatives of foreign powers. Esme Howard, a genial and considerate man, said that Hoover was 'the most difficult American whom I have ever met.'[84] In a conversation with some Hoover associates towards the end of his Washington term, Massey suggested that the president should see diplomats and hostile politicians privately, and was pleased (and amazed) to receive shortly afterwards an invitation: 'lunched with Mr Hoover tête à tête on the verandah of the White House and had an hour's good talk with him.' Massey concluded that Hoover's failure to deal with criticism either from within his own party or from the progressives arose from his insensitivity to human nature. He thought that the attitude of the progressives 'was made up principally of vanity and a destructive sense' and should, therefore, be treated with contempt. Massey concluded: 'He knows things better than man. He is inclined to regard a man who opposes his policies as a personal enemy ... The failure to understand men, the incapacity to relax, the over-intensity of mind and lack of good comradeship – enough to overcome political differences, a certain touch of peevishness – all these threaten to impair the success of a man who has a fine intellect and a disinterested desire to do his job, power of leadership, as far as those of kindred mind are concerned, and broad vision.'[85] The analysis is shrewd and compassionate.

The second American of genius was Henry Ford; in many ways he dominated the twenties no less triumphantly than his Model T Ford. Massey's summary of his qualities may well stand for his assessment of popular America: 'he combines in one person the maximum number of American qualities: altruism and idealism, touched with emotionalism and sentimentality; a belief in mechanical organization, the Puritan mind, with its traditional inhibitions, boundless energy, eager curiosity combined with hurried judgments and shallow thinking, fundamental decency and friendliness, an unconquerable confidence in the United States.'[86]

His assessment of popular America was not very different from that of Sinclair Lewis, who in *Arrowsmith* (1925) had written about how the cleansing and involving qualities of the scientific spirit could, in American society, arm a typical young midwestern doctor against materialism, and in *Dodsworth* (1929) had differentiated between the thoughtful American business executive and the horde of Babbitts. 'Samuel Dodsworth was, perfectly, the American Captain of Industry, believing in the Republican Party, high tariff and, so long as they did not annoy him personally, in prohibition and the Episcopal Church ... He was not a Babbitt, not a Rotarian, not an Elk, not a deacon. He rarely shouted, never slapped people on the back, and he had attended only six baseball games since 1900. He knew, and thoroughly, the Babbitts and baseball fans, but only in business. While he was bored by free verse and cubism, he thought rather well of Dreiser, Cabell, and so much of Proust as he had rather laboriously mastered.'[87] Massey knew many Americans who were just as idealistic as Martin Arrowsmith, just as tolerant as Samuel Dodsworth, and greatly superior to either of them in intellectual endowment. Besides his friends of the *New Republic*, there were those who thought of the practice of law as a demonstration of reason in action and a bulwark of justice – Clarence Darrow: 'His consuming passion is a feeling for the underdog which dominates all else in his mind and often his sense of balance. He has stood persecution without the bitterness';[88] Louis Brandeis: 'learned and wise with a rare combination of fine feeling and liberal mind. Not too concerned with ideas to be unmindful of men';[89] and above all Oliver Wendell Holmes: 'a most wonderful old man, liberal, chivalrous, human, aristocratic, mischievous, lovable, and terrifying in his learning.'[90]

The American institution where Vincent Massey felt most at home, and where he believed that the country revealed itself in its most attractive guise, was the university. His farewell speech was given at a university, at the annual commencement of the University of Michigan on 23 June 1930. He observed that during the last three and a half years he had visited some twenty American universities and that 'there are no institutions in your great Republic which are more typical of the best in American life, or which are more interesting to the visitor, or which give him a warmer or more generous welcome.'[91] Of the twenty-four speeches from this period that he selected for inclusion in the volume *Good Neighbourhood*, seven were given at universities, and several others to bodies with an academic orientation. He was clearly at home in his academic speeches. Those to business groups and official societies have an uncomfortable rigidity and a stereotyped structure: first, a facetious disclaimer of personal adequacy for the occasion, then a series of congratulatory and laudatory remarks directed towards his hosts, and, finally, the body of the speech – laboured analogies or commonplaces presented with a decorative flourish. But the university speeches have an easy, relaxed quality; the quotations appear to come easily and are apt; the words have the ring of authority, and the argument is personal and, occasionally, provocative. The ideas now seem familiar, but they were perhaps not so familiar when they were presented in the twenties; and at any rate familiarity does not mean that they have become invalid. They are presented in the form of a series of dualisms that, Massey believed, can be eventually united. Ideas have power in their own right, but to be truly effective they must find their way into action. Specialized learning is indispensable, but it can become mere pedantry without the sense of perspective given by wide reading in the humanities. Massey expressed a polite regard for the American multiversity with its elaborate structure, but emphasized the crucial role of the individual, whether teacher or student.[92] As a diplomat, he talked a good deal about the international role of the university. This could be effective only if the university stayed close to its national origins. He objected to a 'colourless cosmopolitanism,' and, as an ex-academic, scorned the idea then being seriously advanced of the university as a source of tribunals for international disputes. 'I have had enough experience of academic life to know that the college cloister is often too much in need of diplomacy to have much to spare.'[93]

Vincent Massey, supported by able colleagues, represented Canada's political and commercial interests competently. As a cultural representative, a role that he assigned to himself, he was an extraordinary success. He understood and appreciated the cultural and intellectual life of the United States, and, at the same time, he demonstrated that a Canadian could have an urbanity and an intellectual grasp not usually thought to be national characteristics. Two unusual tributes from the American intellectual world attest to this.

Massey addressed the annual meeting of the American Historical Association on 29 December 1927 (the speech has not, unfortunately, been recorded), and in its issue of April 1928 the *American Historical*

Review published this eulogy: 'The principal speech, by common consent, was that of the Canadian minister, the Honourable Vincent Massey, who spoke of the uses of historical research and the qualities of historical writing with the full appreciation of one who, in young days a university professor of history, had since read much history and seen much of public life and large affairs, had contemplated all with a cultivated mind, and could touch upon all with equal insight and urbanity ... He made his hearers feel the value of that rare combination of discriminate knowledge, sympathetic insight into the human mind, and artistic temperament and skill which constitutes the supremely excellent historian.'

Early in May 1930, the Masseys were on holiday in Virginia when a telegram arrived from the prime minister saying that he had informed London of Vincent's appointment as high commissioner to Great Britain. Shortly afterwards, the official announcement appeared in the press, telegrams of congratulations poured in, and the British and American press warmly welcomed the decision. The *New York Times* and the New York *World* made this the occasion for retrospective editorials on his Washington tenure. It is doubtful whether even the great British ambassador to the United States, Lord Bryce, received such measured and solemn praise. The *New York Times* editorial on 5 May 1930 thus commented:

... no one among all members of the diplomatic corps has been more sought for and honoured by cities, universities and learned societies as a speaker on high occasions ... Mr Massey has recommended himself to us not alone by his speech of 'high sentence,' from ancient sources, enriched by the adventurous and commodious colloquialisms of the lands that are still new. He has shown practical sense in dealing with the complexities of border relations in commerce and politics. It has been remarked of a cultivated Englishman that he is either an Aristotelian or a Platonist. Mr Massey is both in the sense that he is an Aristotelian realist, as shown by his business and war record, and a Platonic idealist, as evidenced by what he has done for art in various forms. With it all he knows how to guide men's minds to action, which Plato called 'rhetoric.'

The New York *World* editorial of the same date had a peculiar interest for Vincent. The *World* was edited by his old friend Walter

Lippmann, and, in a subsequent letter to Vincent, Lippmann explained that he had written the editorial himself 'with great restraint, for my personal feelings would have been warmer than the cold, anonymous, institutionalized praise of a newspaper.'[94] There was nothing, despite Lippmann's assertions, 'cold, anonymous, institutionalized' about the editorial. No diplomat could have had a more satisfying pronouncement on his work, or wished for a eulogist of greater eloquence and authority.

... The selection of Mr Vincent Massey, the Canadian Minister in Washington, to represent the Dominion in London amounts to a decision to use his fine capacities at the most important post affecting Canadian interests. He has served Canada brilliantly in the US. No one in the history of the two countries has done so much to make plain to the willing but often careless minds of Americans that Canada is a great nation, a prime and individual factor in the politics of the world. Mr Massey's mission to Washington has, without one trace of propaganda or preaching, taught us much that we urgently needed to know.[95]

Vincent Massey's Washington years were important both for Canada and himself. He impressed a wide range of Americans in politics, business, and education. He was a Canadian nationalist who did not belittle America, and he expressed himself with a grace and wit that were not often present in native orators. At the same time, America had a great effect on him. Some of his critical assumptions were substantiated, luridly dramatized by the dour provincialism of Calvin Coolidge, the elaborate hypocrisy of prohibition, and the dullness and materialism of public display. But there was another America, living in the perspective of history, accepting (and enjoying) candid self-criticism, and responding to the authority of great ideas. Canada had not produced critics as tough and eloquent as Croly, Lippmann, and Frankfurter, or a novelist as uncannily perceptive as Sinclair Lewis; and Canadian politics were not responsive to ideas as American politics, on occasion, were. Vincent's three years in Washington constituted a course in American civilization. Henceforth, without abandoning his English bias, he would be an informed and sympathetic student of the United States, and, during his active career in politics, a staunch supporter of American ideas.

CHAPTER SEVEN

The Squire of Batterwood

When Vincent Massey returned to Canada in the summer of 1930, he took up residence at his country home, a few miles northwest of Port Hope, Ontario, near the little hamlet of Canton.

The Masseys had owned a home in Toronto from 1913 to 1926, at 71 Queen's Park Crescent, immediately in front of Victoria College. The house had been built in 1890, at roughly the same time as Victoria College and the Ontario Parliament Building, a sombre Richardsonian mass a few hundred yards to the south. The area was an attractive enclave for the wealthy who wanted to break away from the solid concentration of mansions on Jarvis and Sherbourne Streets. A short distance to the west from the Massey home stood the great house of Sir Joseph Flavelle, with four towering Corinthian columns commanding the entrance to the street, and six at the rear contemplating the university grounds to the south and west. A block to the west of Sir Joseph's house, which was known as Holwood Hall, was Sir Edmund Walker's house, built in the high Victorian fashion, with a cluster of triple chimneys and an elaborate, broken exterior.

Compared to these, the Massey house was modest in size and unpretentious in design. It was built of red brick, and the only conspicuous mark of the late Victorian taste for the splendid was a turreted tower of modest height that broke the front facade. Vincent was happy in the house and in the area. It was an escape from the suffocating grandeur of Jarvis Street. During his brief period as dean at Victoria and university lecturer he was conveniently close to his work, and Hart House, particularly its theatre, was a short walk away, so that he could casually drop in on rehearsals or adjourn a small dinner party to attend a performance. His interest in the university was shared by his eminent neighbours. Like him, Sir Joseph and Sir Edmund were members of the board of governors, with dedicated service that long preceded his own appointment. As a young undergraduate, he had been a visitor in Sir Edmund's home and was delighted to find that the chief executive of a bank was also a discriminating collector and supporter of the fine arts. With Flavelle the relationship was more intimate. By the turn of the century, when Vincent was a school boy, Flavelle had become one of the city's leading financiers. He was also, like so many of the city's successful businessmen, a triumphant Methodist, and this inevitably brought him into association with the young Vincent – a wavering Methodist, it is true, but still the undoubted heir of the Massey tradition of piety and public service.

When Vincent went to Washington early in 1927 he rented 71 Queen's Park completely furnished. He could not be certain of his return. The Washington appointment had no terminal date, and the London opening, which he passionately desired, might come at any time. Whatever happened, however, he would need to retain his Toronto associations. He would continue to be bound to the city by ties of family and business, and by the close association with the organizations supported by the Massey Foundation. But he began to wonder about the city as the best place for his Canadian residence. He had incurred the wrath of the business community by casting in his lot with the Liberals. Senior associates in the Massey-Harris Company were bitter about his desertion of the gospel of the high protective tariff. He recorded with cynical disgust a sudden repudiation by the Toronto Board of Trade. In the annual elections to the council of that body he had been defeated in 1926 – following his entry into the Liberal cabinet and his candidature in Durham – although just the year before he had headed the poll. 'Thus,' he concluded, 'are moderate tariff liberals punished in Tory Toronto.'[1]

Absence sharpened his critical attitude towards the city. The diplomatic society in Washington could be petty and constricting, but Washington also commanded representatives of great distinction, like Sir Esme Howard, the British ambassador, who had held major posts in

Europe, and Paul Claudel, the celebrated French playwright whose plays had an international reputation for profundity; and on weekends the Masseys were often guests at the great country houses of the American aristocracy of wealth. Brief returns to Toronto and to its formal social life aroused a sense of dispiriting contrast. After a dinner party in their honour he wrote that 'Lal and I were struck by the fact that the guests as a whole, many whom we know, although they were all well-bred and some of them well educated, were all entirely local in their range of interest.'[2] At the Toronto Club, redolent of age and expensive dignity, it was 'difficult to pick up a good conversation among its members.'[3] Of a tea given by his neighbour Flavelle, he observed drily that there was 'a high standard of increment-earned and unearned represented by the average guest.' And then he added, 'had some difficulty in avoiding my Dentonian cousins but did so to my satisfaction and no doubt to theirs.'[4] The last comment briefly illuminates his increasing separation from his own family. Walter's widow, Susan, was a strong-minded woman, who was not sympathetic to Vincent's new course in politics and diplomacy, and attributed to him the public impression that the Massey Foundation was his personal fief.

Toronto society – whether within or outside the family – now had few attractions, and Vincent's general comments about the tone and appearance of the city became increasingly harsh. During a Christmas break, he 'was much struck in driving about Toronto to see how low our standard of taste is. Even when we do something in the name of beauty we are [sure] to make an error of taste e.g. the absurd gothic wedding cake which serves as a war memorial to Saint James Churchyard or the sentimental replica of Peter Pan at the corner of St Clair and Avenue Road. No city of its size in the world is so devoid of urban dignity. We have no doubt excellent moral qualities but we seem to think that ugliness is on the side of the angels.'[5] On another visit, the Masseys stayed at Toronto's latest architectural splendour, the Royal York Hotel, massive and dignified, an embodiment of Anglo-Saxon decorum. Even Vincent was impressed by the exterior, but he found the interior 'garish and tasteless and the furnishing unspeakable.'[6] Usually they stayed at the house of the principal of Upper Canada College, presided over by Alice's sister, Maude.

Vincent began to think seriously of abandoning the city of Toronto as a place of residence. Perhaps, in view of his likely absence abroad for many years in the future, he should establish a country home, which would be his Canadian residence, but, in fact, a place for relaxation away from official duties. There was no thought of deserting Toronto; despite the increasingly caustic tone of his comments, he could not imagine himself as living apart from the city. It might be a place of many depressing associations, of the garish family enclave on Jarvis Street, the heavy effrontery of the Massey tomb in Mount Pleasant cemetery, the unpleasant mixture of piety and recently acquired wealth in the church of his forefathers, the general atmosphere of prudery and philistinism; but it was also a city where a new life was sprouting, with a university that revealed a great world beyond the routine of daily living, a city slowly, hesitatingly, but with increasing assurance finding satisfaction in music, art, and the theatre.

The final decision to turn his modest country home into his principal residence was made in the spring of 1927. He had been first attracted to the area in the summer of 1917. The Masseys had gone to stay with Vincent's old friend, George Wrong, who in 1917 had acquired property where the Ganaraska River formed a small lake and then plunged over a dam on its final course to Lake Ontario. The property – some forty-five acres – had a flour mill that was still operative and, near the road, the miller's house, a substantial structure of red brick built in the early part of the nineteenth century in a simple Georgian design. Vincent was impressed by the site and the location, and by the prospect of joining a university community. Besides Wrong, C.T. Currelly, the enterprising director of the university's archaeological museum, had a summer place in the area. Vincent and Alice immediately addressed themselves to the question of securing property. 'Have set our heart on the Herman Peters farm across the Mill Pond from the Wrongs',' he wrote in his diary on 3 October 1918, and three weeks later he had 'more or less fixed things up for the purchase.' It was a splendid site, on rising ground above the river; behind the farm house, to the north, rose the graceful Ganaraska hills; to the south the house looked across rolling fields towards Lake Ontario, several miles away. During the following twenty years the Masseys gradually acquired more property adjacent to the original farm until the extent of their holdings was approximately four hundred acres. The final purchase was the mill house that in 1932 George Wrong, financially constrained by the depression, reluctantly sold to his old student.

The general situation – geographical and social – had a natural appeal to Vincent. Toronto was sixty-two miles away – a short trip by motor, so that, with improved roads and faster cars, commuting became increasingly easy. The farm was in Hope Township, the earliest settlement – 1792 – in the county of Durham. The town of Port Hope, five miles to the southeast, had an atmosphere of unpretentious self-assurance. It had distinctive links with religion and education. St Mark's, one of the Anglican churches, had been built in 1819 entirely of wood, and had miraculously avoided the fires that regularly devastated Ontario towns. The Masseys became members; no doubt Vincent reflected with deep satisfaction on the contrast between the simplicity of St Mark's and the grandeur of the cathedral of Methodism in Toronto. Port Hope was the home of a private school, Trinity College School, established there in 1868, and sometimes described, with colonial pride, as 'the Eton of Canada.' Finally, and of commanding interest to Vincent, the area had strong family associations. The town of Newcastle lay a few miles to the south and west. Here in 1847 Vincent's great-grandfather had built a one-storey foundry and machine shop that had been the beginning of the Massey-Harris Co. A few miles to the east, near the village of Grafton, was the site of the first Canadian Massey settlement.

For a number of years Vincent was content to play the role of the amateur, largely non-resident, farmer. The diary carefully reports farming activities, usually undertaken with visitors – associates at the university, Charles Cochrane, of the department of classics, Walter Bowles, first warden of Hart House – and with members of the family, brother Raymond and brother-in-law Jim Macdonnell. Archibald the bull was 'solemnly introduced' to his new yard, wandering chickens were rounded up in the apple orchard and put in a new chicken house. At the Canadian National Exhibition in 1919, Vincent addressed himself to the selection of a boar for the farm.

For several years the family contented itself with a simple, L-shaped house. In 1922 Vincent consulted his old architectural associates for Hart House, Sproatt and Rolph, about changes, but these resulted only in the building of a balustrade at the front. In March 1927, during a visit from Washington, he launched a new and ambitious scheme of alterations and additons. He had now moved to the architectural firm of Mathers and Haldenby, rapidly gaining prominence in the city, soon, with Vincent's endorsement, to become the principal architects for Upper Canada College and the University of Toronto.

The decision to shape Batterwood into a country house of generous proportions coincided with Vincent's firm establishment as a man of large resources. He had, of course, never known financial constraints. Following the election of 1925, he had complained to Mackenzie King that his income had dropped by one-fifth as a result of resigning directorships; but this was clearly not a serious deprivation.[7] When he left for Washington he sold his Massey-Harris stock, and realized, according to current newspaper estimates, a little over $500,000.[8] His father died in July 1926, and Raymond and he divided equally almost the whole of the estate. In 1927 the National Trust became his financial agent. In 1930 it reported holdings of $1,086,251.90.[9]

From 1926 on Vincent was, as the American newspapers liked to point out, a millionaire. But to designate him narrowly as such is to create an essential misunderstanding, much like describing Pierre Trudeau as a Montreal millionaire. In the first place, his personal resources were, by comparison with the new breed of Canadian millionaires, modest. Moreover, he had none of the driving acquisitive instincts of the genuine millionaire. Given the generous style in which he chose to live, his and Alice's love of entertaining, and the natural wish to give security to his family by preserving his capital, he did not have the personal resources to make large benefactions. The association of the Vincent Massey name with great wealth came from the conspicuous donations made by the Massey Foundation, into which grandfather Hart had poured most of his fortune and which Vincent, as chairman, effectively controlled.

When he began his conversations with the architects, he was in a position to plan a house in the grand manner. Quite apart from his large new resources, he had from the sale of Queen's Park a sum that would go a long way towards covering the costs of the new construction. Victoria College, at first hopeful that its former dean would give the house to the college, then shocked by the asking price of $50,000 recommended by Vincent's real estate brokers, had finally capitulated. The cost of construction, including architects' fees, was only $20,000 more than the sale price of the Queen's Park house. This was a large sum for the time, but not an indication of conspicuous extravagance.

Architecturally, it is easier to say what Batterwood House is not than what it is. Vincent wanted to avoid any suggestion of the monumental or the pretentiously imitative, to eliminate any hint of the homes of the wealthy that he had know in the Toronto area – of Sir Henry Pellatt's dizzyingly vast parody of a Scottish castle, of Sir Joseph Flavelle's school-book illustration of the *beaux arts* approach, of R.S. McLaughlin's home in Oshawa, a few miles to the west of Batterwood, that Vincent described with sweet irony as the 'perfect Hollywood house.'[10] Although the existing house was swallowed up, it did, in a very real sense, dictate the general appearance of the new. The external structure of the original house was preserved, with large additions made to it – a wing on the southeast to match the existing wing on the southwest, and large additions along the main line of the house to both east and west. The original house had been about fifty feet in length; the new was three times as long. But the Mathers and Haldenby plans emphasized the preservation of the original design, which became the inspiration for the additions – a central door with two panels and a semi-circular fanlight (to which were added a more formal Georgian structure, fluted columns on each side, and a broken pediment above enclosing the Massey arms); tall, rectangular, twelve-panel windows, symmetrically arranged, one centrally placed on each side of the door, an identical window above each on the second floor, with a third above the doorway. The same style of window was continued in the additions. Boston hip-style roofs on the additions preserved the low line of the original roof. 'The house,' observed Hugo McPherson, 'reflects the New England colonial style more than the British.'[11]

Inside too, the new Batterwood was built around the original house. The entrance hall, extending the whole depth of the house, had been fashioned from the original dining room and was the focal point. Above the fireplace in the entrance hall was inscribed in gold letters

> *Give all thy day to dreaming and all thy night to sleep:*
> *Let not ambition's tyger devour contentment's sheep.*

The words are by James Elroy Flecker from his poetic drama *Hassan*. They do not seem to have a distinctive Massey ring. Vincent had seen a performance of *Hassan* in London, and had shown little enthusiasm for it. The sentiments are almost a sharp ironic comment on the constant drive of both Alice and Vincent to occupy positions of more and more responsibility and conspicuousness. But the easy rhythms and the hazy romanticism of the lines appealed to his Edwardian taste in poetry.

The ground floor followed a simple plan – the new eastern wing was given over entirely to the living room, forty-four feet in length. On the west of the foyer was the dining room, formed from an existing room slightly expanded. Beyond it, the new extension to the west provided facilities for the kitchen, various small rooms for the servants, and a children's room. The second floor preserved the central corridor of the original house with bedrooms opening off it; the west wing had sleeping quarters for the servants, and the east wing had two suites – each consisting of a large bedroom, a dressing room, and a bath. After Mrs Massey's death, one suite, following a royal visit, was known as the queen's suite. The third floor was unfinished, and was used for storage. In later years there was assembled there the less resplendent of the vice-regal presentations – crude wooden figures of RCMP constables, formidable moose and morose bears, a lamp fashioned out of deer's antlers, a fruit bowl in the form of a maple leaf. Vincent referred to the room in which these mementoes were assembled as his 'horror chamber.'

The flanking extension at the front of the house, seventeen feet wide and twenty-seven feet long, was entirely given over to the library. It was entered directly from the entrance hall, and was usually the first room that visitors saw, serving both as library and as informal reception room. Book shelves from floor to ceiling lined the sides of the room. Vincent had been a book collector from early boyhood, and the collection steadily grew to some six thousand volumes. Its basis was history, chiefly British, Commonwealth, and Canadian, with an emphasis on biography and memoirs. Literature was dominated by the novel, heavily nineteenth century, with collected editions of Scott, Thackeray, Dickens, Trollope, Stevenson, and Meredith. The twentieth century novel was represented conspicuously by H.G. Wells,

Aldous Huxley, Evelyn Waugh, and a substantial collection of detective stories. The basic English poets down to the end of the first world war were there, but few beyond that date. Painting and architecture rivalled history as a major subject, with numerous illustrated monographs, surveys, and histories. Here there was no slighting of the contemporary, and Matisse, Picasso, Wyndham Lewis, and Stanley Spencer mingled on the shelves with Piero Della Francesca, Lorenzo Lotto, Watteau, and Dürer. All the major Canadian artists were represented, chiefly by catalogues. Books had been acquired not for their rarity but to satisfy personal tastes and needs.

Batterwood was surrounded by, indeed almost encased in, a series of gardens. To the south was a rose garden, from which a cedar-hedged path led to a pergola; beyond the pergola was a sunken garden enclosed by a border of perennials and shrubbery. To the north beyond the terrace was a lawn, and then a series of rock and pool gardens on a slope that descended to the little lake. Here, too, to the west, was a swimming pool, carefully sunken and approached by a pathway lined on each side by a row of lime trees. Farther to the west were two tennis courts, and an indoor badminton court. The entrance gate was on the side to the east, as if the house were to be approached casually and then to reveal itself suddenly.

Batterwood was very much the creation of Vincent and Alice. Indeed the gardens, the architects explained in a letter about an article for the *Royal Architectural Journal*, were so much the work of the Masseys that it was not really necessary to mention the name of the landscape architect. Although all the work was done while they were in Washington, every detail was pursued either in correspondence or during visits. If they had a model in mind, it was 'the small, red-brick English houses of the early eighteenth century,' a period during which, Vincent observed, 'charm and comfort were happily blended.'[12]

If Batterwood was, in many respects, an English country house set down in Upper Canada, it had in the transfer acquired some strong native hues. Almost all the paintings in the house, which grew rapidly in number during the early years of occupancy, were Canadian. There were some fine exceptions: an Epstein landscape, Augustus John's pastoral portrait of Dorelia, Keir van Dongen's *Bullocks by the Water*. Otherwise Batterwood was a gallery of contemporary Canadian painting, probably at that time the finest collection in Canada: landscapes by James Morrice, the best of the early twentieth century Canadian painters; the major members of the original Group of Seven – Tom Thomson (represented by thirteen sketches), A.Y. Jackson, Lawren Harris, Fred Varley (*The Green Shawl*, a superb portrait, for which Alice had been the model), Arthur Lismer; later associates of the Group of Seven – Edwin Holgate and L.L. FitzGerald; two contemporary individualists – Emily Carr and David Milne; and the young painters of the thirties who had begun to emerge, most of whom the Masseys knew as friends and supported as patrons – Pegi Nicol, Charles Comfort, Will Ogilvie, Lilias Newton.

The pictures in the Queen's Park house had been almost exclusively European, derived largely from his father's collection. That collection was made up of 'the works of minor painters of the Barbizon school, or of Dutch artists of his day.'[13] Vincent had no interest in preserving the collection, and a year after his father's death almost all the pictures were sold at auction. It was as if these pictures represented a world that Vincent wanted to forget – a provincial world that was satisfied with what its parent culture no longer relished. Without, Batterwood may have had unmistakeable European associations, but within it celebrated the colour and assertiveness of the new land.

Once Batterwood had been conceived and the work begun, Vincent, as usual, was eager to have it completed. He hoped for completion in a year, by the summer of 1928, and when this failed to happen, 'Lal and I turned ourselves into "clerks of the works" and no doubt saved weeks of delay by dealing with details on the job.'[14] On Saturday, 22 September the Masseys gave a party for the workmen and their wives, as they had done on the completion of Hart House and as Vincent was to do many years later for the opening of Massey College. But the real possession of Batterwood did not come until they left Washington. Even then, in June 1930, it was to be an incomplete possession: books and pictures had been packed for London, and Vincent, with some nervousness, waited the result of the Canadian election of 27 July. The election resulted in disastrous defeat for King and the Liberal party. Vincent wrote to R.B. Bennett, the new prime minister, to get his decision on the London appointment, then took the whole family on a week's canoe trip (with three Indian guides) in northern Ontario. It was, so to speak, a ceremonial beginning for a return to Canada, its ritual delights noted and celebrated – 'The dip in the cold and very soft water *en nature,*' 'the lazy fishing,' 'the furious appetites,' 'the paddle on a smooth and silent lake after sunset,' 'the camp fire and northern light.'[15] He returned to face a confrontation with Bennett, and finally on 15 August to submit his resignation.

The shattering of their London plans was a bitter disappointment, but the enforced five-year stay in Canada had many happy results. The Masseys could now possess Batterwood and make it their Canadian home, not simply a summer retreat. An immediate shift to London would have meant a long and continuous absence from Canada and the inevitable weakening of ties. Now they could resume interests only fitfully maintained in Washington, and assume new ones. And, after the feverish and fragmented life of the diplomat, they could take stock of themselves and the family. This, for all practical purposes, consisted of the two boys, Lionel, now fourteen, and Hart, now twelve; Alice's mother, Lady Parkin, advanced in years but still vigorous; Alice's sister Maude, her husband, William Grant, and their four children, Margaret, Charity, Alison, and George (there was a continuous going and coming between the principal's residence and Batterwood); and Alice's second sister resident in Canada, Marjorie, her husband, Jim Macdonnell, and their three children, Anne, Peter, and Katherine (the Macdonnells, living in Montreal, were less frequent visitors). Raleigh Parkin, Alice's brother, and his wife, Louise, joined the Batterwood group at Christmas time, but they too were Montreal residents and Vincent and Alice saw them only occasionally.

Vincent's family on the Massey side disappeared from the inner circle: the Vincents – his mother's family – lived in various parts of the United States, and while Vincent was proud of their attainments in church and university, he saw them infrequently; his brother, Raymond, was now firmly established in London as an actor, and rarely returned to Toronto. Vincent's turning towards his wife's family no doubt arose from preference and affection. But the Parkins also reinforced his English bias. The Parkins were both deeply English and deeply Canadian. Sir George Parkin had been a Canadian of humble origin, but he had made his mark in England. He had not, like so many Canadian expatriates there, made money, but his credentials from his success with the English governing class were impeccable.

Lionel and Hart had both attended a private school near Washington, and were now enrolled at Upper Canada College. Their uncle was the principal, and Vincent, appointed a governor in 1927, had begun to take a strong, active interest in the school. Lionel was a sturdy, good looking boy, keenly interested in the farm and its economy, with a sound manly interest in motor cars. (In his Christmas verse greetings for 1930, Vincent hailed Lionel as a 'fine chauffeur underage.') Hart had artistic interests and skills. He collaborated with his father in drawing a sprightly map of Batterwood and its area, illuminated and framed, and hung in the vestibule of the house. His talent as a painter developed so successfully that he had a canvas accepted in the Royal Canadian Academy show of 1934, submitted under the pseudonym of Clayton Norfield. He was as enthusiastic as his parents about the paintings of David Milne, which had been bought *en masse* by the Masseys. Alice was moved to write to Milne about her young son. 'There is much I will some day tell you about him. He had a very bad operation when he was six years which affected the pituitary gland, which as you know controls growth. This means that as a boy of sixteen he remains very, very, small. He is very healthy, has quite a brilliant mind, plays a violin, and we think has a distinct gift for painting. All these things are compensation for the lack of growth. He is the most fascinating person, and his love of your pictures is a most touching thing to see. He has two of them in his room at school. You couldn't help but be interested in him and like him (forgive a mother's confidence – I just wanted you to know about him). He is the best companion in the world.'[16]

Vincent now had more time to devote to the problems of his sons. Hart had been operated on by the great Boston surgeon, Harvey Cushing.[17] Cushing continued to treat Hart, and, in addition, Vincent sought the advice of a wide group of medical authorities, among them J.B. Collip of McGill University, who had played an important part in the development of insulin, a brilliant young scientist named Hans Selye, also at McGill, who was later to win international fame for his studies of stress, and, in England, Arthur Ellis, who was engaged in fundamental research related to Hart's ailment.

Lionel was healthy and vigorous. His problem was minor, but vexatious to parents of high educational attainment: he was an indifferent student who preferred the active life to the mastery of books. In 1934, as he approached the time when he would write his university entrance examinations, it was evident that he was in difficulties. A group of Lionel's teachers at Upper Canada College decided that it would be best if he undertook technical agricultural studies and prepared himself for the supervision of the Batterwood farm. This was clearly where his interests and satisfactions lay. But other counsels prevailed, stimulated no doubt by Vincent's refusal to accept the suggestion. His eldest son must go to university – not to any university prepared to admit him, but to father's old Oxford college, Balliol. That fall arrangements were made for Lionel to go to Kingston, where he would stay at the home of the deputy minister of education, Duncan McArthur, and would be tutored in the principal academic subjects, English, French, and mathematics, by Queen's University professors under general arrangements made with the principal of Queen's, Hamilton Fyfe. The specific task of the tutors was to prepare Lionel for the Balliol entrance examinations. This was successfully accomplished, and in 1935 Lionel was admitted there.

Raymond's departure from the family circle was not because of any temperamental difference between Vincent and his brother. In his memoirs, Raymond has suggested that Vincent took a cool, supercilious attitude towards his decision to train as an actor. The greater likelihood is that Vincent, a gifted actor himself, approved of the decision and helped to smooth Raymond's way with their Methodist father. He carefully followed his brother's career. He was present when Raymond made his début in a West End performance, playing two minor rôles in the first production of Shaw's *St Joan*.[18] He made a special trip to England in the summer of 1925 in response to a request from Raymond, presumably to discuss financial matters, and was there when Raymond's first child, Geoffrey, was born. For the next three years Vincent was immersed in politics and in the setting up of the legation in Washington. In 1928 Raymond reversed the transatlantic meetings. He came to New York to look for a play that he might produce in London, and to escape briefly from a marriage that had collapsed. The meeting with his brother was not a happy one. Vincent wrote that Raymond was 'full of troubles – difficulties of all kinds – financial, legal, medical, marital.'[19] From this low point, Raymond's fortunes rose rapidly. In November 1930, Vincent and Alice met Raymond's new wife in London and were charmed by her. She was

Adrianne Allen, who was enjoying great success at the time in Noel Coward's *Private Lives*. Vincent was delighted to hear praise of Raymond on all sides, from, among others, Bernard Shaw. In the summer of 1931, again in London, Vincent and Alice saw Raymond and Adrianne regularly. Raymond was now the embodiment of success, as producer, director, actor, both on the stage and in the cinema.

When Raymond finally returned to Toronto in 1934, he did so in the full splendour of his professional status. Prior to its New York opening, he brought a new play, Keith Winter's *The Shining Hour*, for a week's engagement at Toronto's only professional theatre, the Royal Alexandra. The venture was completely Raymond's: he had already appeared in a play by Winter, a young English dramatist who had a talent for pairing Gothic romance and realistic social drama, and he had commissioned the play that became *The Shining Hour*; he was both director and leading man, and his wife appeared opposite him. The theatre, Vincent observed, 'was packed with a very smart audience, almost the atmosphere of a London First Night.'[20] It was a great occasion in a city where the professional theatre was confined to touring companies from London and New York, usually performing plays long-tested in those cities. Vincent and Alice presided over what was, at the very least, a splendid social event. The governor-general, Lord Bessborough, an enthusiastic supporter of the drama, and Lady Bessborough, the lieutenant-governor, Herbert Bruce, and Mrs Bruce, attended the opening; Vincent and Alice sat in the vice-regal box, and gave a formal dinner party after the performance.

Raymond never made another professional return to his native city. Although the first-night crowds were ecstatic, and the theatre was packed for the entire week of the run, the critics found the play slight and harshly melodramatic and predicted failure in New York. The judgment of the provincial city was reversed by the metropolitan centre. After the opening there, Vincent and Alice attended a supper party for the cast given by Ogden Reid, publisher of the *Herald-Tribune* and a friend from Washington days. During the evening Reid called up his drama critic, Percy Hammond, to find out what he would say about the play, and reported a notice of enthusiastic approval. Vincent made no comment about the play in his diary. It is possible that he shared the Toronto critics' opinions, and had been apprehensive of the New York reception. But he was relieved that New York thought well of the play, and he rejoiced in his brother's success.[21]

Outside of the immediate family, Maude and William Grant were the closest to Vincent and Alice. Before their marriage in 1911, Alice wrote to William about her delight in the coming event: 'You know Maude is my very special sister ... You have no idea how happy we are at the thought of your being one of the family. There is absolutely no one who will so naturally become one of us as so much affection is already there for you.'[22] Maude and Alice had first known William Grant when he was Beit lecturer in colonial history at Oxford from 1906 to 1910. Vincent's acquaintance went farther back, to his schoolboy days at St Andrew's, when for two years, from 1902 to 1904, Grant was his history teacher. William recalled Vincent as his favourite pupil, and Vincent had equally warm memories of his teacher. Years later Vincent wrote to William, 'I do not forget the years during which I subjected you to the ruthless examination to which most schoolboys subject their masters. Few schoolmasters have escaped their trial with such a whole-hearted acquittal as you received from your future brother-in-law.'[23] Vincent and Alice were married in the home of the Grants, William at that time being the professor of colonial history at Queen's University. In 1917 Vincent played a crucial role in William's appointment as principal of Upper Canada College: William was overseas, recovering from a severe injury sustained during manoeuvres, and Colonel Massey was asked to secure his acceptance of the appointment before the board of the school made the official proposal. From this time on the closest relations existed between the Grants and the Masseys. When the Massey Foundation was established in 1918, William became one of the directors, and exerted a profound influence on foundation policy.

The relationship between William Grant and Vincent Massey was more a matter of intricate counterpoint than of full harmony. There was, within a fundamental alliance based on respect and affection, a complex of differences. In part, these grew out of age and experience: William was fifteen years older than Vincent, and neither could altogether forget their initial association as student and teacher. Their educational background was similar – a Canadian undergraduate degree (William graduated from Queen's in 1894) and then an Oxford degree. But William was a better and more disciplined scholar (he took a first class in *Literae Humaniores*) and later pursued postgraduate studies in Paris. Over the years he published a number of volumes in Canadian history, but, after leaving university work to be a school principal, he became more of an influential critic of contemporary society than a serious scholar. William's roots were deeply and firmly Presbyterian: his father, George Munro Grant, had been an eminent Presbyterian clergyman, first in the pulpit in Halifax, and then as the principal of Queen's University. Unlike Vincent, William never deserted his early faith, although he accepted the modifications that came with the years. In a letter written during his Oxford days he had referred to Presbyterianism as 'the most intellectual and ethically sound of the religious bodies,'[24] and the intellectual and ethical content of religion always remained his primary concern.

There was a touch of Presbyterian austerity in the Grant outlook; and the habits of a public school headmaster were, under any circumstances, bound to be more circumspect than those of a diplomat in a national capital. From Washington, Vincent sent this Christmas message to William.

> *Dear Brother William, Alice and I*
> *Have racked our brains in an effort to find*
> *What we could steal or borrow or buy*
> *To comfort your body or please your mind.*
>
> *We find ourselves at a hopeless task,*
> *You have no vices – at least not known*
> *Such as respond to a pocket flask,*
> *Or the treasured freight of an 'I'm alone.'*
>
> *One cannot interpret abstract virtue,*
> *Such as yours in terms of a Christmas gift;*
> *The choice of a thing might only hurt you*
> *Did it not enable, or else uplift.*
>
> *So we have severed the Gordian Knot,*
> *Nor yet endeavoured the fates to taunt;*
> *Accept the enclosed with our love – a lot*
> *And buy whatever you darn well want!*

The verses, although light-hearted, were a comment on the staunch Presbyterian from the emancipated Methodist and Anglican neophyte. But William's austerity did not extend to important matters. He was no pinched puritan. He, for instance, warmly praised Frederick Philip Grove's early novel *Settlers of the Marsh* (1928), which had been abused and proscribed for its realistic treatment of sex; and when his brother-in-law Jim Macdonnell attacked him for defending H.G. Wells's 'glorification of raw lust,' he replied that he did not believe 'in the new negative purity of virginity' and that 'the desire of man for woman is to him – and to me – heaven-born.'[25] Vincent would not have differed with William on this particular question, although he would have been more reticent about expressing his views.

On general social issues, William was far more outspoken than Vincent. During his undergraduate days at Oxford, Vincent had gloried in the spacious social life of pre-war England without looking at its hideous underside of poverty and human degradation. William saw this underside and reacted in fierce disgust. 'The condition of the lower classes in the cities is appalling, and the drain from the country to the cities still goes on. The hopeless degradation of vast masses of the population is terrible ... to go through the streets and see the thousands of pinched undersized vagabonds, useless morally and physically, who cadge a living, makes one wish to find who are responsible for it all, and hang them every one.'[26]

William was outspoken, too, in his protest against the anti-semitism that ran through polite English Canadian society, especially in Toronto, like an invisible but powerful disease. (Vincent was naturally attracted to individual Jews because of their intellectual and artistic attainments, but the diary suggests, from time to time, an acceptance of the common attitude towards the generality.) When a young man, a member of a prominent Jewish family who had been a student at Upper Canada College and subsequently had become a Rhodes scholar, experienced great difficulties in getting established, William wrote: 'It makes me feel almost communistic when I think that the depression, and our medieval anti-Semitism may bring about in his case a repetition of the old tragedy of the ardent young Jew who comes up against a dead end and leads a useless life.'[27]

The ideas and attitudes of William and Vincent coincided most closely in two areas that were of constant and primary concern to both of them: education, and the Canadian outlook. When Grant wrote to the principal of Queen's University, explaining why he was leaving his professorship to head a boy's school, he emphasized the opportunity that he would have to change the course of Ontario education. 'Secondary education in Ontario has reached a high level of mechanical efficiency, and great sacrifices have been made for it. But it is loveless and unbeautiful.'[28] The implication was that from his central position in a great private school he could play a crucial role in humanizing the educational system. Ten years later, he used almost the same words in writing about Vincent's contribution to education: 'His ambition was to make Ontario education, which was efficient but unlovely, more beautiful.'[29] Both men were devoted to the idea of changing formal education from a mechanism for acquiring a body of useful knowledge into a civilizing process. They believed that formal schooling should exist within a wide context of informal discussion, the practice and enjoyment of the arts, and a consciousness of the moral and social issues of the day.

Neither William nor Vincent had any problem in identifying and expounding the Canadian outlook. Canada to them was a European country in a North American environment. (By European they meant, first of all, British. Vincent had a livelier sense of the French heritage, but his bias was still unmistakably British.) But towards both European heritage and North American environment, Canada should demonstrate a constant wariness. William could be abrupt and corrosive in his comments on anglophile extremism. About Sir George Parkin's Empire gospel, for instance, he wrote, 'I don't think that he got God and Oxford and the British Empire wholly separated.'[30] In a letter to Sir Maurice Hankey, secretary of the British cabinet and of the committee of imperial defence, with whom he corresponded regularly, he complained about 'The mid-Victorian stuffiness and hauteur with which the [British] Foreign Office is said to treat the press, more especially the chief Canadian and American representatives,' and recommended that Hankey consult Vincent Massey about the superior manner in which the American Department of State dealt with foreign correspondents.[31] He had no desire, however, to see Canada assimilated to American ways. When he was an Oxford lecturer he received, by mistake, a letter from the American consul asking him to register as an American citizen. Grant replied, 'Yours of June 3 received. Your informant is incorrect. I am not, and never shall be, an American citizen'[32] and he meant it with every fibre of his being. Wariness of undue influences was not enough, however, to define Canadianism. The positive qualities both William and Vincent would have emphasized were a distaste for extremism, a belief that a consciousness of tradition is necessary for an authentic style, and a feeling for the beauty and power of the land, especially as it was being interpreted by the new school of landscape painters.

In his correspondence, wide-ranging and salty, one of William's favourite subjects was Vincent Massey. He wrote about Vincent as a headmaster would write about an able but complex student, emphasizing first the student's strong points, but scrupulously noting his deficiencies. In 1918, when Vincent was a civil servant in Ottawa, William described him as uniting 'power of hard work with business and political sagacity.'[33] In 1926, William was still full of praise for both Vincent and Alice, but success had revealed a weakness. In a letter to Sir Maurice Hankey, he included a series of sketches of the Canadian delegates to the 1926 Imperial Conference. He gave a devastating account of Mackenzie King, and a brief factual statement about Lapointe. Vincent received the most detailed treatment. There was a suggestion of the light that failed, of the superbly endowed young prince with a fault that could prove to be fatal.

... the new Canadian Minister to Washington, Vincent Massey. I have known him well ever since he was my favourite pupil at school, and he is my brother-in-law, having married my wife's elder sister, the daughter of the late Sir George Parkin. She is some years older than himself, but is still a woman of good looks, charm, and mental and social distinction. They are very deeply devoted to each other, and she is accompanying him to England.

Massey has a natural distinction and quickness of mind, and wide interests, social, political, dramatic, and religious. Thus, though a Canadian, he went to Oxford University, and took a very good degree in Honour History. Though his parents and his grandparents were prominent Methodists, his aesthetic and dramatic good taste has made him a member of the Church of England. He is wealthy and has been an enlightened patron of education, the drama, and music.

During the war he was one of the dollar-a-year men in Ottawa, and was the only one of them to show that mixture of political and administrative ability so essential to success. At Washington he will be admirable, having a real flair for that imaginative administration which is akin to statesmanship. He is a strong believer in the British Empire, and in the British spirit.

The one defect both of himself and his wife is that they are extremely accessible to subtle and well bred flattery by anyone whom they regard as an intellectual equal, more especially if the flatterer has a title. Thus, when the Devonshires left they were inconsolable, and looked for little from the rough soldier who succeeded. Byng was very charming to them, and within a month they rated him even higher than they did the Devonshires. This is an intellectual and aesthetic snobbery, not a social. Set some able, sympathetic and well bred people to be nice to them, and in a week they will adopt your American policy.[34]

In the extensive literature of abuse that King inspired, Grant's contribution in this same letter has a place. Grant wrote that 'it is very difficult to make a permanent impression on him [King] for two reasons. 1) He is as selfish a man as I have ever known, the selfishness disguised by a thick smear of sentimentalism. He will, therefore, sacrifice anyone or anything to his ambition, and then sob about it. 2) He has a mind as lacking in edge as a jelly fish. Fortunately for you he has a real fund of dignified, though rather windy eloquence, and will do little harm if given plenty of speeches to make.'

Jim Macdonnell, Vincent's other Canadian brother-in-law, was not as close to him as William. After Queen's and Oxford, he had entered business, and in the thirties was an executive with the National Trust. Like Grant, Macdonnell was a Presbyterian, with the same combination of idealism and moral integrity. Tall, spare, his expression verging on the severe, he gave an impression of austerity that was not entirely misleading. He had uncompromising ideas about responsibility and duty. During the war he served in the front lines, and he despised those who managed to avoid active war service. He wrote to Grant from France, 'Every man who is not prevented by physical unfitness or some other good reason and who does not volunteer is going to have a bad time with his conscience in later years.'[35] (The thought occurs that he may have resented Vincent's unbroken home front service.) But the severity concealed a relaxed, light touch. He remarked once to Grant,

'We both lack that sure earmark of gentle blood – a liking for whiskey and we both succumb to that lower middle class liking for sweets.'[36]

Jim Macdonnell was, like William, a subject for Vincent's light verse, with the same general theme – Presbyterian austerity.

> *D'you know him?*
> *Smile is prim*
> *Jokes are grim*
> *Morals are trim*
> *(Irreducible – each limb!)*
> *One of the longer seraphims –*
> *Attenuated Cherubim*
> *and also Presbyteri-im*
> *That's Jim.*

At the Christmas party at Batterwood in 1930, Vincent hailed his brother-in-law again:

> *There's Jim Macdonnell – long in head and limb*
> *A trinity of Johns have nurtured him.*
> *Balliol, Calvin, and Macdonald too –*
> *Under these three his present stature grew.*

The last reference was, of course, to Sir John A. Macdonald, the archetypal chief of Canadian conservatism. Jim, who was later to enter politics and to serve in the Diefenbaker cabinet, was a staunch Conservative; and he had more difficulty than Grant did in accepting Vincent's devotion to the Liberal party. He was particularly unhappy about Vincent's close alliance with Mackenzie King, whom he hated with Presbyterian fervour. To Grant he reported the belief that 'the only people loyal to King were the Honourable Vincent Massey and his wife and Hon. Wilfrid McDougald.'[37] The association of the Masseys with McDougald was a malicious touch, since it was generally believed that McDougald, a close friend of King, used his intimacy for personal gain – a belief substantiated a few years later in the Beauharnois scandal that rocked the Liberal government. Over the years Macdonnel became increasingly cool to Vincent. The story is told that on one occasion, in Macdonnell's presence, a political associate criticized Vincent sharply, then apologized to Macdonnell for speaking ill of his brother-in -law. Macdonnell drew himself up to his full commanding height, and in his best calvinistic manner said, 'Not my brother-in-law – my wife's.'

Two members of the Batterwood family were George Smith, professor of history at the University of Toronto, and Burgon Bickersteth, the warden of Hart House. Each was a frequent guest on his own, and both were invariably members of the Christmas house party. Burgon was now highly visible and influential in the university, and he had become, and was to remain throughout his life, a close friend of Vincent Massey. Since the invitation he had received from Mackenzie King, he had not lost his associations with the great world. In 1932 he was asked to join the BBC in a senior capacity. Vincent was strongly opposed to acceptance: Burgon 'wouldn't like the drudgery' and 'his best qualities would have no chance,'[38] and the invitation was declined. Burgon knew that Hart House was close to the hearts of both Vincent and Alice, and he was sometimes over-zealous in his requests for aid. They were usually granted, although Vincent protested against Burgon's assumption that Hart House automatically qualified for Massey benefactions. He wrote to William Grant that 'It is very easy for the idea to get abroad that the Foundation is a sort of amiable milch cow for everything in Hart House with the Warden as the milkmaid.'[39]

George Smith and Vincent Massey had been contemporaries at the University of Toronto, and Smith had preceded Vincent to Balliol. They were colleagues in the history department during Vincent's brief academic career. Smith had served overseas with the Princess Patricia's Canadian Light Infantry and cherished his regimental associations. By the late twenties he was the senior in the history department. He was a fine teacher, whose lectures were careully prepared (and regularly refurbished). But he had not published, was passed over for the headship of the department, and in 1929 left the department and academic life, with some bitterness, to embark on a business career. Vincent was eager to bring him back into the academic fold. In many respects, he had, during the twenties, been Vincent's closest friend, a constant guest at Queen's Park and Batterwood, a confidant in time of trouble. (He had, for instance, gone with Vincent and Alice to

Baltimore for Hart's crucial operation.) William Grant shared Vincent's high opinion of Smith, and his little sketch of Smith in a letter to Jim Macdonnell would have had Vincent's approval: 'He is academic, and I rate his intellect high, yet he is not without business shrewdness and knowledge of business life. He is a gentleman, and his strongest and most lovable characteristic is his love for and helpfulness to young men.' With a typical blunt shrewdness Grant added that 'there is of course the difficulty that a celibate is always in danger of marrying a fool.'[40] William and Vincent worked together, but to no avail, to have Smith appointed secretary of the Rhodes Trust in Oxford (Vincent proposed to change the title to warden of Rhodes House). Smith left business shortly after, and joined the history department at the University of Alberta.

Another frequent visitor to Batterwood in the early thirties was a young lawyer, Paul Martin, who during his undergraduate days at St Michael's College, University of Toronto, had been marked by Bickersteth for a career in public life. He was increasingly active in politics as a Liberal, and Vincent, now fully committed as King's lieutenant, had enlisted him in the service.

All of the relatives and friends would come together at Christmas. The tradition of Christmas celebrations had grown up at 71 Queen's Park, and included church attendance, a grand dinner, distribution of presents (with Vincent as Santa Claus), and charades in the evening. At Batterwood the celebration could expand into a house party, beginning a few days before Christmas and extending a few days beyond. The badminton court became a theatre, where the traditional charades grew into dramatic presentations. Vincent was the star performer. George Grant recalls brilliant improvisations, usually involving one of the guests. Lady Parkin was a favourite subject. She was a sweet, uncomplicated person, easily moved to tears or laughter, usually a little *distrait*, dropping her handkerchief, recovering it in some confusion. Vincent's impersonation was brilliantly accurate, but so warm and sympathetic that Lady Parkin joined in the general merriment.

In building Batterwood, Vincent no doubt had in mind English country homes that he had known as an Oxford student on vacations, and later as a guest at fashionable weekend house parties. But he never aped the English squire and, even less so, the wealthy Canadian gentleman farmer feeding his agricultural fantasies on prize cattle. Recalling, possibly, Bernard Shaw's description of the Edwardian aristocrat's country home as 'consisting of a prison for horses with an annex for the ladies and gentlemen who ride them,' he never kept a stable of horses, nor rode to hounds (although there were ponies for the children), acknowledging only by attendance at Epsom and the Queen's Plate his respect for this avocation of the fashionable world. He and Alice were great dog lovers; but they thought of their dogs as house companions, and not as creatures of the farm. The loss of a favourite dog was a great blow, as this entry in Vincent's diary shows. 'On returning to Batterwood from Toronto, found really tragic news awaiting us, that poor Beau had been killed by a motor ... L & I were terribly shocked and for two or three days we thought of little else. How extraordinary it is that a dog can wind his little personality so closely around one.'[41]

It was Vincent's monarchical sentiments that could on occasion turn Batterwood into a transplanted English country house. He had always been a supporter of the monarchy, although the theoretical approval of the institution did not rule out sharp comment on royal persons. On at least two occasions, he thought that the Prince of Wales had exceeded the generous limits of tolerance generally accorded to the conduct of royalty. On a Canadian tour in 1924, the prince visited Hart House and Vincent described him as 'very jaded and highly nervous. A decent slightly underdeveloped boy with a natural bent for rather low society, a hatred of his official job, good manners, a horror of boredom and not at all an inconsiderable mother wit.'[42] Three years later, Vincent, as Canadian minister in Washington, was called to counsel the prince against extending his Canadian trip to the United States. He advised strongly against it, particularly with an election in the offing. The prince was irate and exploded, 'Hell, it's a bloody bore.' Vincent commented in his diary: 'Neurotic, jumpy, easily bored and likely to develop a rather touchy temper ... takes his only real enjoyment out of the society of people unworthy of his friendship e.g. ... the numerous very commonplace young women whom he caused to be invited to parties by which he upsets the balance of society in many places.'[43] But when he met the prince in London on official occasions, these harsh provisos disappeared in the brilliance of the occasion and in the glow of the prince's charm. The king never aroused the slightest suggestion of criticism. He was the kindly, patriarchal figure who had given his blessings to Vincent as he commenced his diplomatic career; and he was the embodiment of the idea of monarchy – a compelling symbol and warm *paterfamilias*.

On 6 May 1935, Batterwood became a focal point for the celebration of the twenty-fifth anniversary of King George's ascension to the throne. At 11.30 AM Vincent and Alice attended a town service in Port Hope. The evening they spent in the splendour of a formal dinner in Toronto, at the great chateau-like structure in Chorley Park where the king's provincial representative lived and held court. But on that day the monarchy found an even more receptive home in Batterwood. At one o'clock all the employees were summoned to the house. There they drank the king's health, 'a good sherry cup laced with brandy.' Afterwards Vincent and Alice made individual presentations to mark the great day – 'for the men (their wives included) a pewter cup with the Jubilee medal on the front and the words: "Batterwood 6th May 1935" engraved below and for the children china mugs with the King and Queen's picture and for the elder girls and maids in the house china boxes similarly decorated.'[44] The Batterwood celebrations ended in the afternoon as the entire group listened in reverential silence to the broadcast from London, with its climax 'the unforgettably moving speech by the King.'

Batterwood was a place where he could determine his own company and indulge his hobbies. Besides the inner Batterwood group, he saw old academic friends. Frank Underhill, classmate at Toronto and Balliol, had returned to his alma mater after a long period on the history staff of the University of Saskatchewan, his radical ideas shaped and toughened by his experience in a prairie democracy; he was a guest on several occasions. Vincent observed that it was 'interesting to get in touch with his radical mind again.'[45]

Vincent had now abandoned formal appearances on the stage. He found a relaxing substitute in the making of movies, in which house guests were called upon to play parts. He made three during the interregnum at Batterwood: 'Durham Darling,' a tender love story; 'How Derek Dared,' a tale of heroism in the far west; and 'Hell in Hollywood,' a satirical view of the cinema industry. In the evening guests would be shown the films. His academic friends, Vincent complained, were often bored. But he was elated by the enthusiastic response of the company of *The Shining Hour*, who were staying at Batterwood prior to the Toronto opening, and concluded that only professionals could properly appreciate his work.

He could now devote himself intensively to mastering French. He took seriously a remark he had made in a Montreal speech that bilingualism was an essential part of being a Canadian, and he had, from time to time, taken instruction in the language. Now, in the fall of 1934, he devoted a month to a concentrated course under the supervision of Mrs W.R. Paterson, known affectionately as Madame Pat, a French lady, who had married a Torontonian, taught French at University College, and brought Parisian *chic* to Toronto society. He followed an exacting program: in the early morning the writing of a short French composition, then at 10 AM two hours of conversation with Madame Pat; in the afternoon one and a half hours of reading aloud and conversation, and in the evening another two hours of conversation and instruction, with French alone spoken at both lunch and dinner.

During the first few years after their return, Vincent and Alice were absent for long periods from Batterwood: in the fall of 1930, for two and a half months in France and England; from February to August 1931, when they were accompanied by Hart and Alison Grant, a good deal of the time on the continent; later in the same year for three months in China, where Vincent was the chairman of the Canadian delegation to a meeting of the Institute for Pacific Relations; for most of February 1932, on a speaking tour in the west, where Vincent appeared as an expert on the Far East, and at the same time cultivated political allies. From this time on, the political urgencies were too great to permit long trips, and his absences were confined to brief visits to New York, where he continued to see every contemporary play of note, and dined with old American friends, in particular with Walter Lippmann.

For the first two years of the Batterwood interregnum, his English friends in high places suggested that he should accept appointment in the British service abroad. They were unhappy about the new Canadian prime minister, who had summarily dismissed their favourite Canadian, and who was now causing alarm in British political circles by his aggressive and high-handed tactics. There were suggestions of an appointment as British ambassador to China, or of a governorship in the Dominions. The latter proposal took on a specific form when J.H. Thomas, the dominion secretary, offered Vincent the governorship of West Australia. Vincent was tempted and delayed his reply until he could return to Canada and consult Mackenzie King. King was firm against acceptance. He needed Massey for the reshaping of the Liberal party. Vincent declined the appointment. It had some immediate allure – an automatic knighthood, translation to a higher service, and, thereby, a sharp and telling rebuke to Bennett; but he knew that his Canadian ties were too strong and numerous to be thus sharply severed. Another proposal made a little later and sent via the office of the British high commissioner in Canada was that he should become 'High Commissioner of the League of Nations at Danzig' – a proposal that he had no difficulty in declining. Even at this early stage in the march to war, an appointment such as this could only arouse deep apprehension.

Vincent received an offer of a university presidency. It came from Dalhousie, with the strong endorsement of the chairman of the board and the retiring president.[46] But the Maritimes, for which Vincent was to have an increasing affection, were far removed from his various interests, and he could not consider the appointment even on a short-term basis.

His various interests – education, music, painting, the drama, for the most part concentrated in Toronto – were more assertive now that he was easily accessible. Politics too were becoming more demanding than they had been in the later twenties. His reappointment to London was dependent on a Liberal return to power, and subject to the whim of Mackenzie King. By 1932 he was active in a multiplicity of causes, and Batterwood ceased to be headquarters and became a retreat and a refuge.

Fortunately his health was equal to the strain of a hyperactive life. The diplomatic life with its endless succession of formal dinner parties had not altered his boyish build. He delighted in good food, but was able throughout his life to indulge his appetite and at the same time preserve an appearance of slim austerity. At Washington he had played golf regularly; and at Batterwood he swam, played tennis and badminton, and took long walks. Alice was not so fortunate. Her two boys had been born when she was thirty-eight and forty, and the births had been difficult. She retained immense energy and drive, but often in Washington days she would find it necessary to retire from the official life and seek a complete rest. In the summer of 1932 she had periods of acute illness. The illness returned in the new year; there were anxious consultations with doctors, and finally, in June 1933, a decision to operate. The operation took place in New York and was successful.

The Batterwood family suffered two losses during these days. Lady Parkin, since the death of her husband in 1922, had been close to the Masseys, and at the time of her final illness was staying with them. The night before her death, the editor of the Winnipeg *Free Press*, John Dafoe, had been a guest at Batterwood. When Alice told her mother about Dafoe's visit, she said, 'Tell him how much I enjoy that page of his. I love its quality – quality – quality!' 'Those were the last words she spoke,' wrote Vincent, 'not a bad legacy to the grandchildren and all.'[47] A more tragic death was that of William Grant on 3 February 1935. His powers of resistance greatly lowered by his war wound, he was unable to rally against a severe attack of pneumonia. For Vincent, it meant the disappearance of a kindly but unflinchingly critical mentor, who knew his old pupil's strengths and weaknesses. Nobody could take William Grant's place.

CHAPTER EIGHT

A Young Maecenas

Although the period from 1930 to 1935 was to see a great intensification of Vincent's interest in politics, immensely stimulated by his own concern for political survival, he never at any time allowed politics to crowd out his interest in the arts and education. Politics was his official profession that he attended to assiduously and with some personal satisfaction; the arts and education were his passion, never to be slighted even under the most acute distractions and pressures, and to be nurtured single-mindedly when the clouds of politics lifted. At Washington his concern for the two Hart House creations – the theatre and the quartet – continued. McFarland, the administrative watch-dog for both, kept him informed regularly of developments financial and cultural. From Washington, he and Alice arranged for the appointments of directors of the theatre, Carrol Aikins from 1927 to 1929 and Edgar Stone from 1929 to 1934.

These appointments constituted a shift to directors whose experience and training had been in Canada. Aikins came from a prominent Manitoba family that had attained senior positions in business and politics. He was a romantic individualist, who chose to be a fruit farmer in the Okanagan Valley, but directed most of his time and his resources (and the resources of his affluent relatives) to building a little theatre on his property. Vincent knew and admired his work, and had been in touch with him before his appointment as director was made. Edgar Stone had worked on some of the Hart House productions. He was employed by the Ontario government in its motion picture branch, and was enthusiastic about the new medium of radio. His strength as a director was in the handling of technical problems. Both Aikins and Stone continued to draw upon the considerable number of acting talents that had grown up around Hart House Theatre, and each had his triumphs, Aikins with *Juno and the Paycock* and Stone with *Peer Gynt*, the theatre's one hundredth production. But, on the whole, for the theatre this was a troubled period. The depression reduced audiences, and thrust the arts into the background. Vincent was never inclined towards generous subsidies; he wanted audience receipts to bear most of the costs, with the Massey Foundation entering only when careful planning and rigid accounting failed to achieve a balanced budget. The balanced budget required a middle-brow policy in the choice of plays and a firm hold on expenses. There were thus inevitable conflicts between Vincent and the directors. He wrote to Aikins urging 'a continued care on the financial side which need not in any way detract from our artistic achievements.'[1] It is doubtful that Aikins, with his romantic concept of the divine mission of art, took these sentiments seriously. In addition to this, Hart House Theatre, in the university but not of it, was an intense, introverted world, with its share of sensitive people responsible to no authority except their own talents, constantly comparing what was present and often irritating with what was past and beatified by time. Edgar Stone no doubt suffered from comparison with the British-trained directors of the twenties.

Vincent had moments of pessimism about the theatre. On a return to Toronto in the spring of 1929, he went to see Carrol Aikins' production of *Antony and Cleopatra*, a play that has usually escaped the grasp of even the most accomplished performers. He reported 'a fairish production but a miserable house. A depressing evening on the whole because "Ichabod" seemed somehow to be written on the proscenium.'[2] The theatre survived and even revived under the direction of Stone. By 1934, however, the old malaise returned, and Vincent and Alice decided to entrust it for the 1934–5 season to a number of directors.

(The glory that Vincent gloomily saw departing in 1929 did not return to the theatre until after the second world war when the university finally assumed, although without enthusiasm, the role of the Massey Foundation and appointed a full-time director, Robert Gill. In the early fifties Hart House recaptured the excitement and repeated the success of the early twenties. Just as the early Hart House helped prepare the way for a national movement in the amateur theatre, so the Hart House of the fifties helped to prepare the way for a national movement in the professional theatre. Vincent Massey had launched and sustained Hart House Theatre in its early stages and had not deserted it in the later stages of privation. He had cause to remember with satisfaction the day when he and Alice decided to turn a rifle range into a little theatre.)

The other Hart House creation – the quartet – continued throughout the Batterwood interregnum to be a major concern. Indeed, Vincent was much more deeply involved with it than he was with the theatre. A quartet, he had rapidly discovered, was a balance not only of musical skills, but of individual temperaments. Its members felt free to write to Vincent about the work of the group and about their personal problems – all except Boris Hambourg, who was content to play his cello with untroubled perfection. Increasingly the letters from Harry Adaskin, second violin, and Milton Blackstone, viola, reverted to one subject – the increasing tensions created by the first violinist, Geza de Kresz, undoubtedly a musician of great talents, but often arrogant in his relation to his fellows, and imperfectly loyal to the quartet. Finally, late in the summer of 1935, Vincent was persuaded to write to de Kresz and request his withdrawal. De Kresz accepted his dismissal more in sorrow than in anger. This, in effect, brought to an end the Masseys' close personal relationship to the quartet. A distinguished violinist, James Levey, succeeded de Kresz, but the quartet never recovered 'the glorious sweep of unity' that it had possessed in its heyday.[3]

During its great years from 1924 to 1934, the quartet brought intense joy to Vincent and Alice. All of its members were happy to look upon the Masseys as their generous patrons. At their request the programs prominently displayed the words 'founded in 1924 by the Hon. Vincent Massey and Mrs Massey.' They responded eagerly to requests from the Masseys to perform privately. During Chester's final illness in 1926 they came to the Jarvis Street house to play for him. At the Washington legation and at Batterwood they played for small intimate groups with all the enthusiasm and devotion of court musicians performing for a royal patron. Vincent recorded one such occasion at the legation, where the quartet was dining prior to a concert at the Library of Congress. 'At dinner the quartet became temperamental and declined to eat so instead they played the Ravel quartet to us while we dined. Such music makes one ashamed to eat.'[4] A Batterwood visit turned into an all-day festival. 'The H.H. String Quartet and their wives came down for the day. A feast of music and other feasting. A Haydn quartet in a.m. along with Debussy's afterwards, and in the p.m. Brahms' Quartet with Mrs de Kresz and a quartet by Beethoven afterwards. The servants all came to hear the afternoon concert.'[5]

The Masseys were especially attached to the youngest member of the quartet, Harry Adaskin, and his wife Frances. (Vincent wrote an 'Epithalamium or Nuptial Ode on the felicitous occasion of the eighth anniversary of their marriage celebrated at Batterwood, August 7, 1934,') Two incidents dramatize the relationship. Adaskin wrote to Vincent for advice on sponsorship for a loan to purchase 'a fine fiddle' – a Joseph Guarnerius – which had been reduced from $6000 to $4000. He had been turned down by the bank, which would not consider keeping a violin as security. Vincent did not reply by letter, but, shortly afterwards, he sent a note directing the Massey Foundation to pay $3500 for a violin to be bought by Harry Adaskin on terms arranged with an officer of the National Trust Company. Later on, Adaskin gave Hart violin lessons. The Masseys wanted him to charge regular fees, but Adaskin replied that he couldn't think of charging them anything. No one, Adaskin explained, could ever repay them for their efforts on behalf of art, music, and the theatre in Canada. In his memoirs, Adaskin recounts the affecting sequel. 'Mrs Massey burst into a flood of tears. Her husband put his arms around her shoulder and tried to soothe her spirit. She couldn't speak at first, but since she couldn't stop crying, yet wanted to say something, she spoke through her tears. "No one's ever, ever said anything like that to us, have they, Vincent? Have they? No one's ever said anything like that." And she continued to cry.'[6]

The Hart House Quartet is the best example of Vincent's skills and power as a patron. The financial support, although not great, was indispensable, and, at the time, could not have come from any other source. More important, he was a unifying force, who dealt sympathetically with a long succession of personal crises and administrative obstructions. He was determined that the quartet should gain international recognition and correct the impression of a Canada immersed in wheat, pulp, and politics. In this, the quartet succeeded beyond his expectations.

In the period between Washington and London, Vincent avoided any more personal initiatives in the theatre and music; but, as the one nationally visible figure in the arts, he could not escape involvement. In music the involvement was comparatively minor. In 1932 he accepted the presidency of the Toronto Symphony Orchestra. The new director was Ernest MacMillan, whom Vincent greatly admired and whose advice in musical matters he had often sought. He reported an 'amazing transformation' in the orchestra under MacMillan's direction;[7] after hearing the Montreal orchestra some months later, he wrote 'pretty dull compared to ours.'[8] There were, nonetheless, suggestions of the emotional problems that plague artistic enterprises. He had MacMillan as a weekend guest at Batterwood to recover from the psychological shocks of Toronto society. He had become, 'poor fellow, fed up with intrigue and indifference in Toronto, a difficult community for a sensitive man.'[9] But Vincent himself kept aloof from this intrigue. His involvement with the theatre was far more demanding and important.

The Dominion Drama Festival was conceived by the governor-general, Lord Bessborough, who had succeeded Lord Willingdon in 1931. A man not conspicuously animated either in private conversation or on the public platform, and with no great range of cultural interests, he yet had a passion for the theatre. At his country seat in Hampshire he had built a fully equipped theatre, and had brought in professionals for his productions. He was determined to use his vice-regal office to stimulate the Canadian theatre. When, in September 1931, Captain Alan Lascelles, the governor-general's private secretary, sent Vincent a proposal drafted by His Excellency for a national dramatic competition, Vincent had no choice but to respond. He looked upon the office of governor-general as an essential part of the monarchical system, even more important in the new Commonwealth than in the old Empire. From early manhood he had been a guest at Rideau Hall, and had known all the governors-general who had served since that time. Now here was a governor-general who shared his own passionate concern for the theatre. His sense of duty, his reverence for the crown, and his concern for the development of the Canadian theatre all neatly cohered. The long letter of advice that he wrote in January 1932 combined endorsement of the idea with some judicious comments on its implementation. He counselled a cautious approach, pointing out that dramatic activity was not automatically accepted in Canada as desirable. This was particularly true of Canadian drama. In a recent speech to the Royal Society, on 'Art and Nationality in Canada,' he had remarked that 'a little experience with the amateur stage would suggest that the public seems to combine an insistent demand for Canadian plays with an almost religious abstention from the performance.'[10] He accepted Bessborough's suggestion that competitions should be divided into set-piece declamations of classical soliloquies and dramatic performances, and of the two he thought that the former would meet with most public approval, especially from provincial departments of education. Fortunately, this schoolmasterish idea was abandoned. For one who had fought so long and hard for a Canadian theatre Vincent's adherence to the idea is curious. Perhaps he merely wanted to show his respect for the royal concept, or unconsciously was intent upon reducing the scope and importance of the competition. His other suggestions were sound. The competition should be national in scope, not confined, as the governor-general suggested, to the two central provinces. A central committee should be made up of experts, not of a gathering of political and educational dignitaries. And no grand meeting should be called until a definite scheme had been worked out by a few; 'otherwise there are apt to be useless questions and objections raised through misunderstandings, or, on the other hand, an unintelligent acquiescence.'[11]

Vincent was elected chairman of the Dominion Drama Festival at the inaugural meeting on 29 October 1932, and from then until he left for his posting in London in November 1935 he was continuously in touch with festival problems. The active administrator was the director and vice-chairman, Colonel Henry Osborne, an old friend of Vincent and his nominee, so that communication was easy and rapid. The Massey Foundation provided the major initial financing, and Vincent, besides dealing quickly and judiciously with a succession of problems – regional and provincial sensitivities, the choice of adjudicators, the nature and number of awards – presided at the Ottawa finals in 1933,

1934, and 1935, and the lengthy meetings that followed, the last occurring when his political preoccupation was at its most intense.

Lord Bessborough's strategy for a national campaign had been sound, and Vincent Massey was the effective field commander. Despite their common devotion to the theatre, the two men never approached intimacy. Vincent was far more enthusiastic about the courtly Willingdon, or the blunt, soldierly Byng. Perhaps he sensed the solid businessman beneath the imposing vice-regal presence (Bessborough's fortune had come from the manufacture of margarine). After the Bessboroughs' final visit to Batterwood, during which court protocol was meticulously observed, Vincent made these summary comments: 'Their Exs both most friendly and welcoming but he is always very self-conscious and "buttoned up," and she although with much superficial charm shows beneath it a Latin dogmatism which tends to affect the intelligence which she undoubtedly possesses.'[12]

In the theatre and music, during the Batterwood years, Vincent either continued earlier initiatives of his own or put his influence and administrative abilities at the service of good causes initiated by others. It was painting that aroused fresh initiatives. The sale of the Queen's Park house and, along with it, most of the traditional art inherited from his father, and the move to a new house and new surroundings in the Canadian countryside, seemed to release his interest in Canadian painting. He had not been indifferent hitherto to the Canadian art scene. He had acquired some Tom Thomson sketches as early as 1918. Friendship with Lawren Harris and membership in the Arts and Letters Club had brought him into association with the members of the Group of Seven, particularly with Fred Varley and A.Y. Jackson. He had been responsible for four Varley portrait commissions, of himself, his wife, his father, and his father-in-law. Alex Jackson became a close friend, and acted as an advance agent in the building up of the Massey collection. Canadian painting seemed to Vincent to be far more varied and vigorous, and certainly far more patently national, than Canadian music or drama. The latter were largely a matter of peforming the works of Europeans; there were few native dramatists and composers, and these few received a frosty reception from native audiences. But Canadian painters, even if they were immigrants and had received their early training abroad, had to come to grips with the landscape, and the landscapes of the most adventurous painters had a quality not to be found elsewhere – at once realistic and abstract, rock and forest and water set to strong rhythms and colours.

The new group of landscape painters – 'The Group of Seven' as they were called – aroused passionate opposition. They concentrated on barren and austere landscapes, untypically remote, and they used colour with what seemed deliberate lavishness and violence. McGillivray Knowles, an accomplished landscape painter in the traditional manner, recounted this story about the response of an English viewer to paintings by the Group of Seven: 'A lady observing some pictures from Canada, hung at Wembley, stated, "What a strange country; surely I would not like to emigrate to such a place!" A lady companion replied, "Oh, I have been in Canada; it is a beautiful country; these pictures must have been painted by the Indians."'[13] There were accomplished portrait painters among them – Varley was unsurpassed in this field – but they largely neglected human subjects, and scorned the allegorical and historical themes favoured by some nineteenth century Canadian artists.

Vincent found himself in the middle of this controversy. In 1925 he had been appointed to the board of trustees of the National Gallery. Mackenzie King had made the appointment not out of sympathy with Vincent's advanced artistic tastes but as a first step in winning over a prominent Toronto industrialist to the Liberal party. The board had been established in 1913 to give the gallery a degree of independence, but the appointments had hitherto been uninspired, and the director, Eric Brown, turned to Vincent Massey with relief as a source of support and encouragement. Brown's chief interest was building up the collection of old masters, but he was keenly aware of what was going on in Canadian art and receptive to the new trends. Repeatedly he was attacked by groups of artists for giving preferential treatment to the Group of Seven in overseas and national exhibitions. He could expect little support from the board. Its chairman, Dr F.J. Shepherd, was, according to Brown, intent on making him 'a continual scapegoat for imaginary gallery shortcomings.'[14] Another recent appointee Brown described as 'a busy, active kind of man who has bought doubtful old masters in the past and has a house full of them.'[15] But Brown's chief adversary on the board was Newton MacTavish, a Toronto journalist, aggressive and cantankerous in the expression of his views. MacTavish had some grounds for his convictions; he had written a study called *The Fine Arts in Canada*, and he had been a friend and supporter of James Morrice. But he was out of sympathy with recent trends in Canadian art; and in trustee discussion he was morosely opposed to expenditure on either the old masters or members of the Group of Seven. He championed the cause of John Russell, who had been a disciple of Morrice but now concentrated on painting sensuous nudes. With Shepherd's death in 1929, Brown hoped that Massey would succeed as chairman. But given Massey's commitment to diplomacy, this was impossible. The new chairman, H.S. Southam, was, however, a man of administrative vigour and wise tolerance; he and Massey worked harmoniously together to protect the director, not always an easy man to defend, and to deflect the attacks of what Massey described as 'the bellicose artists.'

Vincent was no doubt always aware of the shadow of the prime minister in the background. Whether it was Mackenzie King or R.B. Bennett, the board could expect little sympathy in that quarter for modernist views. King's aesthetic sensitivities, never greatly developed, did not encompass anything beyond Victorian sentimental didacticism and Bennett's only documented artistic enthusiasm was for the flamboyant illustrator Arthur Heming. Certainly neither King nor Bennett, particularly when depression clouds appeared and rapidly darkened, responded to appeals from the gallery for additional financial support. As the chairman of a special committee to press for a new gallery, Vincent wrote cheerfully to King in January 1929 urging that the proposed site should receive government confirmation and that the trustees should be permitted to undertake the preparation of preliminary sketches.[16] The prime minister sent Massey a routine acknowledgement, and the question was not to be seriously raised again for three decades.

Vincent's position on the board of trustees, and his close association with Eric Brown and the associate director of the National Gallery, H.O. McCurry, gave him an enlightened perspective on Canadian painting, and helped him to build up a fine personal collection. In December 1934 he consented to exhibit a selection from his collection at the Art Gallery of Toronto. Simultaneously the gallery was showing contemporary paintings by artists of the United States. Alice Massey wrote with nationalistic pride to one of the Canadian artists exhibited. 'My husband and I have seen the American paintings and to our mind there is no comparison between what the Americans are doing and the really lovely work of Canadians.'[17] Alice's correspondent was David Milne, who was represented in the Massey's home by twelve canvases, more than any member of the Group of Seven except A.Y. Jackson, who also had twelve. Milne was an artist to whom the Masseys were peculiarly devoted. They had, indeed, become his patron. The relationship between the Masseys and Milne is a fascinating story.

Milne, born in Bruce County in 1882, five years before Vincent Massey, had spent most of his active creative years in the United States (except for a brief non-combatant sojourn in the Canadian army in 1918 and a subsequent period as a Canadian war artist in France). He had returned to Canada in 1928, but between then and the Massey exhibition in December 1934 he had lived in isolation, making no attempt to sell the pictures that he was painting with steady, disciplined concentration. In March 1932, the Masseys came upon a Milne painting in Toronto, liked it instinctively, and bought it.[18] The purchase of this painting set off a correspondence that continued throughout the thirties, and constitutes a precious record of the inner life of an artist almost as subtle and sensitive in his use of words as he was in his use of colour, line, and hue.

The correspondent on the Massey side is almost always Alice. She is the real patron, who brought warmth and affectionate concern to the relationship. Her opening letter set the tone of her correspondence – brief, direct, brimming with humble admiration for the work of the artist:

We have never met but my husband and I had the delight of discovering at the National Exhibition one of your pictures, and now it hangs in an honoured place in our dining-room. I cannot tell you what a delight it gives us – it is full of subtle charm that fascinated us from the moment we saw it. It is a great pleasure to us both to send the enclosed cheque for One hundred and seventy-five Dollars, and we are most grateful, both of us, to be the possessors of this picture which we take great delight in. I hope some day that we may have the pleasure of meeting you.

For three years the correspondence continued without a meeting between the Masseys and Milne. Mrs Massey was perpetually solicitous about Milne – then living alone in a tar-paper hut on Six Mile Lake, near the Severn River, a hundred miles north of Toronto. She sends him bundles of art magazines, critical notices from Toronto, Ottawa, and Montreal papers as his work becomes better known, plants for his garden (dutifully planted and immediately eaten by marauding animals), and tidbits from the Batterwood kitchen. She invites him to spend some time in Durham House, the original mill house on the Batterwood estate, where 'our friends the Adaskins, he a violinist, she a pianist, are camping for the summer. They would love to have you over there. We would love to feel that for a while you were there. Why can't you shut up camp and come?'[19] She tells him about her son Hart, who is beginning to paint and loves Milne's paintings, and Milne offers to help the boy if he will come and stay with him in his cabin. She has a sudden onset of romantic escapism. 'Your description of some of your north country life makes me often in the midst of what we seem to have to do these days long to drop in on it and spend a day or two away from all the "hurly-burly".'[20] Milne replies, giving a detailed account of how to get to his cabin, with some wry prefatory comments. 'You speak of breaking out of civilization for a little and trying the north country. You can imagine how delighted I would be to see you up in this country. I probably won't be satisfied now until I get you trapped in mosquitoes, heat, starvation, and geography.'[21] Milne resists the repeated invitations to visit them at Batterwood: he is reluctant to break 'the thin thread of painting' and he reminds Mrs Massey that Wordsworth found 'Yarrow Unvisited' just as entrancing as 'Yarrow Visited.' But an opportunity finally arises in October 1935, not long before the Masseys are to leave for their ten-year stay in London. Milne writes thankfully: 'The visit to the Masseys still warms me. Practice seems to have given me the knack of knowing people by letter. The Masseys in person were just exactly the same kindly, interested and interesting Masseys of the letters.'[22]

Alice Massey was homely and maternal in her letters. Milne responded by writing amusingly of the only other human being he saw in the woods, Scotty Angus, a dour and scathingly philistine factotum at Port Severn, and sympathetically of the animals who disturbed his nights and raided his garden. He also wrote constantly about his art. The Masseys were the recipients of his single most comprehensive statement on the nature and theory of his art and the personal and environmental influences that had shaped his development – twenty-six typewritten pages, single-spaced, generously illustrated with work sketches of great beauty. In this long letter of 20 August 1934, he wrote objectively and penetratingly about his work. He pointed out that his canvases are not pictures of objects: they have 'little sentimental appeal;' they are simplifications of line and colour, intended to produce an 'authentic thrill.' He discussed his use of blank space in his pictures: '[The artist] can reproduce his emotion aesthetically by placing on the lower part of his canvas an area of detailed shapes – varied enough to engage and tire the eye quickly – and above this a larger dominating area, perfectly blank, no detail, no gradation, unteased, unnoticed, without interest in itself, merely an area of rest, or refuge.' In a biographical section of the letter he related his theory of art to his Scottish peasant heritage. 'I have never done much manual labour, yet I have the broad, short fingers of the peasant. I have, too, the taste for few and simple things, extending to an almost abnormal impatience with possessions that go beyond necessities. I like to think that my leaning towards simplicity in art is a translation of hereditary thrift, or stinginess, into a more attractive medium.'

When he was sent critical reviews of his paintings, he rejoiced in the more analytical ones. He commented, for instance, on a notice in the University of Toronto undergraduate paper, *The Varsity* (it was by Alan Jarvis, a second year philosophy student, soon to be a great supporter of Milne, and many years later to become director of the National Gallery). 'I don't know how much credit should go to the writer but in using the word "anemic" he gets very close to the heart of things. The word is a little startling in the connection, but it is apt. Probably the critic had nothing more in mind than a contrast with the lusty art of the Group of Seven, but it goes much deeper than that, and explains the sparing use of color, the scratchy sparse way of putting on paint and the general whittling down of things in the pictures.'[23]

When Mrs Massey sent Milne $175 for a single picture, it was the largest sum he had ever received for his work, perhaps, indeed, a sum that exceeded his total income to that point from the sale of his paintings. He reported that from the more than a hundred exhibitions in which he had participated he had sold two paintings for $45. Milne was moved to make an extraordinary suggestion. He estimated that he had now accumulated three hundred paintings since his return to Canada, and that there were about seven hundred left behind in the United States. He proposed that the Masseys should buy them all.

To set some sort of bounds to my proposal, I have put a price of five dollars each on them, good or bad, as they come, possibly five thousand dollars in all. This is purely arbitrary. It isn't large enough to have made their painting a profitable, or even possible, enterprise. Yet it is enough to ensure years of continuous, undisturbed painting for the artist with simple tastes. The aim is to trade twenty-five years of painting that is past for five or ten years in the future. It may seem an unusual way of going about things, but it is in just some such way that much of the art which has influenced our time has passed from the hands of its makers. The best work of Cézanne, Degas, Renoir ... went to helpful and discerning patrons, often at prices well under a hundred dollars. Yet those transactions are the ones that have to do with the making of an art. All the millions spent on Holbeins, El Grecos, Rembrandts and the work of other masters after their death did nothing except to move their pictures around a bit.[24]

Milne had second thoughts about the pictures in the USA. It would be difficult to retrieve them, and the Canadian government insisted on payment of duty. The final proposal was for the three hundred pictures painted in Canada and a small group of thirty or forty left with a friend in Buffalo, all for $1500. The Masseys said in reply that they would keep some for their own collection, give a few to public galleries, and arrange with dealers to sell the rest, any surplus 'above the original purchase price of the group we are buying from you (together with selling costs, framing, etc.)' going into a fund to buy further examples of Canadian art and to provide Milne with a share (unspecified) in the appreciated value of the canvases. Milne replied that he had no interest in further payment. 'It would be unfair to the enterprise,' he wrote, 'besides I am being fully and generously paid for the pictures, and that closes the transaction. If the pictures can be used to give other Canadian painters a chance it will be an additional pleasure to me.'[25] Later on Milne agreed to let the Masseys have any new work he completed. The Masseys, for their part, arranged exhibitions in Toronto, Ottawa, and Montreal, and by the end of 1936 pictures to the value of approximately $2500, at an average price of $40 or $50, had been sold. But, when expenses were carefully accounted for, there was still no surplus, and Milne uncharacteristically expressed surprise and disappointment.

From the vantage point of hindsight the arrangements with Milne appear hard and self-serving. The $1500 for three hundred Milne paintings would today constitute a down payment on one, and the Masseys recovered even that modest sum from later sales. A more charitable interpretation would be that, since at that time Milne was an unknown painter with no recognized market value, the Masseys could not be expected to exceed the sum that Milne asked for and that for him represented economic security for the imaginable future. The exacting accounting system that was adopted was, in all likelihood, the work of the National Trust, the trustees of the Massey estate, a firm that had a rigorous, methodistical approach towards the accumulation and disbursement of money.[26]

Vincent and Alice had not succeeded in persuading Milne to spend a summer with them at Batterwood. But they did gather together, in the summers of 1933 and 1934, painters – Will Ogilvie, Pegi Nicol, Lilias Newton – and two musicians, Harry and Frances Adaskin. The little art colony was put up in Durham House, but came to Batterwood, a short distance away, for general festivities. The two women painters were particularly close to the Masseys. Pegi Nicol had, at Alice's request, done sets for a Hart House production. She was a talented, exuberant artist, who tried, in bold expressionist style, to render the excitement of people and places. Lilias Newton was a fine portrait painter, two of her subjects being Vincent and Alice. She was particularly grateful to the Masseys for the purchase of a picture that was more controversial than her portraits. This was a striking female nude that Montreal galleries refused to show. She wrote to Alice: 'I can't begin to tell you how happy I feel about your wanting it. I had really felt terribly discouraged about the ban on it and to have it all so splendidly vindicated is wonderful.'[27] The Masseys selected the Lilias Newton nude for the exhibit at the Art Gallery of Toronto, but that gallery too refused to hang it. Vincent was greatly annoyed. 'When,' he asked, 'will Toronto grow up?'[28] Canadian taste in the thirties could accept female nudes provided they had an allegorical or classical aura, and were placed in a remote and vaguely romantic natural setting. But Lilias Newton's nude was impudently realistic (the lady's sole attire was a pair of shoes), with no solemn text to come between the eye and full enjoyment.

Vincent's interest in and support of the arts gave him a great satisfaction. The actual financial support that he directed towards the theatre, painting, and music, almost entirely from the Massey Foundation, was not great, although in every instance it was crucial and not available from any other source in Canada. But he realized that his grandfather's principal interest had been in education, and that the major contributions from the foundation should be in that field. Now his educational interests concentrated on Upper Canada College, whose board of governors he had joined in 1927. Family associations alone were sufficient to give the school a special priority. His father-in-law had been a principal, Alice had briefly served as matron of the new prep school before her father took up his appointment with the Rhodes Trust, and Alice's sister Maude had married the man who had now become the principal. Vincent had played an important role in William Grant's coming to Upper Canada, and he was bound to William by fond memories of his old schoolmaster and now by a reliance on him for advice. Under Grant, Upper Canada had become a far better school than it had ever been, but it had also become a vital part of the city's life. Grant had the remarkable talent, the highest and rarest given to educational administrators, of combining a robust individualism and a delight in new and adventurous ideas with a skill in attracting the support of the rich and the powerful. Attending college events or going to a reception at the principal's house were social occasions not to be lightly valued. Royal associations and a strong bias to the Church of England gave added social weight to the college, and Vincent was not indifferent to such matters. In a speech he made in 1929 at a dinner for the school's centenary, he recited the virtues that Upper Canada celebrated along with its English models: 'good sportsmanship, *esprit de corps*, loyalty to tradition, corporate discipline, and above all, a sense of public service.' By contrast, his old school, St Andrew's, had a Presbyterian austerity, and now, moved to a new location far beyond the city limits, had ceased to be part of the social life of the city. Besides, it had found a generous benefactor in Sir Joseph

Flavelle, and did not need the financial nourishment that was required for Upper Canada's continued existence.

In 1929 Upper Canada faced the necessity of renewing and expanding its physical plant, either at its existing location on Avenue Road within the city, or at a new location to the north in open country. Vincent Massey and William Grant were both in favour of a move. Vincent was pleased at the prospect of leaving the old buildings, erected, as he said, in 'neo-asylum style,' and starting a new life in buildings designed by his Batterwood architects, Mathers and Haldenby, in impeccable Georgian. The cost of the new buildings would be met by selling the existing site to the city and raising money from the public. Vincent, through the Massey Foundation, promised $100,000 provided the buildings were started in two years' time. This was later raised to $400,000, provided a matching sum could be raised from the public. But as the depression deepened, the public, which was of course the old boys of the school, did not respond. The city was not prepared to offer a sum of an appropriate magnitude for the property. Vincent then proposed that the college content itself with the renovation of the main building and the erection of two new houses. Since the Carnegie Corporation proposed to make a grant of $150,000 and two old boys had given $50,000, there would be sufficient money, with the Massey $400,000, now offered without condition, for this modified building program, with a substantial residue for scholarships and masters' salaries. The board gratefully accepted the solution. The work moved ahead rapidly, and was completed in five months in time for the opening of the new term in 1932. All this had demanded many hours of negotiation and correspondence in the middle of Vincent's complicated transition from Washington to Batterwood. But he obviously enjoyed the planning and manoeuvering, and he took great satisfaction in changing, as he had before with Hart House, the course of a major educational institution.

Before he left for London in 1935, Vincent was responsible for another major decision in the life of the college. He was the chairman of the selection committee to find a successor to William Grant; he favoured the choice of a Canadian, and of one particular Canadian, Terence W. L. MacDermot, an associate professor at McGill University. Terry MacDermot was a typical Massey man – a Rhodes scholar, an historian active in public affairs (he was national secretary of the League of Nations Society), reticent and scholarly, but with strong opinions supported by an incisive wit. The selection committee duly endorsed Massey's nominee. MacDermot had a tonic effect on Upper Canada, but he was too acerbic a critic of the old boy emphasis on athletics and good form to be warmly embraced, and he left the college in 1941 for government service.

Upper Canada College had replaced the University of Toronto as Vincent's primary educational interest. When he left for Washington, he had served for five years as chairman of the property committee of the university's board of governors. This was an important committee, which, by its selection of old buildings to be renovated or of new buildings to be erected, influenced the whole course of university development. In Washington he had kept in constant touch with the university. At his request, the Massey Foundation continued its contributions there, all to Hart House – $50,000 for extensions to the kitchen, and a new sitting room for the warden; $14,000 for additional rehearsal room and quarters for the costume department of Hart House Theatre; and an annual grant of $1000 to the warden for support of music and art. But when, on his return to Canada, he resumed his attendance at meetings of the university governors, Vincent found a spirit and an attitude that was disquieting.

Hart House had been established with a high degree of autonomy within the university, and the university, he hoped, would achieve a high degree of autonomy within the state. Certainly the University of Toronto Act of 1906 was designed to bring to an end a long and debilitating period of direct government control. A lay board was granted ultimate power, and was to be a bulwark between government and university and between the public and the university. But the board that emerged was not so much bulwark against government and the public as a conduit by which government and the public could directly reach and influence the university. Almost all the appointments, which were made by the government, came from the upper reaches of business, and many of the members were close to the government in power. They thought of the university, not as an intellectual and cultural centre with its own independent life, but as a government organization for providing an essential professional training and for turning raw adolescents into respectable citizens.

These simple, crude assumptions were certainly not held by the chairman of the board, Henry John Cody, who was a distinguished cleric, with a capacious and active mind, and a genuine understanding of the academic community. But he was closely associated with the provincial Conservative government, and with the dominating figure in the Conservative party, Howard Ferguson, premier from 1923 to 1930. In the election of 1926 Cody had spoken eloquently on behalf of the Conservative proposal to institute government control of the sale of intoxicating beverages, and had swung thousands of wavering voters to the Conservative side. 'Harry,' said Ferguson, affectionately referring to Cody by his undergraduate name, 'makes me look respectable. I benefit by the leavening of his holiness.'²⁹ As chairman of the board, Cody was determined to keep the university from any bruising collision with outside authorities. Autonomy was the fruit of discretion and prudence. In this he did not differ greatly from the president, Sir Robert Falconer, who believed that university autonomy could be maintained only if academics kept clear of politics and avoided controversial statements about public issues. Vincent Massey had a more robust attitude towards university autonomy. He thought that an academic had the right to speak out on controversial issues, even if he thereby ran counter to official government policy, and that a major responsibility of a lay board was to protect the staff against the occasional brutality of state and public. An issue arose in the early thirties that luridly dramatized these differences, and convinced Vincent that the university was governed by men who were prepared to defend autonomy only if it meant spineless indifference.

A violently reactionary Toronto Police Commission set out to crush the small but vocal Canadian Communist party by denying its members the right to hold public meetings. This was bad enough, but the commission interpreted Communist meetings to be those held in languages other than English or sponsored by religious societies with radical views of the meaning of Christian democracy. This aroused sixty-eight professors at the University of Toronto to sign a letter published in all four city papers, deploring the abrogation of free speech and affirming their belief 'in the free public expression of opinions, however unpopular or erroneous.' The professors were violently denounced by all the Toronto papers, except the *Star*, as arrogant intellectuals who would deprive Christian society of its defences against atheistic bolshevism. The board of governors, led by the chancellor, Sir William Mulock, and supported by the influential Sir Joseph Flavelle, joined in the chorus of vilification. The board met in long sessions; rumours grew that the professors would be severely disciplined, even dismissed. What emerged, however, after a final meeting on the issue, was 'a resolution which dissociated the university from the action taken by some of its employees, but contained no judgment of that action.'[30] Cody was relieved. He had no doubt spoken against extreme measures, and urged a face-saving compromise. Massey had made no public statement, but his diary makes clear that he was profoundly disturbed by the whole sorry affair. After attending the first board meeting on the question, he wrote with uncharacteristic savagery, 'Toronto shares with Moscow and Rome a dislike of free speech as an absolute virtue.'[31] After the board's pallid compromise had been worked out, he went to see the chancellor about a donation to Upper Canada College. Sir William ignored the request and launched into a tirade on the 'free-speech' issue. 'I had "surprised and disappointed" him by my attitude on the subject in the Board of Governors. As a matter of fact I had during the discussion been in a very small minority – sometimes one – in an effort to resist the authoritarian and repressive point of view held by the other members. Sir William like many of them sees red on the subject. What a silly form of mental distortion Bolshiphobia is. We *all* hate Bolshevism, but some of us simply invite the extension by the method resorted to.'[32]

Up to the 'free speech' issue his relations with Cody had been cordial. Cody had been a guest at the Washington legation, and Vincent had commented favourably on the speech Cody had made to an American society. When the question of his appointment as high commissioner to Britain arose after the election of 1930, he had consulted Cody about his response. He 'found Cody most sympathetic and anxious to help. Very keen that I should go. His strong advice that I should not resign.'[33] Shortly, however, the diary references to Cody become sharp and critical. Vincent no doubt thought of himself as a strong contender for the presidency, and it became increasingly clear that the government plan called for the chairman of the board to succeed Falconer. Alice was characteristically direct about her husband's ambitions in a letter that she wrote to Maude:

Poor V. had another blow the other day in a letter from Rowell. The latter had had a talk with Sir Joseph Flavelle about the University of Toronto and V. succeeding there – which between ourselves V.'s whole heart would love – a real job to do for Young Canada – but Sir J. says Cody wants it and must evidently have it ... My beloved man doesn't seem to have many friends amongst the powers that be. V.'s friends are among the inarticulate group. I think the U. had grown in V.'s mind as such a real job to do and that he might have a chance to get it. Now poor dear I think he feels Canada will never give him anything real to do ... think how we might make the U. of T. live.[34]

Vincent's interest in the presidency of the University of Toronto never surfaced in his diary or correspondence. His volume of memorabilia for the period, however, makes a bitter comment on Cody's election. The front-page headline in the *Globe* for 10 October 1931, 'Cody chosen University of Toronto President,' occupies a whole page, except for a heading in smaller type inserted just below – 'New Tory Swindle.'

From 1931 to 1935 there are only two references to the university, both expressing a gloomy attitude towards the new regime. On 10 March 1932, he describes a meeting of the board of governors as 'an increasingly uninteresting occasion now that Cody carries out instructions from Queen's Park and turns the rest of us into rubber stamps.' A year or so later he writes that 'I rarely attend meetings of the University Governors in consequence of the atmosphere which prevails because of certain people in high positions and the hopelessness of getting anything done.'[35]

On a national scale, Vincent's public activities concentrated more and more on the fortunes of the Liberal party. His interest in the work of the National Council of Education gradually waned and disappeared entirely. The council had been an effective catalyst in the twenties, but in the thirties, with the depression and the rapid breakdown of even the semblance of an international society, it ceased to command attention, and wandered into dangerous bypaths. The national bodies that enlisted Vincent's interest and support were directed towards broad political issues. They were non-partisan and attracted representatives from all political parties, although the bias was left of centre. In the autumn of 1931 he went to China as chairman of the Canadian delegation to a meeting of the Institute of Pacific Relations – a meeting that took place under the shadow of the impending Sino-Japanese war. He had by this time acquired impressive credentials as a spokesman for Canadian foreign policy: besides the Chinese experience, a pioneer trip to Russia and, during his years in Washington, a privileged seat for watching the international diplomatic ballet. Following the British Commonwealth Relations Conference, 11–21 September 1933, which was jointly sponsored by the Royal Institute of International Affairs and the Canadian Institute of International Affairs, and was held in 'the magically sequestered precincts of Hart House,'[36] he was elected president of the Canadian institute in succession to Newton Rowell. The conference provided a lively introduction to the besetting problems he would later face in London. It was concerned with Commonwealth communications; there was a good deal of sympathy with the contention that Commonwealth commissioners in London should have full diplomatic status, which would give them access to the Foreign Office as well as the Dominion Office, and would insulate them from political changes in their native countries. Logical conclusions such as this reached in free debate by scholars and experts would often, he was to discover, be distasteful to practical politicians.

A second national educational body that attracted Vincent was concerned with a particular issue that was just beginning to emerge, and had not yet become, as it was to become later, an issue for universal concern. The body was the Canadian Radio League, founded in October 1930 by two young men, Graham Spry and Alan Plaunt, who had strong convictions about how the new medium could best serve the Canadian public, and were prepared to fight to see them triumph. Vincent's years in the United States had given an advance impression of the strength of American private interests in the exploitation of broadcasting. As a member of an international body to assign radio frequencies, he was aware of the determination of the American government to satisfy the demands of her radio entrepreneurs. He responded very quickly to the Radio League argument that unless Canada elected for government control of radio, Canadian broadcasting would simply become an extension of powerful American stations and networks. When in 1928 the King government decided to set up a radio commission, Vincent suggested two out of three of the commissioners – Charles Bowman, editor of the Ottawa *Citizen*, and Sir John Aird, the president of the Canadian Bank of Commerce.[37] Vincent also contributed to the cost of bringing out Gladstone Murray, a Canadian who was director of publicity and public relations for the BBC, to give evidence before a parliamentary committee on radio that Bennett established after coming to power. Murray was the key witness, who made the committee aware of the importance of broadcasting and of the necessity of giving any controlling body a high degree of independence.

All these activities – in music, drama, painting, education, and in what was to be known as the mass media – had to be combined with a pre-eminent commitment to diplomacy and politics. They no doubt constituted a relief from a world reverberating with the clashes between men obsessively bent upon power. But for Vincent they were more than relief. They were at the centre of his life; they justified the hours spent on the business of the nation. In politics he was broker, consultant, at best a frustrated leader; in the arts and education he was originator, director, publicist, critic, and, occasionally, practitioner, as well as patron. In this area he was acquiring an authority that would, in due time, enable him to preside over a major transformation in Canada's cultural life.

CHAPTER NINE

The Return to Politics

From his relaxed retreat David Milne viewed with cynicism the Masseys' increasing involvement in politics. 'I have kept my faith in Santa Claus,' he wrote to Mrs Massey, 'and the tinsel on the tree but am beginning to have faint doubts about the church and politics. So I never go to church and seldom vote. An election is just a chance to say – to myself, nobody else bothers – that we are overdeveloped politically, and so to infer that we are among the backward people in some other things – Literature, for instance, below the French, the English, the Irish, the Americans, below the Italians, Russians, Scandinavians, Spanish, and maybe the Japanese, Chinese and Ethiopians.'[1] Both Alice and Vincent were as deeply concerned about literature and the arts as Milne. They would not, however, have taken as gloomy a view as he did of the Canadian achievement in these fields, and they were certainly less contemptuous of politics. At Balliol Vincent had learned that politics, at least in the United Kingdom, could attract the ablest minds and the finest spirits; and if Canada fell short of this, no one, at least, could deny the importance of politics, especially as more and more of the nation's life came under political control. Alice too had not been disillusioned by the Durham defeat; she had become an uncompromising partisan, devoted to the Liberal party and more prepared than her husband to accept Mackenzie King as her rightful leader.

But Vincent knew at first hand that party politics often brought out the worst as well as the best in human nature. It could be a form of warfare, no less destructive because it attacked the mind and the emotions, and not the body. It could elevate bitterness and revenge into virtues. In the summer of 1930, following the July election, Vincent was peculiarly aware of politics as the guerilla warfare of the spirit. Through articles and editorials in the press, he quickly realized that he was looked upon as one of the most glittering prizes in the Conservative victory. Editorials in the *New York Times* and *The Times* of London, praising his work in the United States and warmly commending his appointment as high commissioner, made no impression on the triumphant Tories.

As he contemplated his situation late that summer, Vincent realized that personal considerations were not likely to moderate the attitude of the prime minister. Bennett knew and admired Sir George Parkin, but little of the admiration was passed on to Sir George's most eminent son-in-law. The feeling was mutual. There are no references to Bennett in the Massey diary until he became leader of the Conservative party in 1927; but for the next eight years, until Bennett's defeat in the election of 1935, he is the subject of a steady trickle of derisive comments – not an emotional luxury that Vincent often permitted himself. Shortly after Bennett became party leader, Vincent wrote congratulating him on his election and inviting him to come to Washington for a visit. Bennett did not reply to the letter, and when Vincent saw him later at a state dinner at Government House, Bennett observed curtly 'that he wouldn't have time to come to Washington.' 'Such an attitude,' wrote Vincent, 'takes the pleasure out of any service one may be trying to render Canada. Bennett is apparently a bit of a cad in this particular at least. He is such an uncontrolled egocentric sort of fellow that I feel that under the provocation which lies ahead of him as leader he will not last about a year in that capacity – and no more.'[2] The dislike of Bennett, hardened and sharpened after the 1930 election by what Vincent thought of as a grievous personal affront, finally erupted creatively, as we have seen, in a long satirical poem, which never emerged beyond a private circle, but was composed with a savage gusto not unworthy of a minor eighteenth century satirist.

For a few weeks after the election, Vincent did nothing, ignoring the chorus of 'resign' from the Conservative press. He decided to take high ground, to point out that he was a member of the diplomatic corps simply being transferred from one post to another, and that as such he was above politics. By telephone and interview he organized a network of influential support: Mackenzie King, who was happy to have an issue on which he could take a high moral stand; influential journalists like Charles Bowman of the Ottawa *Citizen*, John W. Dafoe of the Winnipeg *Free Press*, and Wilmot Lewis, *The Times* of London correspondent in Washington. But Massey must have realized that although he occupied high ground, it was ground from which he could easily be dislodged. The high commissionership was, as Bennett argued, different from ministerial appointments in Washington and Tokyo.[3] After a stormy session with Bennett on 13 August Massey realized that he had no alternative except to resign.

Bennett's letter of 16 September, accepting Massey's resignation as high commissioner, set out clearly the position he took. '... the present Conservative Government considered it proper to adhere to the spirit of the statute creating the office of High Commissioner for Canada in Great Britain, and to affirm the policy which has developed under it, by appointing as its representative one who through conviction could fully subscribe to the declared views of the Government relating to the conduct of the affairs of this country in Great Britain.' Massey remained unconvinced by Bennett's explanation, and in his autobiography remarked, 'I find it hard to believe that Bennett had any clear understanding of the issue, apart from the fact that he did not wish me to represent his government either in London or Washington.'[4]

For a short time Vincent thought he might be asked to return to Washington. He had not formally resigned as minister, and, according to Bennett's doctrine, he was not, by reason of his Liberal bias, ineligible to represent a Conservative government in that capital. But Bennett declared that he had signed Massey's recall and he had no intention of reversing himself. He went on to say that although he had someone in mind for London – it was presumably the Ontario Conservative premier, Howard Ferguson, who in a short time was to receive the appointment – 'he had no idea who [Massey's] successor would be in Washington.'[5] In this assertion, he was being disingenuous. He undoubtedly had clearly in mind who the Washington nominee would be, and knew that revealing the name at this time would greatly increase the distress Massey already felt and would make Bennett vulnerable to another attack from King.

Bennett's choice as Vincent's successor was William D. Herridge, an

Ottawa lawyer who had suddenly emerged in the election as a close Bennett adviser. He had no previous political experience, and was unknown outside of Ottawa and the legal circles in Canada and the United States, where he moved with the ease that comes to those who unravel the affairs of large corporations. What brought acute distress to Vincent was that Herridge – always referred to in the diary as 'Bill' – was an intimate friend, so intimate that in 1929 Vincent had named Herridge in his will, in the event of his and Alice's death, as one of the guardians 'of my infant children.' (The other two guardians were William and Maude Grant.) Bill Herridge was a year older than Vincent. They had been at the University of Toronto at the same time, and may have known each other then; but the friendship flourished during Vincent's years as minister, when each would stay with the other during visits to Ottawa and Washington. Herridge was a magnetic figure: he had been a war hero, decorated with the MC and the DSO; he had achieved success as a patent lawyer, and he was known for his social charm, his easy fluency of speech, and his wide interests in literature and politics. He was a widower, and it was assumed that on her death his wife, who was a granddaughter of John R. Booth, the Ottawa lumber king, had left him financially independent. He was not known as a political partisan, but a number of factors pointed to Liberal sympathies, particularly an early and close association with Mackenzie King. Herridge's father had been minister for forty years at St Andrew's Presbyterian Church, of which King was a devoted member throughout his entire Ottawa career; and for a brief period in the early 1900s King had formed a romantic attachment for the elder Herridge's wife, the first of a long succession of respectable liaisons with married women. One result of the affair was a friendship between Bill Herridge and King. 'For some time, it seems,' wrote Charles Stacey, 'he regarded King almost as an elder brother, and it seems likely that King was responsible for his joining his own fraternity, Kappa Alpha, at the University of Toronto.'[6]

Herridge's appointment was a greater blow to Vincent than the denial of the high commissionership. He must have known of Herridge's increasing intimacy with the Conservative leader, shortly to be given a sacramental blessing in a marriage to Bennett's sister. But he had no inkling of the Washington appointment in August when he had his grim sessions with Bennett. In September, he began to sense the reality. George Smith reported from Ottawa a 'conversation with Bill Herridge which left me still unable to understand that extraordinary situation.'[7] Herridge's official appointment came early in March 1931. Bennett accompanied the announcement with remarks that were a testimony to Herridge and a condescending dismissal of Massey's work. He emphasized 'that the most important task developing [sic] upon Canada's diplomatic representative at Washington is that of maintaining close intimacy with the business mind of the American nation. To reserve an influential and dignified place in America's social and intellectual spheres was only of secondary importance.'[8] Vincent had one final meeting with Herridge, in London where Herridge had accompanied Bennett to the Imperial Conference. The diary duly records a polite but icy session at which there was a silent agreement to end the friendship. 'Bill Herridge to lunch with us at the Berkley. Protestations of affection from B. but not a reference to our affairs, nor evidence of any interest in them. Can friendship continue with so little that one can talk about (His affairs being equally tabu)?'[9]

Up until 1930 Vincent Massey's career had proceeded from one triumph to another (the Durham defeat excepted) with what seemed like smooth inevitability. Now it had come to a sudden halt amid recriminations, direct and covert attacks on his conduct, and the shattering of a close friendship. No doubt his long trips abroad during the next year were part of a program of self-therapy. In England he sought and obtained sympathy from friends in high places and, what was even more comforting, confirmation of his low opinion of Bennett. In his diary he lovingly reported the anti-Bennett remarks, and noted with satisfaction that the British attitude towards Bennett was not simply a reflex of party. Thus the attitude of Brendan Bracken, a Conservative MP, is 'one of blasphemous disgust.'[10] Gladstone Murray of the BBC and Adrian Boult, the eminent conductor, joined in the chorus of disapproval: 'His manners are inconceivably shocking as for instance when J.H. Thomas sent him a note of apology after his speech in the house (the "humbug" speech) he didn't even reply.'[11] And Vincent listened with satisfaction as a Canadian journalist, a representative of the Southam Press, recited a catalogue of Bennett's sins – 'ineptitude, clumsy diplomacy, and atrocious manners.'

Despite such evidence of support and sympathy, Vincent was, for a time, depressed by the harsh interruption of his diplomatic career, and was tempted to turn elsewhere. He would, no doubt, have accepted the presidency of the University of Toronto if it had been offered him. There had been considerable public discussion of the appointment, in which Massey's name was frequently mentioned. The magisterial *Saturday Night*, not well disposed to Liberals, especially if they supported their leader, thought well of him as a candidate. He had, the magazine declared, 'shed lustre on his *alma mater*,' which was indebted to him 'in an enormous degree'; his appointment, the paper concluded, 'would be regarded with widespread favour.'[12] But public discussion was pointless, since the decision had been made privately between the board of governors and the government. During the next five years newspaper speculation about Massey appointments occurred with regularity: he was to become the leader of the Liberal party in Ontario; he was to be the head of the new Radio Commission or the new central bank; he was to go to a senior post in the League of Nations. None of these had any substance. Another university presidency attractive to Vincent became a possibility in 1934 following the death of the incumbent, Sir Arthur Currie. Mackenzie King recorded a visit from Sir Edward Beatty, the chancellor of McGill, to discuss the principalship. 'He wanted to sound me out as to Massey. I told him he would make I thought, a good Principal, but that he was interested in London, & if we were returned would be sent there. Beatty thought he would be excellent for the post.'[13]

King was always convinced of Massey's suitability for the London post, and never seriously considered any other person. When Larkin died, early in 1930, King wrote to Massey assuring him of the succession: 'As you know I have never had anyone else in mind for London but yourself. Others may have their preferences and desires, but I believe that Canadian opinion will be more of one mind on who should go, than on anything I have known in the way of an appointment. For this, you and Alice have only yourselves to thank.'[14] Assured of King's support, Vincent contemplated a period of relative calm, during which he could pursue in his own time his various interests, while acting as King's confidential adviser. But King had other and more active plans for him. It was not a question of extracting service in exchange for the London appointment. It was a question of whether or not King would be in a position after the next election to make any government appointments at all. For some time he had been unhappy about the casual and ineffective attitude of the Liberal party towards organization and publicity, and now this attitude had helped to precipitate a disaster of a dark and foreboding character.

The disaster was the Beauharnois scandal of 1931. Blair Neatby, in the second volume of the life of King, began his chapter on the scandal in this way. 'Mary Tudor, Queen of England, said she would die with Calais written on her heart. For Mackenzie King the word was Beauharnois.'[15] It is a happy way of dramatizing the tumult in King's self-obsessed mind. The Beauharnois Corporation proposed to develop power from a canal that would receive water diverted from the St Lawrence River. The diversion had been authorized by an order-in-council passed by the Liberal government in 1929, and the order-in-council could be defended, given the complexities, federal, provincial, and international, of power politics, as a good Canadian compromise. But it was alleged that the company hoped to have the entire flow of the St Lawrence diverted to the canal, and that it counted on the support of the Liberal government. The chairman of the board of the Beauharnois Corporation was W.L. McDougald, a friend whom King had appointed to the Senate, and a member of the National Advisory Committee on the St Lawrence Seaway. A special House of Commons committee reported at the end of July 1931 that the Beauharnois Corporation had given a large sum to the Liberal party – between $600,000 and $700,000 – presumably for favours rendered and the expectation of other favours to come. Moreover, Senator Andrew Haydon, who was still the active head of the national Liberal organization, belonged to a legal firm that received an annual retainer for legal services of $50,000 from the Beauharnois Corporation. King protested his innocence: the order-in-council authorizing the diversion to the Beauharnois canal rested on its own merit, and he, King, was ignorant of the large Beauharnois contribution to Liberal funds; he deliberately kept aloof from party finances. But unfortunately for his peace of mind, he discovered that he was in fact personally involved. He had gone on holiday with McDougald to Bermuda, and McDougald had paid his hotel bill. King had thought this the generous act of a friend, the kind of act that King always accepted with humility and gratitude. In the evidence before the House of Commons committee, it came out that McDougald had charged the hotel bill to a Beauharnois expense account. King the innocent, or the naïve, found himself deeply involved, his honour at stake. In his long speech of defence in the House of Commons, he could not dissipate the dark shadow that enveloped the Liberal party. At the end he rose only to the humility and pathos of the repentent sinner: 'The party is not disgraced but it is in the valley of humiliation.'[16]

For the rest of the year King devoted himself to preparations for a rejuvenated Liberal party organization. The Beauharnois scandal had arisen because of the existing nature of the organization – lacking a strong national base, concentrated in a small committee, relying upon contributions from wealthy individuals, indifferent to mass support. King ruthlessly dropped both McDougald and Haydon; his friendship for McDougald vanished into the murky depths of Beauharnois, and Haydon, who had served his party faithfully for many years and was probably innocent of any direct involvement, ceased to be a King familiar. In a speech to the Ontario Liberal Association on 31 August, King, unwisely in the opinion of many of his followers, publicly talked about the Beauharnois scandal, and declared that the Liberal party must create a new non-parliamentary organization so open and widely based that no scandal could ever touch it. The overriding consideration in the success of such an organization was securing a head who was politically untainted and enjoyed wide public support. King rapidly came to the conclusion that the ideal person was Vincent Massey, now providentially without a job.

There was a network of reasons, personal and political, for the choice. On a personal basis, King's relationship with Massey was still untroubled. True, King would not now emphasize, as he did in 1925, the identity of their ideals, and see in Massey a friend bound to him by spiritual ties. Some of these spiritual ties had become frayed during Massey's Washington years. And although King always stoutly defended Massey in his public speeches and comments – and was to continue to do so throughout his career – privately he criticized Massey's aggressiveness and interest in self-promotion: his insistence on what King thought was a large personal staff (whereas King saw himself as selflessly labouring for the country without any help); his persistence in asking for an ostentatious building for the Canadian legation; his perpetual speech-making on Canadian achievements, a subject that King presumably thought should be reserved for the prime minister. But these were minor irritations that never swelled into confrontations. On the other side, references to King in the Massey diary during the Washington years breathe almost filial devotion. They have a frank talk about Massey's extensive speaking tours; King mentions the criticism he has heard from Liberal members in the House, but does not press the matter and tells Vincent to make his own judgments about the nature and number of his speeches. Vincent concludes, 'What a wise person the P.M. is.'[17] After a general talk about his work, he commented that King was 'very appreciative of what we are trying to do at Washington.'[18] Vincent rejoiced in this close association. His personal letters now begin with the salutation 'Rex,' the nickname that King had acquired at the university and that only intimate friends used, and even then rarely.

King obviously realized that any relationship with Vincent could not exist apart from Alice. Vincent's attitudes and ideas bore her imprint. She must always, however, be considered as a person in her own right. She combined a warm, affectionate nature with a tough, realistic pragmatism. She was quicker than her husband to read King's moods, and, in particular, to sense when benevolence was about to modulate into a tyrannical ruthlessness.

The personal relationship between King and Massey was, then, in 1930, an easy and friendly one. But the choice of Massey to reorganize the Liberal party outside of Parliament rested more on broad political than on personal grounds. King wanted somebody who, untouched by scandal, not known as a fierce Liberal partisan, could obliterate the stigma of Beauharnois. Vincent was now five years away from his brief sortie into politics, and, apart from Conservatives who still bitterly resented his 'betrayal of Meighen,' few thought of him as a politician. Two public images dominated: the philanthropist devoted to the advancement of education and the arts, and the diplomat who had been a model of urbanity, charm, and erudition and had helped to change the American image of Canada as a rough and immature country faintly visible in a wilderness on the northern horizon. If the outer mask was angular and solemn, it proclaimed an inner integrity, and recalled the generations of puritan ancestors who had laboured resolutely in the service of man and God. If Vincent Massey was thought by many to be more English than Canadian, that was, for the job King had in mind, an asset, since Canadians had the illusion that British politics were more high-minded, certainly less corrupt, than the politics of the United States and of Canada.

Finally, King wanted a wealthy man for the head of the new Liberal organization, one who could inspire others by his generosity, and address himself with zest to a national campaign for funds. Massey's qualifications under this heading were not as great as King imagined. Massey was not, for instance, a millionaire in the same class as the rest of Toronto Methodist millionaires; his resources were invested soberly, and were not likely to multiply in the miraculous fashion of corporate profits. He was not in a position to make a large donation to the Liberal party, and, under any conditions, he was not disposed to give generously from his own resources. The foundation that he controlled could not, of course, under its charter, make a contribution to a political party. Moreover, he was not on easy terms with the very wealthy, whose tastes he often deplored and whose interests he did not share. He was not averse to raising money for unexceptionable causes, as he demonstrated at this time in a successful campaign for a convalescent hospital in Toronto for the sisters of St John the Divine of the Church of England. But he was uneasy about approaching the rich for political donations. After one such endeavour he wrote, 'What a hateful job cadging is.'[19]

Although King was certain that Massey was his man, Massey was not easily persuaded. He felt confident about eventually becoming high commissioner: why not, then, wait patiently, and confine himself to old interests that he had revived and to new ones that he had acquired? King realized that he could not make peremptory demands. He must proceed slowly and with circumspection. It took almost two years.

It was not until August 1931 that King launched his campaign. Until then Vincent had played the role of senior adviser and discreet political activist; it was a role that satisfied his self-esteem and did not interfere with his personal plans. He was active in promoting Charles Dunning, then wavering between politics and business, as party organizer, and helped to collect for a 'Dunning Fund' – in the event never used, since Dunning, for the time being, elected the business life. He was prodigal of advice to King when Bennett called a special session of Parliament in the fall of 1930, and reported with satisfaction that on one occasion King came out of a party caucus to receive his telephone call. He kept in touch with the Ontario situation, which was crucial to any Liberal recovery. He cultivated the new provincial Liberal leader, Mitchell Hepburn, and, like all Liberals, was initially enchanted by the forceful young man. He and Alice 'liked him immensely and think that his faults are clearly the faults of quality.'[20] He took part in high-level discussions about party organization along with the prime minister, Dunning, and the two men then responsible for party organization, Senator Haydon and Charles Stewart.

King did not hold a high opinion of Stewart, an Albertan and former cabinet minister, who had taken over the major responsibility for fund-raising and party organization, and at this point he began to think of Massey as the real successor. His approach was, at first, studiedly oblique. When Massey gave a subscription of $1000 to the Liberal party – an unusually generous gift for him, and, in the Liberal financial desert, a refreshing sign of revival – King wrote to him: 'I am convinced that this work is even more important than anything that can be done in parliament. I am equally certain that without it, all that is attempted there will be of little avail.'[21] While Massey was on a long European tour, from 21 February to 3 August 1931, King wrote him a thirteen-page letter reviewing the political situation. He reported a new spirit of buoyancy in the party, as the result of his call to the younger members to take on responsibilities and leadership. The question of organization was not yet settled, but he was optimistic about a resolution. He ended the letter with a detailed analysis of the Herridge appointment, in which he accused Herridge of a callous betrayal of his friends and Bennett of nepotism – an analysis calculated to strengthen Massey's conviction that he was the innocent victim of a calculated plot.

When Vincent returned from his trip, he consulted King about the offer of the West Australian governorship, and, according to his own diary, was advised not to accept on the grounds that 'I was needed in reorganization of Lib. party.'[22] King's diary has a far less bland account of the interview. When Vincent asked whether an Australian appointment would make it difficult for King to appoint him to London, King replied, 'I said most decidedly so. That I felt that those who left the party in its time of need would get no recognition later on ... That I felt if he were away it wd be impossible to appoint him to London later on.'[23] For the first time in the dialogue on Massey's role, the glint of naked power momentarily appears beneath the façade of praise and flattering confidentiality.

King now began to press his case on Massey and ask for a decision. On 22 August he spent the night at Batterwood and conferred with Vincent and Alice on the following day. In his diary Vincent laconically noted King's visit, and recorded as the only matter of substance his convincing King 'of the advisability of holding a National Liberal Convention in 1932.' For King, however, the meeting was a great turning point, the definite enlistment of the Masseys – Alice was a party to the agreement – in the cause of the party. On 3 September King wrote a long emotional letter to Massey, now departed on his Chinese trip, in which he hailed the agreement that he believed had been reached:

I must thank you above else for new hope and peace of mind you have both helped to bring to me. Since August 1930, and very often before, I have almost despaired of being able to carry on the leadership of the party, with the absence of any real organization or any publicity department ... I must say that what you and Alice have volunteered to undertake in the way of helping to get something in the way of effective cooperation in the party's tasks outside of parliament, has given me very great heart and hope. You must have seen the visible effect upon my spirits, for your words were like the breaking of the sun rays through clouds of gloom, if not despair, which has well-nigh enveloped me.

The letter concluded with a passage of florid prose in which King saw Massey as one who, like himself, although in a lesser degree, had suffered much from man's cruelty, but had come through the ordeal renewed and strengthened. It was King in one of his *Parsifal* flights, and to Massey, who despised ostentation in all its forms, the passage in both style and sentiment must have brought acute discomfort.

Perhaps it is well that we should all be disillusioned somewhat before the battle of life is over; and I am quite sure that suffering and sacrifice, if not too great or too frequent, are essential to our real development. We pass by these arid and rocky places on to more fertile plains and finer vistas, and if we endure are the gainers in the end. That has been my experience, so often, already, that I begin to fear when the good continues too long. It is true, as well, that adversity helps to bring into being the friendships that are most worth while – and indeed, to reveal what alone is worth while. So that so long as we view our portion here as a pilgrimage we may even thank our misfortunes, and the turn in the road of life which takes us for a season away from the roar of its traffic and the bewildering distractions of its lurid sights and sounds into the quiet of the fields, and gives us an open sky for contemplation by night as well as by day, till our spirits regain their own power and truer vision. We have both shared so largely in experiences of a kindred sort, that I feel I can write with a sense of companionship, in this way. It is that which makes the decision of Alice and yourself to stay with Canada, with the Liberal party, with its needs, as well as the great opportunities, mean so very much to me. How much, it would be quite impossible to say.

Despite the fervour of his letter, King realized that Massey's conversion was not complete. Vincent still suspected that his task would be essentially a financial one, and for this he had no appetite whatsoever. Accordingly, King wrote to him shortly before his return from China to assure him that the financial burden was not to be his. 'Having in mind what you said to me about not wishing to incur responsibility with respect to the financial side of the party's affair, I have felt it might be just as well to have this phase dealt with before you return. After you get back, we can bring together any group that may appear to be desirable in order to get underway the work that you and Alice were kind enough to say you would make more or less especially your own.'[24]

The way to Massey's mind and heart was, King realized, to emphasize the high status and the broad educational impact of his proposed position in the Liberal party. For Christmas 1931, he sent Massey a copy of J.A. Spender's recently published biography of Sir Robert Hudson. Hudson had been the secretary of the National Liberal Federation in the United Kingdom from 1893 to 1927, from the stirring days of Gladstone and Home Rule to the secession of Lloyd

George and the rapid disintegration of the Liberal party. King, who had been impressed by the book, knew that it would have a great attraction for Massey, and might give him a pleasing vision of what could happen in Canada. King had, as usual, acted with great shrewdness. The book, Vincent observed, was 'a bit of an inspiration for anyone about to take on a job in a Lib. organization.'[25]

Robert Hudson was a full-time professional, and he was not, therefore, a model for Massey. But in his life he demonstrated that the work of political organization need not be demeaning. Spender's biography emphasized the atmosphere of candour, idealism, and sweet reasonableness that prevailed at party headquarters. Hudson was far from being a political hack: he was a devout man, with wide literary interests, who made friends in high places, was knighted, and, towards the end of his life, married the widow of Lord Northcliffe, the newspaper baron. All this no doubt impressed Vincent Massey. As the prospective president of a Canadian version of the British organization, he noted with great satisfaction two of its characteristics. In the first place, it was a non-parliamentary group that had a profound effect on party policy, and, on occasion, even determined policy. In the second place, the presidents of the organization were men of stature and notable achievement, some of them, like Augustine Birrell, J.M. Robertson, and J.A. Spender, men of letters, all of them prominent in their communities, and well known nationally. Spender drew the following general profile of the federation's presidents. They were men

who were the political leaders of their localities and had the purely disinterested object of keeping their fellow-citizens in the right path. Most of them were business or professional men to whom politics were necessarily a side-issue, but they were the mainstay of the local clubs and Associations, and gave generously of their spare time and all the money they could afford for the support of the cause, on which they genuinely believed the welfare and progress of the country to depend. The local newspapers treated them with great deference and reported their speeches at length, and it was everywhere recognized that they had to be consulted before a candidate was 'sent down' or any serious development of policy proposed. The dissent of any one of them was recognized at once as a matter of grave import which might entail the loss of a seat or indeed of several seats.

Generally they were Free Churchmen, and when the Nonconformist conscience was aroused it spoke first with their voice, but their emotion was a genuine and honourable one, and many of them had won the respect of their neighbours because they were evidently endeavouring to practise Liberalism in their lives.[26]

Vincent must have reflected that he had some right to count himself a member of such an honourable order. He deviated in a few ways: he was more concerned about directing money to the support of education and the arts than to politics; he was certainly not a Free Churchman, but his withdrawal from the Methodist Church had not seriously disturbed a nonconformist conscience, an inheritance from nine generations of puritan ancestors.

At the beginning of the new year, 1932, King was not yet sure of his man. On Wednesday, 6 January, he was confident that 'Massey is going to stick all right.'[27] A week later the conviction has softened into a devout hope. 'I pray Massey will take hold.'[28] On 2 February Massey departed on a speaking tour in the west. His subject was the crisis in the East, and he was greeted everywhere by large and enthusiastic audiences. In the evenings he gathered little groups of faithful Liberals, who, by now, knew of his probable acceptance of the position of president of the National Liberal Association. The Calgary *Albertan* for instance, had recently welcomed his shift from diplomacy to political organization where 'his powers of organization, his sweet reasonableness, and his ability to inspire confidence' would be effectively used.[29] He began to think of the organization of his office, and, in February, had a preliminary talk with Norman Lambert, who was to become the secretary. Lambert was a native of Ontario and had lived in the west for twenty years. He had had experience in journalism, in business, and in political organization with the United Farmers of Manitoba. He was by temperament friendly and outgoing, but was a shrewd appraiser of men and adept in the ways of politics. He became the mainstay of the Liberal organizaton, a confidant of both King and Massey, even when they were violently at loggerheads with each other. Lambert was an example of Massey's skill in selecting men, whether as associates, as the heads of enterprises in which he was interested, or as students in postgraduate studies abroad.[30]

On his return from his western trip, Massey reverted to his doubts about the organization, and about his taking over the presidency. King was enraged, and soliloquized in his diary about Massey's desire to achieve 'position & gravy without drudgery and risk.'[31] The next day he recovered his faith in Vincent and contemplated the best way to bind him securely to the task. With typical shrewdness, he hit upon an effective device – a joint committee of the House and the Senate that would wait upon Massey and formally request him to take the presidency. 'I met them in my office,' King wrote, '& primed them as to what to say'; no doubt they were 'primed' to emphasize the importance of the position, and Massey's role in clarifying and enunciating policy. The device worked. Massey accepted the presidency. 'Vincent, Alice & Savard [Savard was an officer in the association] went to the office & "began history" by sitting at an empty table in an empty room.'[32]

King was exultant. Two years of agonized doubts and searching had, he thought, come to a glorious end, and the diary entry rises to a tone of biblical jubilation. 'Today the Lenten season of 1932 comes to a close. It has been to me the most wonderful of all, the one to which all others have been leading up through the years. For the first time in my life I seem to be able at last to raise the song of conquest, and to feel that surely I shall dwell in the House of the Lord for ever.'[33]

But 'the song of conquest' could not be sustained. King still detected reservations in Massey's attitude. His acceptance of the presidency of the association was not official, and the association itself was a shadowy structure that had to be reconstituted. Before that took place and Massey was duly elected and proclaimed the first president of the new National Liberal Federation, King felt the need of a final act of persuasion. He set out for Batterwood on Saturday, 28 May, determined to achieve a final resolution. It was to be a warm, relaxed, and friendly weekend. King came in the spirit of a wise compassionate spiritual leader who was intent upon banishing the doubts of a disciple, who was full of respect and devotion for his leader but inclined to waver in the faith. The weather and the place were propitious. King could, when the spirit of '37 briefly descended on him, make savage comments on the garish opulence of the rich. But Batterwood, with its rural setting, its lovely vistas of fields and hills, reminded him of his own rural retreat at Kingsmere although, as he observed with satisfaction, 'the birds did not seem to be quite as numerous or as

"alert" at the time of waking in the morning, as they are at Kingsmere.'[34]

During a long walk on Sunday afternoon and in the evening after
supper, King talked about the glorious opportunities that lay before
Massey if he made a commitment to the Liberal association. He painted
a broad and radiant canvas in which he and Vincent would appear as
dominant figures. He said 'that there was a chance to launch a great
political educational movement which would go on in Canada for
generations, raising the political life of the country. He had started the
diplomatic venture abroad, – the Massey Foundation, the Educational
League, etc. Here was something more potent for good than all these.
Also it was an instrument of political power, between us we could
determine the appointments of the future etc. on right lines ...'[35] The
next morning King had a session with Alice during which he repeated
what he had said to Vincent; he realized that Alice's support and
agreement were an essential condition for Vincent's participation in
any scheme.

This was the final act of persuasion. Massey took King at his word.
Here was his chance to exercise leadership and to wield power, the
leadership and power that had been snatched from him in the Durham
defeat of 1925 and that had returned only in a shadowy form during
his three years in Washington, He now faced his new responsibilities
with relish. His Washington years had given him confidence as a
speaker. He was doubtless aware that he lacked the common touch, but
if King could arouse public support with his heavy prolixity, and his
high-pitched, southern Ontario voice, he could surely do likewise with
his more ordered and polished sentences, and his Canadian Oxonian
accent. Moreover, he was far closer than any of the standard Liberal
spokesmen, King certainly included, to progressive thought in the
United States and Canada. He had, as we have seen, formed friendships with the leading American progressives – with Herbert Croly,
Walter Lippmann, and Felix Frankfurter. They had bitterly questioned
a society that had, in the name of human freedom, made business
success the measure of national welfare, and they had urged that the
state should intervene on behalf of equality and justice. In Canada he
was aware of the wide appeal of the new socialist party, the CCF, that
had just been launched in Calgary. Frank Underhill, who was to play an

important part in the drafting of the CCF platform, was a friend from
college days in Toronto and Oxford. And he was aware that, among
the young generation rising to positions of responsibility and influence, there were many who, although opposed to doctrinaire
socialism, were doubtful that any genuine reform could come through
the old parties. His chief informants here were a group in Montreal
drawn from business, academic life, and the professions, chief among
them Raleigh Parkin, his brother-in-law, a businessman with the Sun
Life Insurance Company, Brooke Claxton, a young lawyer, and
T.W.L. MacDermot, an assistant professor of history at McGill, shortly
to become principal of Upper Canada College. One of his first actions
after accepting the presidency of the Liberal association was to ask
Parkin and Claxton to summon a group to work on a Liberal platform.

MacDermot was the most eloquent and passionate of the Montreal
group. After a number of conversations with Massey, he wrote a
remarkable letter on 2 January 1933, in which he summed up the ideas
and attitudes of 'the average reasonably well-to-do, capable, ambitious,
intellectually unsubtle Canadian man of about the age that took us into
the war as youngish soldiers':

*First we – may I say we – are not party minded. We are if anything anti-party
minded. It is a common-place (ill-founded, I think very often) to say that politics
is the dirtiest of all social games, that it is infested by the half-baked and the
uninspired, that it is a giant humbug in which empty protestations are the only
features that distinguish one party from the other. Hitherto we have ignored this
rather seamy side of our national life. Now under stress we have to take note of it,
and so our negatives are supplemented by some positive demands. We want
politics to be honest and to disclose its honesty. Both parties should, through their
leaders, utter self-denying ordinances, which would publicly and beyond
compromise cut them off from the mistakes and sins of the past. They should
confess to their ignorance past and present, and take up a learning attitude –
without of course any loss of resolution or self-confidence in their ability to learn
and to act accordingly. In fact they will have somehow to shine out in the light of
a genuine re-birth if they are to capture and inspire the young and the younger
men and women. These generations have as you know waved a perfectly
contented farewell to the home conceptions, the morality, the relations of the
sexes, the religion, the classical books (Pilgrim's Progress, Bible, Gulliver, etc.),*

the social grades and categories of their fathers and mothers. And they have replaced them successfully enough, or are replacing them, and without fear or doubt. But they are not allowed to bid farewell to the old and to them meaninglessly outworn political concepts & slogans & formulas, because the parties still sing these old songs, man their old bastions, issue the same defiances. And this is why the CCF with all its pitiful chaos and feeble intellectual output is causing the younger people to turn their faces up. The CCFers are like the sans culottes of the French Rev. or the bootless and ragged soldiers of George Washington — contemptibles to the disciplined and tradition-loaded soldiers of the crowned heads of Europe and the obstinate George III — but ultimately unbeatable, or at least shall be unbeaten.

Well, I ask myself, and I should like to ask you further, how is Liberalism — in which I believe as the truly civilized political level — to capture that fine careless rapture? I think by the building of the organization, every part of it subsisting and growing by the life that dwells within it, which you spoke of, a good deal can be done, but somehow the new organization must be attuned to the despair which is now driving so many people to think.

MacDermot's letter, as did MacDermot himself, had a profound effect on Massey. He accepted the analysis. The problem before the Liberal party was to find a response to the CCF that would enable it to capture the Canadians whom MacDermot had described, and thousands of others far less sophisticated, who were confused and angered by the sudden economic collapse and impatient at official inaction. The Liberal party, Massey reflected, could adopt one of three attitudes. It could oppose with all its might the program of the CCF as doctrinaire and autocratic. The danger in this was that the Conservatives would undoubtedly adopt the same attitude, and the distinction between the two old parties could reduce itself to differences in personalities and in the phrasing of platitudes. At the opposite extreme, the Liberal party could welcome the CCF as allies, a little eccentric and impatient, but fundamentally sound. The danger here was the alienation of the old guard. The third possible policy lay in between: the immediate and definite formulation by the Liberal party of a program of reform that would give immediate relief without questioning the structure of society.

Vincent Massey favoured the third response, but, in his radical moments, could move towards the second. Whether he was supporting the third or second, he was always in danger of offending King. For King did not see the political situation in crisis terms. God was in his heaven and, in due time, would give victory to his centrist elite, the Liberal party, and confound the enemies on both the right and the left, Tories and socialists.

As soon as he had accepted his call, Massey began a campaign to move the Liberal movement to the left. He urged his leader to be 'bold and definite'[36] and warned him of 'the process of compromise and modification which would result' if King waited for the party caucus and a meeting of the federation to gain consensus.[37] 'I quite realize,' he went on, 'that we must listen to all the various groups that make up our party and give them all a voice in the formation of policy, but I am satisfied that they need and desire a pretty bold lead.' But King could not be persuaded or bludgeoned into action. He had no taste for bold measures. As Neatby observed, 'for two years (1930–1932) he would continue to argue that the tariff encompassed most of Canadian politics.'[38] Even if he were convinced of reform measures, King, as a matter of strategy, was unhappy about clear statements of policy. When Massey talked to him about a program 'I told him to be careful, that what was inserted would be misconstrued and everything left out wd. be commented upon as intentional. General principles were about the limit we should go.'[39]

Until the end of 1932, King was not unduly disturbed by Massey's activities. He resented the frequent inroads Massey made on his privacy, and was irritated by the calls for decision and action. Perhaps he was a little alarmed by Massey's first public speech as the designated head of the non-parliamentary party, delivered on 18 November to the Ontario Liberal Association. It was a judicious mixture of the old free enterprise liberalism and the new liberalism that saw the need of government intervention to maintain freedom of choice. But the emphasis was perceptibly on the new version: 'The man who is destitute has little patience when his relief is held back while lawyers discuss the British North America Act.' Moreover, King must have reflected that this was not the speech of a disciple. There were no ringing references to the leader, no appeals to partisan party senti-ment. The speech was carefully constructed, with a sprinkling of epigrammatic phrases calculated to stimulate interest and arouse admiration. 'Participation by the many makes a party real and keeps a party clean'; 'Liberalism is a slave neither to the theory of force on the one hand nor to the force of theory on the other.'

Whatever misgivings King may have had, he kept them to himself. He wrote Massey a fulsome letter of praise that must have struck the recipient as an endorsement of the high line he was taking: 'As I read your address and talked with others of the significance of your address, and the even greater significance of what you are doing in other ways, I could not but help remark upon the parallel which your life and example affords to that of Lord Bryce, Lord Grey, Lord Crewe, and others whose names have an enviable association with British diplomacy, and an even more enviable association with British politics in what they have given, both in and out of parliament, in the way of guidance and support to the affairs of the party with which their entire lives have been identified.'[40] After the launching of the National Liberal Federation, King followed this letter with another one equally congratulatory, equally assuring to Massey that his role was a high and puissant one.

In the time that I have been leader of the Liberal party, nothing has happened which has given like satisfaction and hope to the future – Saturday's achievement is what it is in virtue of the way in which you have co-operated to bring it about. But for your having put your shoulder to the wheel as you did, the party would be still floundering along as it has been doing in matters of organization and publicity for over a decade past.

The establishment of the National Liberal Federation of Canada is a milestone in the history of Liberalism in our country. It is, however, much more than that, it is an onward and upward step in political organization and education which gives promise of being as widespread and far-reaching in its effects as any political or educational movement launched in Canada at any time.[41]

During the next two years, King's attitude towards Massey changed dramatically. Massey became a noxious rival who had to be ruthlessly suppressed, removed from the high position that had been assigned him as a co-imperator of the Liberal empire and reduced to the status of a dependent bureaucrat. The conflict rarely surfaced: its record is to be found in the diaries of King and Lambert (rarely in Massey's diary, which for this period is consistently bland); and even in King's diary, into which he distilled his venom, the references to Massey oscillated between brutal castigation and fatherly approval.

The relationship between King and Massey staggered from crisis to crisis. The first sharp crisis came with a speech that Massey gave before the Essex County Liberal Association on 24 March 1933. The cause was his apparent *volte-face* towards the CCF. In a speech given to the Hamilton Liberal Club little more than three months earlier, on 16 December, he had dealt severely with the new party. It had, he declared, been pusillanimous in not declaring itself to be a socialist party: no doubt the founders realized that 'there are few countries where the principles of real socialism are less applicable than in Canada, or less welcome.' The CCF sought to convince the people of Canada that there are no distinctions between Conservative and Liberal – a gross absurdity, for Liberalism is wedded to reform, and Conservatism to the preservation of the *status quo*. But the most serious indictment of the CCF, said Massey, was that it aimed only to hold a balance between the two parties. 'This movement has the intention of assuming *power without responsibility*. They wish to hold a sufficient number of seats to be able to dictate policy to the party in office without being answerable to the national electorate. What a log-rolling, vote-catching, kaleidoscopic chaos in Parliament would ensue! What a vortex of intrigue and instability we should have!' The conclusion of the speech was that Canada should stick to the two-party system. A resurgent Liberalism, by eliminating the need for a radical third party, would assure this. Now at Windsor, three months later, Massey appeared to welcome co-operation with the CCF. Doctrinaire state socialism his party could not, of course, accept. 'On the other hand, if the word "Socialist" is meant to apply to people who wish the State brought to the service of the individual in an advancing program of social legislation, who want to see the abuses and evils of primitive capitalism checked and controlled in the interests of individual men and women, who want to see a more equitable distribution of wealth, then I say that these views are those of all right-minded thinking men and women and that the Liberal who does not share them is not a

Liberal at all.' It is clear that Massey thinks of the members of the CCF as being this kind of people – bringing a moral passion, a sense of religious mission not present in Liberalism, a contribution that should be welcomed. 'I believe that between the majority of Liberals and the majority of men and women in the new third party movement there is no fundamental difference in approach. Let us have teamwork between them.'

In his diary Massey recorded that at Windsor 'I made a pretty good speech – conciliatory towards the CCF & succeeded in pleasing left and right wing.'[42] Alice, who, as always, was on the platform with her husband, wrote somewhat more emotionally about the event. In a letter to King she said: 'your name got a great welcome and it would have thrilled you could you have seen the audience from which it came. You know the story – out of 100,000 in that district, 35,000 are on public relief. Such an audience, many of them in their oldest and barely warm enough clothes – with their drawn faces hit near the heart. Their suffering and patience humbles one and makes one long for the day that you can lead them out of the wilderness. This is a great cause to be fighting for Rex. Although we are often tired – we are glad to be with you in it.'[43] King must have wondered whether Alice really believed that he was leading a crusade in which Massey was a brother evangelist, or whether, aware of her husband's dangerous dissidence, she was trying to placate King by playing up the special circumstances. King replied with great coolness. He regretted that so much public attention had been directed towards Massey's conciliatory words for the CCF. 'I have come to share the view held by our members that the CCF have not the slightest intention or desire to cooperate with the Liberal party, but are out to destroy us, even before the tories.'[44] The cool words in this letter to Alice were accompanied on the same day by some bitter words addressed in his heart to Massey.

It made me a little indignant reading between the lines I could see it was an attack on the side from what I had said in the H. of C. – reference to old leaders, & Liberalism of Gladstone, Asquith, Laurier, etc. – the reference to religion, & reference to greed etc. – His talk about 'the new Liberalism' & a new platform etc. was gratuitous. His references to the CCF were mistaken politically, his references to myself were little short of contemptuous. I am not sorry, it will help me to put that gentleman in his place. He is a place seeker & time server despite all his high flown motives etc. & all that he said was really an echo of Bowman of the Citizen. Had I gone for inflation etc. as desired when it was uppermost, I wd have been discredited now. Massey has made no end of trouble for me trying to force the pace. He is incapable of working with any one else.[45]

The second crisis in the King-Massey relationship was the Liberal Summer Conference held at Port Hope from 4 to 9 September 1933. Vincent was closely identified with the conference; without him it is doubtful whether it would have existed even as an idea; certainly its organization and enactment would have been impossible. King, on the other hand, initially approving of the conference, became indifferent and basically hostile. The conference dramatized the different approaches of the two men and deepened King's suspicions of Massey's motives.

The idea of a conference where political issues would be discussed by a group of laymen and politicians was at the very heart of King's original concept of the role of the national president of the Liberal Federation. It would be educational in a broad sense. Its constituency would be, first of all, Liberal Members of Parliament and lay partisans, and, beyond them, intellectuals of a liberal cast of mind – academics and writers, and the public concerned with basic issues. Massey outlined the general idea of the conference in a speech delivered to the Hamilton Liberal Club on 16 December 1932. In this early form, it was to be 'a summer school,' obviously based upon the British practice of the major political parties, held regularly each year, and to be concerned with relating 'the thinking which is being done on the subject of politics in this country' to 'concrete realities.' The men who dealt with the 'concrete realities' – politicians and journalists – were not enthusiastic. An editorial in the Ottawa *Journal* described the proposed conference as if it were an Oscar Wilde comedy – a Canadian version, which might have been called *The Importance of Being Vincent*. 'Those who want to may still practice their airs at a certain kind of reception on sawdust-sprinkled floors, but they won't be the ones to save the party. That will be done over tea-cups and lettuce sandwiches at a nice summer school, where real statesmen won't have to rub shoulders with uncouth & perspiring ward-healers.'[46] This was malicious Tory badinage, of which Massey was a favourite target. But there was little enthusiasm in the Liberal party, and what was more serious, in the shadow Liberal cabinet. Thus Norman Lambert described the attitude of Ernest Lapointe: 'Saw Lapointe who was not particularly favourable to summer school & promised to write to V.M. – His view was that with so much hardship about, it would leave a bad impression to have a leisurely conference on political questions held at Pt Hope under the auspices of the Liberal party organization. More attention should be given to practical affairs of organization.'[47] Lapointe and others expressed their doubts to King, now sceptical himself. The surge of discontent with the idea of the conference gathered head and momentum, and Massey was forced to fight hard for its survival. On 11 May he described a 'hectic day occupied in efforts to salvage the Lib. Summer Conference which had fallen foul of the fears, jealousies & prejudices of the parlty party.'[48] He was willing to agree that the conference should be unofficial, not related in any direct way to the party. '[King] consented to allow conference idea to be carried out without asking for sanctions of caucus – in other words the conf. is now regarded officially as unofficial. Bien Merci!'

For a short period, Massey insisted, against Lambert's opposition, in having the national office of the Liberal federation take responsibility for the organization of the conference. 'He [Massey] insisted that our office machinery be used & that printing accounts be carried here, but that the latter should be kept separately from general printing account. He said that unless the office of the Federation could do this, he would take steps to close it up.'[49] Since the conference now had no official relationship to the Liberal party, Massey was completely in the wrong. But this burst of self-righteous arrogance was short-lived. Two months later he was penitent. 'Massey discussed finances & said that it was unthinkable that this office should close now. He wanted Summer School costs to be sent to him & he would send a cheque at once to pay for them.[50]

King's coolness towards the conference arose from the suspicion that it would be a Massey venture, and that he would use it to give publicity to ideas that he had already enuciated on the platform. If King could not stop it, at least he could make it ineffective. King was right in his suspicions, but unsuccessful in his tactics. Its unofficial status gave

Massey a free hand. In the organization he enlisted a group of young men who were sympathetic to the new Liberalism – Paul Martin, soon to be an MP, Stephen Cartwright, Massey's secretary, and Raleigh Parkin, who was closely bound up with the Montreal ginger group. Massey's idea from the very beginning was to draw upon British and American progressives who were also men of indisputable intellectual authority. Such men, he was sure, would support his own concept of 'militant, progressive Liberalism.'[51] He was not notably successful in obtaining a strong British contingent. His first two choices, J. M. Keynes and Sir Walter Layton, were not available, and he had to content himself with two men who were exponents of orthodox Liberalism – Sir Herbert Samuel, the leader of the Liberal party, and T.E. Gregory, professor of economics at the University of London. He was far more successful with his American representatives. He had wanted Walter Lippmann as first choice. Lippmann could not come, but he was helpful in obtaining two of the major spokesmen for the New Deal, Raymond Moley and W. Averell Harriman. Moley was a member of Roosevelt's 'brain trust,' a close adviser of the president during the election of 1932, and for the first year and a half of Roosevelt's first term assistant secretary of state, with a roving commission to investigate a variety of major problems. He had recently resigned to become editor of a national weekly. Gossip attributed this to his resentment of the arrival in Washington of strong rivals for the president's attention; but he retained his ties with the administration. W. Averell Harriman came from an old and wealthy railroad family, was chairman of the board of directors of the Union Pacific Railroad, and held a senior post under Roosevelt's National Industrial Recovery Act. Both men were sympathetic to Roosevelt and the New Deal, but not uncritical supporters.

It was fortunate that such strong spokesmen for the New Deal came to the conference. The program covered almost every problem, national and international, political, economic, social, but the liveliest debates focused on the New Deal. For the 'New Liberalism' it had become a rallying model; it breathed courage and resolute action, and it embodied the principles of federal intervention, control (although not ownership) of industry, and a theory of the organic interrelationship of all parts of the economy. It was the great contemporary example of successful planning. Terence MacDermot contended that 'The New Deal, as I see it, is a valiant effort to protect political liberty, and, simultaneously, through its operation, to hasten the coming of economic liberty.'[52] R.M. MacIver, once head of the department of political economy at the University of Toronto and at this time professor of sociology at Columbia University, saw the New Deal as the blessed harbinger of a new age:

Under the spell of this rugged capitalism the spirit of liberalism slept, and the priests of the prevailing faith, Coolidge, Hoover, Mellon, Ford, and the rest diversely intoned the chants of false prosperity. That spell is broken. The God of Things-as-They-Are has been, for the time at least, dethroned. The sacred liberty of competition in the sweat-shop and the coal-mine has been put under at least temporary arrest so that other liberties might breathe the air. The competitive anarchy of the textile trade, of the oil industry and dozens of others has been curbed ... Whatever be the success of these various experiments, undoubtedly the State has assumed a new role which it will not easily abandon. An example of control has been initiated which will have enduring consequence.[53]

Massey listened to these words with approval. They embodied ideas that he had enunciated. In his most recent speech, delivered the previous month at the Lake Couchiching conference – an Ontario conference on current events that had considerable influence in shaping public opinion – he had argued that the circumstances of the time demanded an economic nationalism; and he had pointed to the experiment in the United States of the planned state carried out 'with such vigor and courage.' King was distressed by all this praise of the New Deal. He had been initially pleased by Roosevelt's election. Roosevelt, after all, was a liberal and many of his ideas, King reflected with satisfaction, sounded as if they had been lifted from the sacred testament, his own *Industry and Humanity*. But by the time of the conference, King had become alarmed by the course of American policy: the federal government had undertaken planning on a sweeping scale; and the great public works program threatened ruinous inflation. Shortly before the conference he had a talk with Dafoe and agreed with him that 'Roosevelt is on the wrong line re labour & industries, – use of arbitrary power to make artificial agreements – also re inflation.'[54] The day before the conference he reflected, 'Massey will be for planning – with young Liberals & University radicals etc. Massey told me the conference wd. develop into a contest between the two. I am all anti-planning – as understood generally.'[55] He was pleased to find one sceptic on the subject of planning, Gregory, who attacked Harriman with great acerbity and turned his speech into a long tirade against the very concept of planning. King 'shuddered' at MacDermot's exposition of the New Deal – 'The mad desire to bring about State Control & interference beyond all bounds'; and Moley's speech 'made [his] blood run cold.'[56] In his mind Roosevelt was moving from liberalism to something akin to fascism. 'I am beginning to think Roosevelt is a little like Bennett in his outlook.'[57] And two months later, 'I am beginning thoroughly to dislike the man, as a dictator, whose policies are absolutely wrong – amateurish, half-baked & downright mistaken.'[58]

King was a guest at Batterwood throughout the conference. It provided a soothing retreat from the exacerbations of the meetings. But he was still restive and troubled. He had a series of disturbing dreams that did not seem to carry a comforting message; and he regretted his occasional capitulation to 'the man of the senses' – a drink or two, and, at an evening party, a few dances, which aroused some vague libidinous feelings.

At the final session on 9 September King made the concluding speech. Aware that much of what had been said during the last six days was, by implication, critical of his own ideas and attitude, he was on the defensive. His speech was an exercise in cloudy circumlocution. What it finally amounted to was an exposition of his method of formulating policy by consensus: in the palace of Liberalism he admitted that there was an obscure cupboard for conferences of this kind, but the spacious rooms were reserved for the caucus and the cabinet.

His own unhappiness about the conference carried over into some subsequent correspondence. Massey proposed to change the title of the book containing the text of the speeches from *The Liberal Way* to *Liberalism Here & Now*. King sensed a typical Massey desire to emphasize urgency and definiteness, and to hint at official endorsement. He replied testily that 'any treatise on Liberalism, which might be taken as related to the work of the Lib. party in Canada, should be issued either under the auspices of the National Liberal Federation or as the result of some party convention, or by the authority of the leader of the party.'[59] King was also unhappy about the choice of the picture of him that would appear in the volume. In the proposed picture he was flanked by Sir Herbert Samuel, and the picture was to be entitled 'Liberal Leaders.' King detected in this an implication that he was an ally of Sir Herbert, and a junior ally at that – all the more demeaning since British Liberalism was in deep decline and Canadian Liberalism would, he was confident, soon assume its natural position of power. He finally accepted one group picture where he is standing beside Harriman, whom he admired. He insisted, in addition, on a separate picture of himself, a picture taken elsewhere under more relaxed circumstances, where he looks like a stout eupeptic grandfather beaming on his grandchildren.

As King reviewed the conference, he came to the conclusion that it was not only a basic criticism of his ideas, but a questioning of his leadership. Moreover it was evident that only one person could possibly challenge his leadership. That person was the president of the National Liberal Federation, whose every public speech was the declaration of a leader and not the soothing endorsement of a disciple. King was aware of the considerable comment in the press that confirmed his analysis. A writer in *Saturday Night* had reflected on Massey's increasingly important role. There is hope in some quarters, he wrote, that Vincent Massey will become 'an almost legendary figure wielding great influence, reshaping the Liberal party from within, until it again assumes form and vividness. There are greater satisfactions than wielding the sceptre and wearing the robes of power: to be behind the throne is more than being on it. Mr Massey might use the respect and esteem in which so many thousands of people hold him to put on power so that he may purge and elevate his party.'[60] The *Canadian Forum* commented in a similar vein. 'Vincent Massey has come to be looked upon increasingly as the man who might bring about a political revolution in Canada by persuading the Liberal party to adopt liberal principles.'[61] Other comment saw Massey as supplanting King. The popular humourist 'R.T.L.' added this comment to his epigrammatic portrait of Vincent Massey: 'If he could borrow some of the bodily bulk which Mr Denton Massey could readily spare, and if he could lose some of his constant culture, he might end up as P.M. whether he wants to or not.'[62] King must have found particularly alarming a Canadian Press story that appeared in the fall of 1933 in a number of papers, among them the High River, Alberta, *Times* of 2 November.

The divergent views of Mr King and the Honourable Vincent Massey, National Liberal organizer, are the subject of speculation among Liberals as to whether the party will get a new leader or a new organizer. Mr Massey has become an outspoken partisan of ideas grown popular among the younger intellectual Liberals of England, the idea that in the interests of human welfare men should meet the challenge of our economic regime in which they are the victims of their own creations, the idea that it is the duty of the heads of States to give leadership in escaping from the ignominy and assisting the organization of a coherent, and controllable economic system.

Mr King still holds to the ideas of Liberalism of the Victorian era ... during his recent tour of the west, he devoted himself to a defence of his old loves, laissez-faire *and* opportunism.

By the beginning of 1934 King had concluded that Massey was conspiring against him and that he must seek a confrontation. The opportunity came in April when Massey and Lambert were planning a trip to the west. King feared that the trip would simply be another opportunity for Massey to give a series of magisterial speeches on policy before sympathetic audiences in the radical west, and he now made it clear to Massey that he must abandon speech-making and attend to matters of party organization. In his account of the interview, King's diary prose, never even at its calmest achieving a high degree of coherence, splutters into angry fragments.

After clearing his throat as he spoke, he said that Lambert & he had been talking over the West, and that while he & Alice wd. not like it, and it would mean a tax to them & expense etc., that they both thought he ought to go out on a speaking trip, to offset the growth of the new ideas etc. springing up, to keep interest in Liberal thought etc. I asked him if Lambert had said that, he replied yes, I waited a moment & then burst forth (my righteous indignation would stand it no longer – I felt he was lying, and that Lambert was being made the goat) and I said then I did not know where I was at, or who I could trust, whether I was walking on quicksand – I said only the day before Lambert had told me the direct opposite, that I had talked with him about it, & said that he Massey had been phoning him to sound me out & to prepare the way for this, and that I had said it would be a great mistake, that I was having a hard enough time to keep the members of the Party in line in the H. of C. & I wd. have all the trouble over again I had as a result of some of his previous speeches that Lambert knew what that trouble had been & agreed what I was saying was true. Vincent then asked me, if his speeches had not been satisfactory. I told him what he had said about planning & the like had not, & that there had been great difficulty – I said if he went, & he wd. have to do as he pleased, I wd. not be responsible for having sent him, or anything he might say, that I thought it wd. be best to wait till after the session when the members & all wd. know just what our attitude on certain questions would be. He then said he wd. not go, if I felt that way. I told him he must decide himself. If he asked my opinion. I wd. say a trip at this time wd. be unwise. – I went on to speak of being amazed at Lambert – he began to try & excuse him, asking if the conversation were over the phone etc. that he thought Lambert of all men wd. be straight etc. I could have spewed him out of my mouth.[63]

To Lambert at a later interview King cut through his tirade with a specific charge. 'He implied that my trips west were for the purpose of boosting V.M. for leadership.'[64]

Lambert had a difficult role to play. He was responsible to both King and Massey, and anxious to preserve the peace and his own position. He knew that King's accusations were well founded. In the summer of 1933 Massey had toyed with the idea of Union Government, not of Liberals and Conservatives, but of left-wing Liberals and the CCF. More recently, he had become more specific, but talked, not of Union Government, but of a spontaneous realignment after the next election, which he, Massey, would lead. On 7 February 'Massey and Mrs M. came to our house. He and she discussed future possibilities & said that after 18 mos. in England as Ambassador, he would be willing to return to Canada to carry on the cause of the New Liberalism. Nothing in his opinion can be done until after an election which will undoubtedly result in King's return to power, but with the realignment of political forces in the background still to be determined. Mrs M. was quite ardent in declaring that "Canada is our first love" and after doing a job of reorganization in connection with the High Commr's. office, they would return.'[65] On 28 February, Massey repeated this account of his plans. Lambert had now become an understanding Brutus to Massey's designing Cassius. 'To establish a new political line up I pointed out the need of a strong press & suggested *Globe – Mail* deal which appealed to him. "Let us work on it," he said.' By 2 March a grand design was beginning to appear. 'Had an interesting call from Graham Spry who told me that the *Farmer's Sun* was going to advocate V.M.'s ideas, or those of the summer school, that Hume Blake & Plaunt were in touch with V.M. & that with the *Canadian Forum* now in the picture with Cartwright, advocating summer school ideas, an effort to put over a new Liberalism with V.M. as chief exponent would be undertaken.'[66]

Lambert had some sympathies with the Massey approach, and may even have encouraged Massey's aspirations. But he had strong ideas of his own: he was a free-trade liberal who believed that Canada could not be self-subsisting, and that she did not have the industrial resources to ape the American New Deal. He sent Massey a long, vigorously argumentative memorandum on the Couchiching speech in which he wrote that 'you and Keynes are presenting the best case possible for a fascist government in Canada.' He was well aware of Massey's tendency, on political tours, to set himself up as a potentate graciously receiving the addresses of his subjects. He protested to King that the proposed western trip was for organizational purposes and that he did not want 'to combine this work with private secyship to the M's who would be making public appearances & having public receptions.'[67] On the other hand, Lambert had no great love for King, whom he found increasingly machiavellian in his dealing with the federation. King had the ultimate power, however, and Lambert concluded that his best course was to wean Massey away from the politics of ideas and persuade him to concentrate on financial and organizational problems.

During the summer of 1934, Massey, bruised by his confrontation with King, ceased to exercise leadership either on the platform or in the committee room. Lambert now became King's spokesman, converting King's dark tirades into specific threats. He told Massey that 'he should take more active part in the management of the campaign (1) because he is being kept in the picture just enough to be identified with it and (2) enough to be blamed for it if things don't go well.'[68] Three months later he was still distressed by Massey's inactivity and passed on a blunt warning from headquarters 'Told V.M. & Mrs M. that King expected him to attend to business end of things & in effect that was to be the price of London appt. Mrs M. said she had been urging this on V.M.'[69]

By the end of the year Massey had decided to follow Lambert's advice. By that time, it was obvious that King's political instinct was, as usual, sound. The country was moving towards the Liberal party, with the inevitability of the tide moving towards the shore. In the summer of 1934 Ontario and Saskatchewan elected Liberal governments just as Nova Scotia and British Columbia had the year before. Of eight federal by-elections held since the Bennett victory, the Liberals had captured seven. The CCF had had little success, except marginally in British Columbia. The possibility of a radical coalition between Liberals and CCF such as Massey envisaged and seemed to desire had vanished. He could now, on both personal and national grounds, address himself to securing the final triumph of the Liberal party.

His speeches from this point on to the Liberal victory in October 1935 were models of party decorum, with increasingly enthusiastic references to the leader. At the second annual meeting of the National Liberal Federation in December 1934, he publicly proclaimed his shift from ideas to organization. 'Ideas,' he said, 'are of little use unless the machinery exists to give those ideas practical application. As time passed and the issues of the forthcoming campaign became clearer, the Liberal attitude toward them established, the task of organization became of paramount importance, with the result that the National Liberal office is now a campaign organization, existing and functioning for the purpose of securing victory for the cause of organized Liberalism in the forthcoming general election.' King, reading the speech in advance, commented that it was 'well prepared & expressed' – high praise from a critic who, on reading previous Massey speeches, had either exploded in anger or rumbled on about the failure to give proper credit to him. By the summer of 1935, with the official campaign launched, Massey had become an unalloyed party man, discreetly lowering his pink flag of protest. Economic revival, not social reform, must come first: 'that revival will provide the truest foundation for those social reforms so urgently needed, and will help to make those social reforms real and effective and enduring.'[70] Aware of

King's increasingly apoplectic attitude towards the American New Deal, he pointedly omitted the United States from a list of countries that had emerged from the depression. King now begins to take on the cast of nobility: he is 'a wise and experienced captain' and 'a chief with a consistent and sincere conception of government and a comprehensive forward-looking policy.' By the end of the campaign, the nobility had acquired a heroic glint. '... The man who as leader of the Liberal party brought Canada through some of its most brilliant years, and now is about to carry it to even greater triumph. If you commence to enumerate the qualities which this Dominion needs in its leadership today you would find yourself describing Mr King.'[71]

In the day-to-day work of the federation Massey was least effective as a money-raiser. He was not happy in giving away his own money or in persuading others to give away theirs. The federation was not conspicuously successful in attracting large gifts from the wealthy or in raising substantial sums by general appeals. The provincial bases of the federation exacerbated the problem. It was not easy to divert large sums to the federal cause when the provincial party was preparing for its own election. Ontario, potentially the largest source, was the most difficult. Lambert reported on a meeting with Albert Matthews, the Ontario chairman, 'who was most disgruntled over finances & did not see how things could go ahead & said he wished he were out of it. V.M. he said could only give orders & was never on time at any meeting.'[72] As the campaign moved to its end, Massey reported to King that the Liberal forces were sadly outgunned on the financial front. The Tories, he said, 'are using apparently $10 to our $1 in their broadcasting & general publicity campaign.'[73]

Massey was much more effective in planning and directing the 1935 election campaign. He did this with the skill and exhilaration of a director of a Broadway play. His diary notes reflect his deep sense of satisfaction. 'The fun of the campaign lay in planning & executing the strategy & tactics – particularly in publicity – selection of slogans, the timing of poster, broadcasts, newspapers, advt. was carefully studied & most successful. "King or chaos" helped to win the election because like all good slogans it epitomized a feeling in the reader's mind.'[74] Massey's fervour was sustained by his deep dislike of Bennett. That dislike was greatly intensified by Bennett's series of radio addresses during

January 1935, in which he dramatically reversed himself, declared the end of *laissez-faire*, and heralded an era of business regulation and social reform over which he would preside. This, Massey believed, was a completely cynical adoption of Liberal ideas. The Bennett speeches, it was reliably reported, had been largely written by Herridge; and Massey must have reflected with sour bitterness that many of the ideas were worked out in long, relaxed discussions that he and Herridge had had in the golden days of their friendship. Massey wrote to King: 'Reform of course is our job as Liberals & I feel fully sure that Bennett dressed up in these borrowed clothes will look like the charlatan he is.'[75]

Massey's private spleen against Bennett, most apparent in his diary at the time of the cancellation of the London appointment, found its way into the concluding section of the satiric verse biography of Bennett, from which I have quoted some calmer introductory passages. Now the politician's righteous indignation takes over, and graceful wit becomes versified assault.

> *One looks in vain within his sounding shell*
> *For aught as constant as a principle.*
> *Unfair you say? He's proved it to the hilt.*
> *Hear ye this airy opportunist lilt*
> *About the virtues of our foreign trade*
> *Who all his life its virtues has gainsaid.*
> *Hear this high-priest of self-sufficiency*
> *Proclaim his zeal for reciprocity.*
> *Hear this reactionary make a bluff*
> *Of his affection for M. Litvinoff,*
> *This acolyte of business uncontrolled*
> *Become reformer, we are calmly told,*
> *Burning to bridle business. How long, pray?*
> *Until the advent of the polling day!*
> *There shall we leave him to the voters' care.*
> *They'll hear more bombast thro' the startled air*
> *More verbal thunderbolts the earth to shake,*
> *But honest citizens will not mistake*
> *The glib and unctuous for something real,*
> *Old dealer's junk for genuine 'new deal.'*

Reform we need. Yes and this land will have it
To those who love reform and won't deceive it.
In short the public — old age down to youth
Has not abandoned its respect for truth.

The campaign began and ended with two 'media' events in which Massey played an important role. On the afternoon of 19 July 1935, King arrived at Batterwood; he had a relaxing evening during which he 'enjoyed a glass or two of scotch,' and the comforting ministrations of Alice Massey's masseuse. (On this occasion, he made no harsh comments in his diary on the self-indulgent life of the rich.) The following day he and Vincent set off for Toronto to see William Gladstone Jaffray, president of the *Globe*. That newspaper, traditionally a Liberal supporter, had been alarmingly indifferent to the Liberal cause, and it was important that it be won over. After an earlier session with Jaffray, Massey had remarked that he 'is always thinking more of heaven than the Liberal party.'[76] This time Jaffray was warmly receptive. After formal discussions in his office, he entertained King, Massey, and his editor at the Old Mill restaurant, to the west of Toronto on the Humber River. King described it as 'a medieval monastic building, with notes of heraldry, chivalry etc. about it,' which he thought of as a fitting background for the new *entente*.[77]

The final concluding 'media' event was a dramatic use of radio. By 1935 the radio had penetrated the Canadian home, and its development had become a national concern. As prime minister, King had appointed a commission to consider the proper way of organizing radio – the Aird commission – and its recommendations for a strong, independent, national body to exercise control had been partially embodied by the Bennett government in the Canadian Radio Act of 1932. There had been a rapid growth of radio stations, both private and public, sufficiently powerful to reach large audiences and to form national networks. Such a network was arranged as a prelude to a great Liberal gathering in Maple Leaf Gardens on 8 October 1935. Each of the eight provincial premiers who were either Liberal or supported the Liberal policy spoke from his own province in commendation of King and his policies. 'The technical achievement of a nation-wide broadcast,' Neatby observed, 'with speakers from coast to coast, assured wide publicity to an occasion which effectively symbolized Liberal promise of government by consultation and cooperation.'[78] Neatby said that the idea was King's. Massey was, however, far more aware than King of the possibilities of radio, and had urged the Liberal party to come down strongly for an independent body that would make radio a national resource. If he did not suggest the national broadcast, he seized the idea vigorously and saw it through to a triumphant conclusion.

From the summer of 1934 until the end of the campaign, much of the tension between King and Massey disappeared. There were idyllic weekends at Batterwood when King became, for the time being, a member of the community, observing Lilias Newton as she worked on Massey's portrait, listening in the evening to impromptu concerts by members of the Hart House String Quartet, visiting Massey's neighbours, Sproatt, the architect, and Currelly, the museum director, settling down in the bosom of the family like a benign uncle, and reading aloud from the works of his favourite Canadian poet, Wilfred Campbell. But the old suspicions of Massey's motives had not disappeared. The diary is still full of bitter comments about Massey's self-seeking and lack of consideration for King's peace of mind. King had carefully noted the verse inscribed above the fireplace at Batterwood:

> *Give all thy day to dreaming and all thy night to sleep:*
> *Let not ambition's tyger devour contentment's sheep.*

The warning against ambition could be an admission of its constant presence. In King's mind the abstract quality was personified, and Massey emerged as an 'ambitious tyger.'

There was one final confrontation recalling in its violence and bitterness that of April 1934. As the campaign moved to its end, Massey, alarmed by the strength of the Conservative appeal, wrote a long letter stressing the need for fresh ideas and the promise of specific action. It was the Massey of the fall of 1933 speaking, implicitly criticizing the leader and telling him what to do. King was called upon to announce that the Unemployment Commission promised by the Liberals would go to work immediately; that a program for housing loans and slum clearance would be launched; and that there would be 'a thorough inquiry and legislation within the power of Parliament for the removal of evils and the reduction of costs in the distribution of farm products and the narrowing of the spread between produce and consumer.'[79] King scored the long letter with underlinings and question marks. Here was the 'ambitious tyger' again, thrusting the leader aside, exalting in the strength of his superior wisdom. King brooded over the letter, and when Massey came to see him on the morning of 5 October, rated him like an enraged housewife.

I had a good rest last night, but was wakened while we were in the station at Toronto by Vincent Massey coming aboard and wanting to talk. I had been annoyed at his 'suggestion' etc last night & also the points he had told candidates to stress, e.g., Bennett's failure – etc etc – but no effort to uphold their own leader. – I had left word not to let him in. Nicol did so, however, and when he began telling me what to do etc I let out at him very hard. Told him he had caused me more pain & concern than anyone or all else in the party besides, that I had never had my privacy invaded as he had, for years. I had had to change the phone, lock the doors etc to be free. I said his insistence on my doing all the [word illegible] has been more responsible for my illness of two years ago than aught else, never once had he suggested a rest, it was always Rex must do this etc also his talk about helping me & 'the cause' was all nonsense, it was himself & London that alone kept him to the party, that I had to tell him, it was only in this way he could hope to be appointed. I said it was all such a pity, as we might have done so much in a great cause with happiness all the way. – It was a scathing review of his selfish actions including telling him frankly he had been quite wrong in his views on most things. He was quite crushed, – perhaps I went too far but it was 'the last straw.' I told him when he was 60, he would come to see I was right – that I thought I knew something about political leadership or would not be where I have been for so long a time.

Massey sent King a handwritten note written in a tone of abject meekness. 'It was good of you to speak so frankly yesterday morning but I felt so crushed that I found it impossible to put my feelings into words. I can only tell you that Alice, I and the boys value your friendship and affection more than words can say. Sometime do let us put it all straight.'[80]

When next they met, King apologized for his outbreak. Following victory at the polls, he invited Massey to come to Ottawa to advise on the selection of the cabinet. He said that Massey was already responsible for the choice of one new member, C.D. Howe: 'I told him that I was taking Howe into the cabinet, and I would like him to feel that Howe owed his appointment to Mr Massey, as President of the Federation.'[81] Next day he told Howe 'that I wanted him to regard his appointment in recognition of the National Liberal Federation and its part in the company, and it was through Mr Massey I had come to know him.' Massey declined the invitation to come to Ottawa as a consultant on cabinet-making. He had had enough of Canadian politics, and his mind was now fastened on London.

The relationship of Massey and King is an example of the ironic tensions that arise when men who are fundamentally different in tastes and outlook are thrown together in a common political cause. The result in this instance was comic with some dark strands. Neither man suffered grievously; suspicion and distrust of the one for the other grew, but the surface of life was not seriously ruffled. On the private and personal plane, there was slight basis for close association. King was never comfortable in Massey's presence. 'What I feel most is being so much alone, & lacking some of the "solid" environment, needed to interest a man like Massey.'[82] Massey seemed always to have just left a sophisticated and cosmopolitan society, whereas King found his heart's content in a quiet evening by the fire at Kingsmere, reading aloud to a close companion from a book of pious reflections or a novel by A.S.M. Hutchinson. King was nervous in Massey's world, a little envious at times, but also contemptuous of what that world stood for. About Englishmen of superior pretensions, King was fond of quoting Asquith's famous phrase about Balliol men – 'a tranquil consciousness of effortless superiority.'[83] He no doubt used the phrase about Massey. Much of what went on in Massey's world was of no interest to King. The Hart House Quartet, in which Massey gloried, he described as an 'interesting orchestra of 4 pieces.'[84] The bedside reading for Batterwood he found exasperating: 'before going to sleep read more of a book entitled "Proust" by Clive Bell, the most impossible thing I have ever read, no sense or meaning in it all.'[85] In one area, King had strong views, and they were diametrically opposed to Massey's. He had a considerable interest in painting, and devoted a good deal of time and effort to supporting his favourite artist, Homer Watson. He had a simple aesthetics: paintings should tell an edifying story, or should render faithfully the surface of nature, but only nature in its most pleasing forms, preferably scenes reminiscent of his own Kingsmere, with or without the ruins. He was violently opposed to 'modern art' – anything that lay outside his own categories of excellence – and he never ceased to rail against contemporary Canadian painting. Here is a typical outburst: 'We attended the Art Gallery opening after. I detested the so-called "Canadian art" – futurist impressionist stuff & barbaric – everyone was complaining of it save Eric Brown, Massey & a few others.'[86]

Even in politics, where their common interests presumably lay, King and Massey were at variance. For King, Liberalism was not so much an ideology as a way of life, a religion that merged with his evangelical Presbyterianism and, later, his spiritualism; a good Liberal, for him, was marked by moral earnestness, a sentimental humanitarianism, and a disapproval of excessive wealth and display. Vincent Massey, too, was reared in an atmosphere of moral earnestness, but it was not, like King's, preserved in a solution of piety. Methodism tended to modulate into action: for the traditionalists, money-making and the support of good causes, like sabbatarianism and winning the war; for the radicals, the propagation of the social gospel. From his early Methodism, Vincent Massey retained the bias towards action, but shied away from extremes, whether to the right or to the left. For him, Liberalism was a middle-of-the-road movement, governed by reason, by a desire for peace and reconciliation in the affairs of men, and by the acceptance of the dominance in public life of an educated elite.

Men have often differed sharply in their ideas of art and politics, but have still found it possible to be friends. But King was incapable of friendship with men. As Neatby points out, none of his colleagues were personal friends. 'As Prime Minister King had always treated his ministers with the detachment of a chairman.'[87] The clue to this characteristic, which made King a lonely man and, at the same time, gave him a peculiar power over others, was the personal cosmology that he had constructed and in which he devoutly believed. In this cosmology King was at the centre, an incarnation of the spiritual force animating the world. He regarded his diary as a holy writ in which he traced 'the ways of God with man.'[88] It was a medieval universe with a series of concentric circles from which benign guides looked down and gave him advice: on the highest level, 'the loved ones,' his father mother, and maternal grandfather; below them, the great apostles of Liberalism who had passed on to glory, Gladstone and Laurier; and at the lowest level, the professionals, not always reliable – spiritualists and readers of signs. The real world outside of King was neutral or evil, and the function of the spiritual world was to enable King to confound the evil and to enlist the neutral on his side. Vincent Massey was sometimes neutral, in which case he could be won over by a combination of flattery and promises; he was sometimes evil, working against King, in which case he must be overcome.

The years from 1930 to 1935 constitute Vincent Massey's last direct involvement in Canadian politics. Some of his friends urged him to stay in Canada and continue his political activity. Brooke Claxton wrote to him as follows:

As it seems more certain than ever that the Liberals are going to get into office I have heard a number of people express the hope that you may stay in Canada rather than go to England as is rumoured is likely. The thought is expressed that you would be of greater service here at the present time, either as a member of the Cabinet or Government leader in the Senate. I have heard this not from one but from several people who were all fully aware of the great service you might be able to render in England and who do not underrate the importance of that post but feel that it is still more important that you should remain to advise the Government in Canada. Many people feel that the Liberal Party will need to have a conscience.[89]

Claxton's suggestion went beyond the realms of possibility. King had no intention of risking his health and peace of mind by giving the 'ambitious tyger' a senior position in the government. And it is doubtful whether Massey still cherished his idea that, presumably in response to a clear summons, he would return to Canada from England to lead the Liberal forces.

How sincere was Massey in his enunciation of radical ideas and how strong would he have been as a leader? The answer to the first question is that he was undoubtedly sincere, and that what he said had its basis in ideas that he had espoused over a long period of time. But to the second question the answer must be that he was not fitted to be a strong political leader; he lacked humanitarian zeal; and, even in politics, he remained an aesthete delighting in the glitter of ideas, and pleased by his skill in presenting them.

From the summer of 1934, with his mind now turned towards London, he began to give first consideration to international affairs. If he was an amateur in domestic politics, he was already a professional in international relations. In June 1934 he began to work, with the assistance of Stephen Cartwright, on a general book on foreign affairs entitled *Canada in the World*.[90] The only controversial speech he gave after the first confrontation with King was a call for Canada to support the League of Nations unreservedly and to 'put an end to the manufacture for private gains of weapons for the destruction of human beings.'[91]

Massey's appointment as high commissioner was made promptly. The few days before he left for London were full of harbingers of a new and happy life. On 31 October King phoned congratulating him on his appointment, and predicting 'a noble chapter in his own life and work and that of our country and the Empire ... When Vincent thanked me, and said he was grateful for the appointment I told him he had only himself to thank.'[92] On Saturday, 2 November, the official swearing-in ceremony took place in the prime minister's private railway car en route to Quebec, and King reflected with satisfaction that it was 'very significant taking place in the Prime Minister's car, which is now mine seeing that when it was Bennett's he had done Massey out of London – after making Washington impossible as well, – a retribution – a nemesis – the working out of the eternal laws of truth and justice.'

At Quebec Massey was one of the official welcoming party for the new governor-general, Lord Tweedsmuir, and one of the few that he recognized. 'When the Gov. Gen. & his lady came down the line of Cabinet ministers, generals etc. and passed me John Buchan cried "Vincent!" & I had to pull myself together to keep from saying "John!"'[93] Massey then returned to Toronto, to attend farewell dinners given by the Toronto Symphony Orchestra Association, a group of private citizens, and the lieutenant-governor. He had a long session on Massey Foundation matters and attended a wind-up meeting of the St John's Hospital Board. On the sixth of November he and Alice took the night train to Quebec, and sailed the following afternoon for England.

A Note on Sources

This book is based primarily on Vincent Massey's private papers. Mr Massey left all the papers to Massey College, and, until my biography is completed, I have been given sole access to them. (Scholars working on related subjects have, however, been given access to particular collections in the Massey papers.) The papers are unusually rich and comprehensive. They can be divided into four parts:

1 / By far the greater part is directed to correspondence, memoranda, notes, and manuscripts of speeches and books. The correspondence contains the personal letters written by and to Vincent and Alice Massey, but it also provides extensive material on the institutions and organizations with which the Masseys were associated.

2 / Vincent Massey kept a diary from 1908 when he was twenty-three and an undergraduate at University College, University of Toronto, until shortly before his death in 1967 (seventy-two volumes in all). The entire diary is in the collection. It is not, like Mackenzie King's diary, uninhibited and confessional; the entries are brief and often amount to little more than a record of engagements. But they are sprinkled with comments on people and events, and are an indispensable guide to the biographer. Where no specific day is given in a diary reference, it comes from a larger journal entry covering an extended period of time. There are actually earlier diaries that were kept in small pocket books and were not considerd worthy of inclusion in the 'official' diary. The first diary is for 1899 (aged twelve); the others cover the years from 1902 to 1907.

3 / Photographs, programs, diner menus, etc. are contained in two sets of volumes, about forty in all.

4 / There are sixteen volumes of newspaper clippings. The sole criterion for inclusion of a newspaper report is the mention of Vincent Massey's name. This

is a happy arrangement for the biographer, since the articles cover the whole range of comment from the hypercritical to the eulogistic.

Numerous collections of papers in the Public Archives of Canada contain reference to Vincent Massey. The indispensable collections for this volume are the papers of the Massey Family (M32A1), the W.L. Mackenzie King Papers (MG 26J) – especially the Primary Series Correspondence (J1) and the Diaries (J13) – and the W.L. Grant papers (MG 30 D59).

Queen's University archives has the Norman Lambert papers, and his diary for the years from 1932 to 1935 is essential for an understanding of Vincent Massey's political role during these years.

Quotations from primary material, unless otherwise identified, are from the Massey papers at Massey College. The following abbreviations are used to identify other collections.

MF Massey Family papers
WLMK King papers
WLG Grant papers

The basic secondary source is Vincent Massey's memoirs, *What's Past Is Prologue* (Toronto: The Macmillan Company, 1963), for which the abbreviation WPP is used in the footnotes. For the period covered by this volume the memoirs are not intensive and detailed. Massey concentrated on his career as public servant and political seer, and gave comparatively little attention to his activities in the arts and education.

PHOTO CREDITS

The photographs of Chester Massey and the infant Vincent, Vincent as a five-year-old, Vincent and Alice Massey during the first world war, George Wrong, Burgon Bickersteth, the Hart House String Quartet, and the family at the Batterwood rock pool all are reproduced through the courtesy of Hart Massey. The photograph of Vincent Massey at Dentonia Park is reproduced through the courtesy of Vincent Tovell, who also helped with other photographs. Robert Lansdale took the picture of the family tomb as it appears today. From the Public Archives of Canada come the portrait of Hart Massey with his two grandchildren (C 86703), the wedding party (PA 113236), and the portrait of Alice Parkin Massey (C 83390). The two photographs related to Hart House are from the University of Toronto Archives (the family: A80-0030; the theatre production: A75-0009). All other photographs are from the Vincent Massey Papers in Massey College and are reproduced with the permission of the master and senior fellows of the college.

Notes

CHAPTER 1

1 Merrill Denison, *Harvest Triumphant: The Story of Massey Harris* (Toronto: McClelland & Stewart Limited, 1948), p. 6. I have been unable to find any reference to Bishop Leckie in contemporary histories of Methodism.

2 The idea of the family in Methodist thought is interestingly developed in William Edward Westfall, *The Sacred and the Secular: Studies in the Cultural History of Protestant Ontario in the Victorian Period* (unpublished PH.D thesis, University of Toronto, 1976), p. 3

3 Quoted in Mollie Gillen, *The Masseys: Founding Family* (Toronto: The Ryerson Press, 1965), p. 76

4 *Ibid.*, pp. 92, 93

5 W.T. Crosweller, *Our Visit to Toronto, the Niagara Falls and the United States of America* (London, privately printed, 1898), pp. 67–70, quoted in Christopher Armstrong and H.V. Nelles, *The Revenge of The Methodist Bicycle Company* (Toronto: Peter Martin Associates, 1977), p. 6

6 W.H. Withrow, *Religious Progress in the Nineteenth Century*, (Toronto: Bradley-Garretsons & Co., 1900) p. 46, quoted in Armstrong and Nelles, *The Revenge of the Methodist Bicycle Company*, p. 5

7 Quoted in Denison, *Harvest Triumphant*, p. 69

8 *Ibid.*, p. 77

9 W.C. McFarland to Hart Massey, 3 May 1886. MF, vol. 1

10 Cameron to Hart Massey, 13 July 1895. MF, vol. 4

11 17 July 1895. MF, vol. 5

12 10 April 1889. MF, vol. 2

13 From the Sarnia Agricultural Implement Manufacturing Co., 3 Feb. 1861. MF, vol. 1

14 Gillen, *The Masseys*, p. 28
15 Sir John A. Macdonald to Hart Massey, 21 Sept. 1889. MF, vol. 1
16 Hart Massey to Chester Massey, 12 August 1886. MF, vol. 1
17 Hart Massey to the Hon. Sir J.S.D. Thompson, 27 Feb. 1893. MF, vol. 3
18 MF, vol. 3
19 Hart Massey to T.J. McBride, Manager N.W. Branch, Massey-Harris Co.,
   Winnipeg, 10 March 1893. MF, vol. 3
20 Hart Massey to Hon. John Carling, 27 Feb. 1893. MF, vol. 3
21 'The Saturday Lecture Course,' *University of Toronto Monthly*, March 1908,
   p. 183
22 'The Man Who Made Chautauqua,' an article from The New York *Sun and*
   Herald, quoted in the *Chautauqua Weekly*, Chautauqua, New York, 13 May
   1920, p. 4
23 Massey Diary, 3 Sept. 1909
24 WPP, p. 4
25 Raymond's account is the climactic incident in his first volume of
   autobiography. In his version, there is a second ironic reversal. When
   informed of Raymond's decision, Vincent remarked, 'What name are you
   going to use?' *When I Was Young* (Toronto: McClelland and Stewart
   Limited, 1976), p. 269
26 13 May 1898
27 15 May 1898
28 10 May 1898
29 12 May 1898
30 16 May 1898
31 WPP, p. 2. Vincent might well have extended the period of intimacy well
   beyond childhood. During St Andrew's and early university days, Ruth was
   a constant companion.
32 15 February 1902
33 6 February 1902
34 27 June 1903
35 6 September 1903
36 Margaret Osmond to Mrs Hart Massey, 20 November 1913. MF, vol. 19
37 Massey Diary, 26 June 1906; 3 January 1907
38 WPP, p. 11
39 Massey Diary, 18 June 1905
40 *Ibid.*, 15 April 1906
41 *Ibid.*, 24 May 1906
42 *Ibid.*, 27 February 1903
43 30 July 1903

44 6 September 1904
45 3 January 1907
46 This is from a letter to Chester (10 September 1903) in which Bishop Vincent summarized the main doctrines of Methodism. Another principal tenet, which throws light on the career of Hart Massey, was: 'I believe that all who are accepted as the children of God may receive the inward assurance of the Holy Spirit to that fact.' Bishop Vincent's letter to Mrs Hart Massey after the death of Anna illuminates the Methodist attitude towards death – the absorption in the final hours of the deceased, the dwelling on death as triumphant release, the elaborate funerals that became sombre celebrations. 'What a singularly beautiful life God's good providence has permitted you to live! Sorrow? Yes. But what compensations! Every time the gate of the grave has opened the gate of Heaven has opened at the same time, flooding your home with light and making your tears to shine. Honour has rested on your children. Success has crowned them. Heaven has claimed them. And from the Massey homestead to the Gate of Heaven a line of light may always be seen.' (MF, vol. 18)
47 11 February 1903
48 27 December 105
49 2 December 1907, MF, vol. 19

CHAPTER 2

1 Michael Bliss, *A Canadian Millionaire* (Toronto: Macmillan of Canada, 1978), p. 143
2 A.F. B. Clark, 'The University College Dinner,' *University of Toronto Monthly*, March, 1907, p. 118. The reporter was the professor of French, and the praise would appear to have been ironical, an interpretation reinforced by Clark's summary of the substance of King's speech: 'He advised students to form lasting friendships while at College.'
3 Massey Diary, 1 January 1910
4 'Address to the Senate of the University of Saskatchewan,' *University of Toronto Monthly*, April 1908, p. 198
5 The aphorism occurred in a speech to the women graduates of the Normal School, Toronto (not, it would seem, the most likely occasion for such acerbic wit), and was published in 'Address to the Women Graduates of the Normal School of Toronto,' *University of Toronto Monthly*, January 1909, p. 115. One undergraduate, Frank Underhill, was so much delighted by the aphorism that he continued to use it thirty years later in his history lectures to Toronto undergraduates.

6 'Address by the Principal of University College at the Annual Reception of the Students of the First Year, on October 2, 1906,' *University of Toronto Monthly*, November 1906, p. 4

7 'University Students at Oxford and Toronto,' *University of Toronto Monthly*, June 1917, p. 217

8 'A Review of the Past Session,' *University of Toronto Monthly*, July 1917, p. 259

9 'Gallicana Quaedam,' *University of Toronto Monthly*, March 1910, p. 272

10 'Gallicana Quaedam,' *University of Toronto Monthly*, April 1910, p. 322

11 *Ibid.*, p. 324

12 Austin Seton Thompson in his *Jarvis Street: A Story of Triumph and Tragedy* (Toronto: Personal Library Publishers, 1978), p. 203, gives this explanation of Vincent's attitude towards fraternities. He describes a conversation with Dr D. Bruce Macdonald, who was headmaster of St Andrew's College during Vincent's attendance, about the fraternity incident. 'Massey had wished to join the Kappa Alpha Society when he entered the University, but had failed to receive an invitation. Since Dr Macdonald had belonged to that fraternity when he was an undergraduate, Massey blamed him bitterly for having influenced the fraternity against him, an accusation that Dr Macdonald emphatically denied.' The conversation took place in 1938, and the passage of thirty-two years may have encouraged a prejudiced interpretation. The diary for 1906 does record regular visits to the 'Kappa Alpha,' of which Vincent's close friend, Harold Tovell, had become a member. But there is no suggestion that Vincent aspired to membership.

13 Alan J. Bowker has an excellent account of Wrong's career in his unpublished University of Toronto PH.D thesis, 'Truly Useful Men – Maurice Hutton, George Wrong, James Mavor and The University of Toronto,' 1975. Bowker lists a great number of societies linking social work and evangelical fervour in which Wrong took an interest. See especially pp. 79–82.

14 Massey Diary, 7 January 1911

15 WPP, pp. 21–2

16 'A College for Women,' *University of Toronto Monthly*, November 1909, p. 7

17 George M. Wrong, *A Canadian Manor and its Seigneurs: The Story of a Hundred Years 1761–1861* (Toronto: The Macmillan Co. of Canada, Ltd, 1908), p. 239

18 'Mr A.L. Smith's Lectures,' *University of Toronto Monthly*, May 1910, p. 423

19 *Arthur Lionel Smith: Master of Balliol (1916–1924): A Biography and Some Reminiscences by His Wife* (London: John Murray, 1928), p. 179

20 The issue of *Torontonensis* referred to is vol. XII, 1910. Vincent's photograph appears on p. 67 and *The masque* on pp. 62–5.

21 This letter is undated but was most likely written in the spring of 1910.

22 'On Thinking and Its Suppression,' *The Arbor*, February 1910, pp. 7–8

23 *The Arbor*, February 1911, p. 168

24 *The Arbor*, January 1911, p. 110

25 Massey Diary, 15 March 1908

26 *Ibid.*, 4 March 1910

27 *Ibid.*, 11 August 1911

28 Charles Rann Kennedy, *The Servant in the House* (New York: Harper and Brothers, 1908), p. 68

29 Discussion of the controversial play was so widespread that Maurice Hutton was moved to comment on it in a speech at the university. He was not impressed. It was, he said, 'a radically melodramatic rhetorical, sentimental play, with grossly unjust caricature in it.' *University of Toronto Monthly*, April 1909, p. 214

30 Massey Diary, 26 May 1910

31 In the diary for 8 July 1911, he refers to a 'meeting which I called at the Robt. Simpson Company to discuss down-town institutional work for the Methodist Church in Toronto.' He lists the members of the committee: Flavelle, Wood, Fudger, Rowell, Warburton, etc., the elite of Methodist millionaire piety.

32 John Mott, *The Evangelization of the World in this Generation* (New York: Student Volunteer Movement for Foreign Missions, 1901), p. 43

33 John Mott, *The Decisive Hour of Christian Missions* (New York: Student Volunteer Movement for Foreign Missions, 1910), pp. 148–9

34 Massey Diary, 25 March 1910

35 *Ibid.*, 24 June 1910

36 Murray Wrong's future father-in-law, A.L. Smith, was deeply impressed by John Mott. Mrs Smith, in her biographical study, described 'the meeting with Mr Mott, the American Evangelist, and founder of the Christian Student Movement' as an 'important factor in her husband's spiritual development.' Mott addressed a crowded meeting in the Hall of Balliol College in 1906 when 'The Hall was hushed to silence.' *A.L.M. Smith*, pp. 225–6

37 Letter to Murray Wrong, 9 November 1910

38 *University of Toronto Monthly*, January 1909, p. 103

39 *The Arbor*, February 1910, p. 54

40 The three quotations come from unsigned editorial comments in the April 1911 issue of *The Arbor* (the magazine was called *The Arbor* during its first

year of publication, but became *Arbor* in its last two years) and appear, respectively, on pp. 316, 271, and 273. Although the editorials are unsigned, the likelihood is that they were written by Vincent Massey; he had graduated, and during these years assumed the chief editorial responsibilities.

41 'The College Room,' *The Arbor*, November 1910, pp. 13–14

CHAPTER 3

1 Keith Feiling, *The Life of Neville Chamberlain* (London: 1946), p. 99
2 Letter to J.H. Ashdown, 11 February 1921
3 The letter is quoted by Vincent Massey in a long letter he wrote to Burgon Bickersteth, 17 January 1929, setting out the full story of Hart House. Chester's estimate of a cost of $300,000 was a typically unrealistic early estimate. The contract between the builders, Page & Company, and the executors of the estate stipulated that the building would be erected at a cost not to exceed $673,000. In his letter, Vincent estimated the cost of Hart House and its equipment at 'just short of two million.' The enormous increase in cost arose, presumably, from the long delay in completion caused by the war, and by the various additions and adaptations introduced by Vincent. The building today would cost, it has been estimated, over $30,000,000. But since the kind of individualized workmanship that went into the decorative features of the building no longer exists, certainly in Canada, thirty million dollars would not be able to duplicate the building.
4 Massey Diary, 23 May 1910
5 *Ibid.*, 9 January 1911
6 *Ibid.*
7 *Ibid.*, 17 February 1910
8 *Ibid.*, 24 June 1910
9 *Ibid.*
10 *Ibid.*, 29 January 1912
11 V.E. Henderson, 'The University Buildings of the Present and Future,' *The Arbor*, March 1910, p. 68
12 Massey Diary, May 1914
13 The letter is undated, but it is clearly May or June 1915. WLG, vol. 43
14 Letter to Vincent Massey, 8 July 1925
15 This is a quotation from a memorandum that Bickersteth wrote on his relations with King. Bickersteth permitted me to read it when I visited him a few months before his death in 1979.

16 Ian Montagnes, *An Uncommon Fellowship: The Story of Hart House* (Toronto: University of Toronto Press, 1969), p. 17

17 The merger of the Massey and Harris interests in 1891 enabled the resulting company to exploit the superior Harris Binder. Lawren Harris and Vincent Massey were as important to the artistic life of Canada as their fathers and grandfathers were to Canadian industry and agriculture. Geoffrey Andrew's quip about the two men deserves preservation. (Andrew married Margaret, a daughter of William Grant, and was thus close to the Massey world). When he was asked at a dinner party about the relation of Lawren to Vincent, he replied, 'There's no relationship. Its just a case of "blest be the binder that ties".'

18 Letter to Carrol Aikins, 21 August 1928

19 Letter to Walter Sinclair, 15 March 1927

20 Professor John Squair, Professor of French at University College, found the Canadian Bill for 1923 unattractive. In his unpublished memoirs he wrote: 'At Hart House two Canadian Plays are being presented this week. Both were very offensive to me, on account of the cynicism contained in them. The Translation of John Snaith by Briton B. Cooke and A Point of View by Marion Osborne. John Snaith is a loathsome creature who betrays a half-breed girl and in the end after being conscripted, steals a Victoria Cross from a dead man. A Point of View is a triangular sex play treated humourously. The amusing person is Jim Cripps, a burglar (Vincent Massey). I felt as if I had been wading in muck all evening.' (23 March 1923)

21 Basil Macdonald, *The New Sin* (London: Sidgwick, Jackson Ltd, 1916), p. 13

22 *Queen's Quarterly*, xxx, 2 (1922) pp. 194–212

23 Massey Diary, April 1912

24 *Ibid.*, 21 July 1910

25 *Ibid.*, 6 April 1917

26 *Ibid.*, 23 November 1920

27 Harry Adaskin, *A Fiddler's World* (Vancouver: November House, 1977) p. 119

28 *Ibid.*, p. 120

29 Letter to Vincent Massey, 10 June 1929

30 The Ysaye quotation comes from an article he published in *L'Action Musicale* and is cited by A. Raymond Mullens in an article on the Hart House Quartet in *Maclean's*, 1 March 1931, p. 41

31 London *Daily News*, 9 October 1929

CHAPTER 4

1 Here is a fair example.

> *The President, courteous and gay*
> *In the Bank lets Sir John have his way,*
> *But at the Museum*
> *That's where you should see him,*
> *Poor Currelly has nothing to say.*

The limerick plays upon a familiar pattern in Canadian cultural life: the domination of the professional by the lay board. Sir John Aird was general manager of the Canadian Bank of Commerce. Sir Edmund Walker was president of the bank and chairman of the board of the Royal Ontario Museum. C.T. Currelly was director of the Royal Ontario Museum of Archaeology.

2 *The Rebel*, launched by two undergraduates in 1916, soon attracted faculty contributions. It was, as the title suggests, much more critical and radical in its stance than *Arbor*. Indeed it was the direct predecessor of *The Forum*, which issued its first number in 1920. (By a slight imaginative leap it would be possible to see Vincent Massey as one of the progenitors of *The Canadian Forum*, given the interrelationship of *Arbor*, *The Rebel*, and *The Forum*.)

3 Massey Diary, 12 January 1911

4 *Ibid.*, 23 March 1912

5 *Ibid.*, 27 November 1920

6 University of Toronto Archives, Falconer Papers, Falconer to Massey, 27 June 1913

7 Letter, 13 March 1913

8 Undated letter, in all likelihood early in 1914

9 Undated letter, in all likelihood early in 1914

10 The original proposal came to the Board of Education of the Methodist Church of Canada from Vincent Massey on behalf of the executors of the Hart A. Massey estate, but this preceded the formal establishment of the foundation by only a few days.

11 *Report of the Massey Foundation Commission on the Secondary Schools and Colleges of the Methodist Church of Canada*, 1921, pp. 11–12

12 Massey Diary, 10 July 1910

13 *Ibid.*, 12 December 1910

14 *Ibid.*, 23 August 1911

15 *The History of the National Council of Education of Canada* (unpublished MA dissertation, University of Toronto, 1974), p. 9

16 *Report of the Proceedings of the National Conference on Character Education in Relation to Canadian Citizenship*, Winnipeg, 1919, p. 84

17 Cochrane was a contemporary of Vincent Massey at Balliol, and a close friend both at Oxford and, for a period, after his return to Toronto. In 1926, when the book was published, he was associate professor of classics at University College, University of Toronto. With the publication of *Christianity and Classical Culture* (1957), he established himself as a major international scholar. Wallace was a Canadian historian who had become a librarian. He was the chief librarian at Toronto from 1923 to 1954, but continued to write frequently and authoritatively on Canadian history.

18 MacMillan was the head of the Conservatory of Music, then a separate institution, apart from the University of Toronto. When it became part of the university, MacMillan (who had become Sir Ernest MacMillan), remained as dean of the Faculty of Music. But his fame arose from his activities outside the university, particularly as conductor of the Toronto Symphony Orchestra. Vincent always turned to MacMillan for advice on musical matters. At one point he discussed with him the possibility of making a full-time appointment of a director of music at Hart House, who would do some work in the university, and be paid in part by the university. But Sir Robert Falconer, the president, could not find a modest sum to supplement the substantial pledge of the Massey Foundation.

19 Michael Sadleir, *Michael Ernest Sadler* (London: Constable, 1949), p. 329. Sir Michael's program at Toronto was unusually demanding. At the actual conference, Wednesday, 4 April to Saturday, 7 April 1923, he made three speeches. On the Saturday evening he spoke to the Hart House Sketch Club. The next day, according to Vincent's diary, he 'preached to an enormous congregation at Metropolitan Methodist Church in the AM and at old St Andrew's in the evening.' On Monday he spoke to the Canadian Club on 'The Cost of Education,' and Vincent described it as 'a superb performance.' It is not perhaps coincidental that on his return to England Sadler presented Hart House with a splendid crucifix, by Eric Gill, for its chapel.

20 Vincent Massey to Fred Ney, 4 February 1925

21 'A Liberal Education and its Cost,' in *Education and Life*: addresses delivered at the National Conference on Education and Citizenship, held at Toronto, Canada, April 1923, edited by J.A. Dale (Toronto: Oxford University Press, 1924), p. 277

22 Both men were related to Vincent Massey. Edward Beatty was a grandson of Hart Massey's sister Elvira. J.M. Macdonnell and Vincent both married Parkin sisters.

23 5 May 1926

24 4 April 1926

25 10 April 1923

26 *Debates of the House of Commons*, Third session, fourteenth Parliament, CLX, p. 46

CHAPTER 5

1 WPP, p. 97

2 Massey Diary, 12 December 1910

3 *Ibid.*, 21 May 1912

4 *Ibid.*, 3 June 1912

5 *Ibid.*, 12 October 1911

6 Quoted in Carroll Quigley, 'The Round Table Group in Canada, 1908–38,' *Canadian Historical Review*, XLIII (September 1962), p. 213

7 Massey Diary, 11 January 1912

8 From a memorandum written by Philip Kerr, a close associate of Curtis, quoted by David Watt in 'The Foundation of the Round Table: Idealism, confusion, construction,' *The Round Table*, no. 240, November 1910, p. 425

9 Lionel Curtis, *The Problem of the Commonwealth* (Toronto: The Macmillan Co. of Canada, 1916), pp. 123–4. The book closes with a long quotation from John Milton's Areopagitica. This is the passage that is emblazoned around the walls of the great hall in Hart House. The date of Curtis's book coincides with Vincent's concern with the details of Hart House and it is not improbable that the idea of the Milton quotation came from the book. Curtis used the quotation to suggest the emergence of the new Empire after the trials and the self-questionings of the war. Vincent said that the quotation was chosen because it suggested the heroic stance of the British people under the ordeal of war. But differing interpretations do not rule out the strong possibility of Vincent's indebtedness to Curtis.

10 Lionel Curtis, *Civitas Dei: The Commonwealth of God* (London: Macmillan, 1938), p. 280

11 *The Blue Book*, p. 300. *The Blue Book* had six issues. It first appeared in May 1912, and lasted until the end of 1913. Vincent's article is on pp. 299–306 of the bound volume containing all the issues.

12 Vincent voted for reciprocity in the election of September 1911, just before he left for Oxford. He derived some satisfaction from the defeat of reciprocity from the reflection that the electorate believed, although mistakenly, that they were demonstrating their loyalty to the crown and empire. 'Father and I voted, I for, he against Reciprocity. Balance of power in hands of Van the chauffeur and he voted Conservative. This is prophetic. The great Conservative victory brought about by a move of fanatical anti-American sentiment which was the result of the annexation bogey operated by our Corporations. It proved, however, our unity and universal loyalty to the crown.' Massey Diary, 21 September 1911

13 The phrase was Benjamin Jowett's and is quoted in H.W. Careless Davis (revised by R.C.H. Davis and Richard Hart), *A History of Balliol College* (Oxford: Blackwell, 1963), p. 177

14 Massey Diary, 21 June 1912

15 *Ronald Knox* (London: Chapman & Hall, 1959), p. 83. William Grenfell was the brother of Julian, who was at Balliol from 1906 to 1910. Julian wrote a poem 'Into Battle,' which caught the spirit of reckless gallantry that characterized the early volunteer army. Both Julian and William were killed in the first year of the war.

16 14 March 1915; in the possession of Mrs C.H.A. Armstrong

17 19 November 1916. The earlier quotation from the memoirs is from p. 47.

18 Massey Diary, 28 December 1917

19 *Ibid.*, 24 October 1917

20 *Ibid.*, 25 April 1919

21 See Michael Bliss, *A Canadian Millionaire* (Toronto: Macmillan of Canada, 1978), for a detailed and convincing defence of Flavelle, especially Chapter 14, 'His Lardship.' Flavelle was reported to have said that Vincent Massey was 'a very valuable discovery from Ottawa combining ... business ability with political instinct' (letter from J.S. Willison to Vincent Massey, 6 May 1918). Vincent took pride in his official status: he recorded with satisfaction that he marched in Laurier's funeral procession as 'one having the rank of Deputy Minister.' Massey Diary, 22 February 1919

22 Merrill Denison, *Harvest Triumphant: The Story of Massey-Harris* (Toronto: McClelland & Stewart Limited, 1948), pp. 270–1

23 Massey Diary, 3 March 1924

24 Letter to Meighen, 22 April 1924

25 Massey Diary, 21 July 1924

26 *Ibid.*, 24 July 1924

27 *Ibid.*

28 *Ibid.*, 11 August 1924

29 Alice Vincent Massey, *Occupations for Trained Women in Canada* (London: J.M. Dent & Sons, 1920), p. 13

30 The observation was contained in an article published in the Boston *Globe*, 26 December 1926, on the occasion of Vincent Massey's appointment as the minister to the United States. The article had a Toronto dateline and was obviously written by a prejudiced insider.

31 Letter to Lord Eustace Percy, 22 August 1922

32 Letter to Sir George Parkin, 4 March 1922

33 *Ibid.*

34 30 January 1924

35 Edmonton *Journal*, 25 September 1925

36 Toronto *Globe*, 19 October 1925

37 Flavelle to J.M. Macdonnell, 1 October 1925 in Queen's University Archives, Flavelle Papers, 8541–2

38 The statement was given wide publicity. This is from the Hamilton *Spectator*, 5 October 1925

39 Telegram to Meighen, 3 October 1925

CHAPTER 6

1 King Diary, 1 November 1925

2 *Ibid.*, 25 January 1926

3 'I brought the discussions on to the question of tendering resignation, not one save Vincent Massey was hearing of it, they were all for holding to office.' King Diary, 2 November 1925

4 *Ibid.*, 13 November 1925

5 *Ibid.*, 14 November 1925

6 *Ibid.*, 5 December 1925

7 Quoted in WPP, p. 110

8 King Diary, 3 July 1926

9 Massey Diary, 15 October 1926

10 *Ibid.*, 21 November 1926. In view of Mosley's later career – withdrawal from the Labour party and espousal of a blatant form of fascism – Massey's comments were perceptive.

11 *Ibid.*, 18 November 1926

12 *Ibid.*, 16 October 1926

13 *Ibid.*, 26 October 1928

14 *Ibid.*, 4 October 1924
15 *Ibid.*, 24 October 1926
16 WPP, p. 117
17 Massey Diary, November 1926
18 *Ibid.*, 26 November 1926
19 Imperial Conference, 1926, *Summary of Proceedings*, p. 14
20 The secretary of state was T.F. Bayard, and the phrase occurs in a letter to Sir Charles Tupper, 31 May 1887. It is quoted by H. Gordon Skilling in his book, *Canadian Representation Abroad* (Toronto: The Ryerson Press, 1945), p. 185. My account of the background of Vincent Massey's appointment is based largely on Skilling's chapter, 'Mission to Washington: Canada's First Legation (1905–1939),' pp. 184–233.
21 *Ibid.*, p. 199
22 Toronto *Globe*, 15 October 1926
23 12 November 1926
24 9 October 1926
25 26 December 1926
26 11 November 1926
27 This portrait appeared in the Kansas City *Star* (30 November 1926), the Montreal *World Wide* (11 December 1926), and the Toronto *Daily Star* (20 December 1926).
28 Massey Diary, 5 February 1927
29 *Ibid.*, 16 February 1927
30 *Telegram*, 16, 17 February 1927
31 Letter to Mackenzie King, 21 May 1927
32 O.D. Skelton to Vincent Massey, 23 May 1927
33 Massey Diary, 30 May 1929
34 Letter to Claude Bissell, 12 July 1976
35 Hume Wrong's letter to his mother as he prepared to leave for France, 2 November 1915, is a moving document. It is in the tradition of Julian Grenfell and Rupert Brooke, an exalted dedication to a higher purpose: 'Mother dear, you mustn't worry about me. If anything does happen to me it is not going to happen for a long time yet. The whole thing is a great adventure which I am not looking forward to much, I must admit, but it has to be gone through sometime, and might as well come sooner as later. On the whole, I am glad the call came so suddenly, proud to be chosen, and eager to be as good a soldier as I can be. I am nervous about my own capabilities, but confident that I can do a good deal better than many of the officers I see around me. No matter what happens to me

please think that I am content.' The letter, and subsequent Wrong
letters in this chapter, are in the possession of Mrs C.H.A. Armstrong, a
sister of Hume Wrong.

36 'It is good news about Vincent. I hope he sticks at Niagara,' and 'I hope
that Vincent's job is a permanency.' Letters to George Wrong, 2 August 1915, 26 September 1915

37 Letter to Mrs George Wrong, 15 April 1927

38 Letter to Mrs George Wrong, 24 April 1927

39 Letter to Mrs George Wrong, 26 September 1929. The Massey routine
of leaving Washington for the summer was standard practice among
diplomats, most of whom escaped to the coast from the hot and humid
Washington weather. The legation was left in charge of a junior, either on
the staff or sent especially from Ottawa. Thus in the summer of 1929
Lester Pearson, who had recently joined the department of external affairs, took charge of the legation. *Mike: The Memoirs of the Right Honourable Lester B. Pearson*, vol 1 (Toronto: University of Toronto Press, 1972), p. 73

40 Letter to Mrs George Wrong, 24 November 1930

41 Massey Diary, 1 January 1930

42 *Ibid.*, 12 April 1927

43 H.B. Neatby, *William Lyon Mackenzie King, vol. 2: The Lonely Heights 1924–1932* (Toronto: University of Toronto Press, 1963), pp. 258–9

44 WPP, p. 128

45 *Ibid.*, p. 166

46 Neatby, *Mackenzie King*, p. 260

47 Massey Diary, 14 September, 3 October 1927

48 *Ibid.*, 4 November 1927

49 *Ibid.*, 28 December 1927

50 *Ibid.*, 26 January 1928

51 18 December 1926

52 18 December 1926

53 Eustace Percy, *Some Memories* (London: Eyre, Spottiswood, 1958), p. 9

54 *Ibid.*, p. 30

55 The diary reports visits and talks with Frankfurter on 8 April 1917 –
Harold Laski, recently arrived at Harvard from McGill, is also mentioned on this visit – 22 August 1918, 24 April 1923. On 5 June 1919, he
wrote, 'Went to see Herbert Croly and *New Republic* and had a good
talk with him.' Lippmann is not mentioned during these years, but he was
to become the closest associate of the three.

56 *The Promise of American Life* was published in 1909 by the Macmillan Com-

pany. The copy in Vincent Massey's library was a later edition, dated 1912. Presence of a book in a private library does not necessarily indicate familiarity with its contents, but pencil markings in the Massey copy are *prima facie* evidence of concerned reading.

57 *The Promise of American Life* (Cambridge: The Belknapp Press of Harvard University, 1965), p. 196
58 *Ibid.*, p. 256
59 *Ibid.*, p. 259
60 *Ibid.*, p. 410
61 *Ibid.*, p. 420
62 Walter Lippmann, *A Preface to Politics* (New York: Mitchell Kennerley, 1914), p. 191
63 Mark Schorer, *Sinclair Lewis: An American Life* (New York: McGraw-Hill, 1961), p. 268
64 Massey Diary, 22 November 1928
65 *Ibid.*, 22 February 1927
66 'Advertising in Canada,' speech at the annual convention of the Association of Life Insurance Presidents, New York, 13 December 1928, in *Good Neighbourhood and Other Addresses in the United States* (Toronto: The Macmillan Company of Canada Limited, 1930), p. 197
67 'L.A. is without form and substance. It is a city of two dimensions – no background, no shades and all glittering light with no relief. Easy money, idle people, no traditions – this combination makes it a home of extravagance, religious nostrums, medical panaceas and fads of every description.' Massey Diary, 25 March 1928
68 *Ibid.*, 27 March 1928
69 *Ibid.*, 14 November 1929
70 *Ibid.*, 5 February 1930
71 Esme Howard, Lord Howard of Penrith, *Theatre of Life* (Boston: Little, Brown, & Co., 1935),vol. 2, p. 564
72 Massey Diary, 25 July 1929
73 *Ibid.*, 23 April 1930
74 *Ibid.*, added 14 September 1930 to an original note of 28 April 1927
75 *Ibid.*, 4 March 1929.
76 Sacco and Vanzetti, two humble Italian workmen, were accused of murdering a paymaster and his guard. Both were devout anarchists, and the case against them, never conclusively proved, was greatly influenced by the current hysteria against radicals. The crime took place in April 1920, and after many delays, and the appointment of a special commission to review the case, they were executed on 22 August 1927. The case

reached its emotional crisis during Massey's first few months in Washington.

77 *Ibid.*, 20 April 1927
78 *Ibid.*, 22 December 1927
79 *Ibid.*, 19 November 1929
80 *Ibid.*, 20 November 1929
81 *Ibid.*, 10 January 1928
82 *Ibid.*, 16 November 1929
83 Joseph P. Lash, *From the Diaries of Felix Frankfurter* (New York: W.N. Norton, 1975), p. 22
84 Howard, *Theatre of Life*, vol 2, p. 569
85 Massey Diary, 29 May 1930
86 *Ibid.*, 24 June 1930
87 Sinclair Lewis, *Dodsworth* (New American Library, 1965), pp. 17–18
88 Massey Diary, 20 January 1929
89 *Ibid.*, 16 January 1929
90 *Ibid.*, 7 February 1930
91 'The Amateur Spirit,' in *Good Neighbourhood and Other Addresses in the United States* (Toronto: The Macmillan Company of Canada Limited, 1930), p. 344
92 He did not, of course, use the term 'multiversity,' which was a creation of the sixties, but his description of the distinctive contemporary American university could well fit the new terminology: 'You have broadened the meaning of this word [university] in your country until the term can now conjure up a vast organization guiding the studies of many thousands of students, distributing knowledge direct to all who seek it – individuals, municipalities, business corporations – and dealing in all branches from Greek philosophy to municipal engineering. It presents a fine picture – this great engine of modern knowledge which you have created in so many places.' ('The University as an International Link,' in *Good Neighborhood*, p. 51) The language and sentiments are amazingly close to Clark Kerr's in his *Uses of the University*, generally recognized as the classical description of the multiversity.
93 'The University and the International Mind,' in *Good Neighbourhood*, p. 150
94 Walter Lippmann to Vincent Massey, 20 May 1930
95 Massey had uniformly good relations with the American press. After an interview in Atlanta he remarked: 'saw the Press as usual – a nice group of fellows as they usually are.' (Massey Diary, 25 November 1929) He was particularly fond of the Washington press, and in one of his

retrospective entries he noted that 'the press in Washington is given a position of unusual prestige and prominence. Enhanced status, however, generally brings with it a heightened sense of responsibility and I always found newspaper men there uniformly reliable and cooperative.' (This was written 15 September 1930, although it appears opposite the entry in the diary for 19 February 1927.)

CHAPTER 7

1 Massey Diary, 25 January 1926
2 *Ibid.*, 20 December 1929
3 *Ibid.*, 10 March 1932
4 *Ibid.*, 20 December 1929–3 January 1930
5 *Ibid.*, 22 December 1929
6 *Ibid.*, 24 June 1929
7 King Diary, 1 November 1925
8 Toronto *Telegram*, 15 February 1927
9 Letter from S.C. Randall, estate officer, National Trust, to Vincent Massey, 28 October 1930
10 Massey Diary, 11 June 1932
11 'The Resonance of Batterwood House,' *Canadian Art*, 90, March–April 1964, p. 97
12 WPP, p. 178
13 *Ibid.*, p. 4
14 Massey Diary, September 1928
15 *Ibid.*, 17–24 August, 1930
16 Alice Massey to David Milne, 12 November 1934
17 Vincent recorded in his diary a dramatic scene that took place in the Washington legation on 3 May 1928. The Masseys were entertaining an old friend, Dr Frederick Banting, the co-discoverer of insulin, and an American acquaintance, Mrs Robert Bacon. 'The latter's small girl had been cured by insulin and she was produced after lunch for Banting to see. Later Harvey Cushing came to tea and saw Hart for the first time since the operation. Therefore in the Canadian Legation in one day a Canadian doctor met an American child whose life he had saved and an American doctor met a Canadian child whose life he had saved.'
18 Massey Diary, 6 June 1924
19 *Ibid.*, 6 December 1928
20 *Ibid.*, 4 February 1934
21 When *The Shining Hour* came to Toronto, I was an undergraduate at

University College, University of Toronto, and attended one of the performances. My impressions were similar to those of the Toronto critics, but when the New York critics chorused their unanimous approval, I concluded that the play had subtleties beyond the comprehension of a provincial audience. A recent reading of the play convinces me that the Toronto critics were right and that the New York critics had been taken in by the glamour of the transatlantic actors. (Gladys Cooper played the *femme fatale* and Adrianne Allen the ingénue.) The play is set in an old Elizabethan farmhouse in Yorkshire, and the story unfolds against a rural background of perpetual eating and much talk about horses and the hot, humid weather. The play consists of brittle chit-chat, punctuated by lurid melodrama. The characters are conceived in crassly romantic terms. The stage directions set the tone. The *femme fatale* 'combines the nervousness of a child with the assurance of a woman. There is something wild about her, but there is also something very still.' When the ingénue resolves on suicide in order to release her young husband for the great love that has suddenly come to him, 'there is about her a power almost embarrassing in its certainty. She is calm too – deathly calm.' Keith Winter, *The Shining Hour* (London: Samuel French, 1934); the quotations are from pp. 44 and 56.

22 Alice Massey to William Grant, 15 August 1910. WLG, vol. 6
23 Vincent Massey to William Grant. WLG, vol. 6
24 William Grant to George Macdonald, undated. WLG, vol. 6
25 William Grant to J.M. Macdonnell, undated. WLG, vol. 7
26 William Grant to Edward Peacock, 22 December 1906. WLG, vol. 8
27 William Grant to O.D. Skelton, 2 February 1934. WLG, vol. 9
28 William Grant to Principal D.M. Gordon, 3 August 1917. WLG, vol. 4
29 William Grant to J.M. Macdonnell, 12 March 1928. WLG, vol. 6
30 William Grant to E. Robertson, 2 December 1929. WLG, vol. 6
31 William Grant to Sir Maurice Hankey, 18 April 1929. WLG, vol. 5
32 3 June 1908. WLG, vol. 5
33 William Grant to Sir George Parkin, 25 November 1918. WLG, vol. 8
34 William Grant to Sir Maurice Hankey, undated, in all likelihood October 1926. WLG, vol. 5
35 J.M. Macdonnell to William Grant, 20 February 1915. WLG, vol. 7
36 J.M. Macdonnell to William Grant, 12 February (no year, likely 1925). WLG, vol. 8. I recall a personal incident that illustrates this combination of severity and humour. Macdonnell was the chairman of the Rhodes selection committee before which I appeared in 1935. At one point I had rashly recited a number of uncomplimentary definitions of the Rhodes

scholar. When I paused, Macdonnell interjected, 'You forgot one defini-
tion – a young man who had a future.' I did not get a Rhodes.

37 J.M. Macdonnell to William Grant, 21 June 1927. WLG, vol. 7
38 Massey Diary, April 1922
39 Vincent Massey to William Grant, undated, probably June 1931. WLG, vol. 6
40 William Grant to J.M. Macdonnell, 28 December 1927. WLG, vol. 7
41 Massey Diary, 30 October 1934
42 *Ibid.*, 16 October 1924
43 *Ibid.*, 6 August 1927
44 *Ibid.*, 6 May 1936
45 *Ibid.*, 23 January 1931
46 *Ibid.*, 20 February 1931
47 *Ibid.*, 20 August 1931

CHAPTER 8

1 Massey Diary, 24 June 1927
2 *Ibid.*, 25 April 1929
3 The quoted phrase is from a letter to Vincent Massey from Harry Adaskin,
  24 June 1932.
4 Massey Diary, 2 February 1928
5 *Ibid.*, 27 December 1931
6 Harry Adaskin, *A Fiddler's World* (Vancouver: November House, 1977),
  p. 227
7 Massey Diary, 30 March 1932
8 *Ibid.*, 27 January 1933
9 *Ibid.*, 1 December 1934
10 *Transactions of the Royal Society of Canada.* Third series, XXIV, 1930, p. 70
11 Vincent Massey to Capt. Alan Lascelles, 4 January 1932
12 Massey Diary, 28 April 1935
13 McGillivray Knowles to Eric Brown, 31 December 1924
14 Eric Brown to Vincent Massey, 3 April 1926
15 Eric Brown to Vincent Massey, 2 January 1926
16 Vincent Massey to Mackenzie King, 9 January 1929. WLMK, vol. 165, pp.
  140303–4. The proposed site was Green Island, which lies at the
  confluence of the Rideau and Ottawa rivers – a lovely site later taken over
  by the Ottawa City Hall.
17 Alice Massey to David Milne, 29 November 1934
18 In her letter to Milne, 28 March 1932, Alice Massey wrote that they found
  the picture 'at the National Exhibition.' Vincent in his memoirs put the

time of discovery as 1930 or early in 1931, and the place 'an art dealer's shop in Toronto' where there was 'a collection of pictures, by various painters, that were offered for sale.' wpp, p. 87

19 Alice Massey to David Milne, 19 July 1935
20 Alice Massey to David Milne, 14 June 1935
21 David Milne to Alice Massey, 1 July 1935
22 David Milne to Alice Massey, 17 October 1935
23 David Milne to Alice Massey, 10 February 1935
24 David Milne to Vincent and Alice Massey, 20 August 1934
25 David Milne to Alice Massey, 10 October 1934
26 The tangled story of Vincent Massey's financial relations with Milne came to an end in 1958 when Vincent was governor-general of Canada. The bizarre story is told in C. Blair Laing's *Memoirs of an Art Dealer* (Toronto: McClelland & Stewart, 1979), pp. 63–4. Laing was asked to come to Rideau Hall to arrange the purchase of Massey's remaining Milne pictures. Lionel Massey was the intermediary in the discussions. 'Lionel ushered me into an enormous ballroom, where spread upon the floor, unframed, and many without stretchers, were what seemed to me acres of Milnes.' There were 166 pictures, and Laing paid $33,000 (an average of less than $200 for each picture) for all of them. There is dramatic justice in the speculation that, in the light of the eventual price of Milne paintings, Massey received in 1958 about as much comparatively for his Milnes as he paid Milne for them in 1934.
27 Lilias Newton to Alice Massey, 17 January 1934
28 Massey Diary, 7 December 1934
29 Peter Oliver, *G. Howard Ferguson: Ontario Tory* (Toronto: University of Toronto Press, 1977), p. 274
30 Michiel Horn, 'Free Speech Within the Law,' *Ontario History*, LXXII, 1, March 1980, p. 39. The article gives a full account of the 'free speech' issue of 1931.
31 Massey Diary, 22 January 1931
32 *Ibid.*, 18 February 1931
33 *Ibid.*, 31 July 1930
34 Alice Massey to Maude Grant, April 1931. wlg, vol. 43
35 Massey Diary, 22 November 1933
36 The phrase comes from Arnold J. Toynbee, who edited the proceedings. 'Introduction,' *British Commonwealth Relations* (London: Oxford University Press, 1934), p. 13
37 The third member was Dr Augustin Frigon, an electrical engineer from Montreal. Vincent lunched with Bowman on 14 April 1928, and in his diary

added a note, dated 25 September 1930, that they talked about a radio commission and 'this was ultimately appointed with two members whose names I proposed – Sir J. Aird and C.A. Bowman.' A detailed account of the radio issue at this time will be found in the early chapters of Frank W. Peers, *The Politics of Canadian Broadcasting* (Toronto: University of Toronto Press, 1969).

CHAPTER 9

1 David Milne to Alice Massey, undated, probably 3 March 1935
2 Massey Diary, 25 January 1928
3 King's argument that Lord Strathcona, a Conservative, held the position of high commissioner for fifteen years during Laurier's regime had an antique flavour. (House of Commons Debates, 15 May 1931, p. 1795)
4 WPP, p. 177
5 Memorandum by Vincent Massey of a conversation with the Hon. R.B. Bennett in the latter's office at Ottawa, 13 August 1930
6 C.P. Stacey, *A Very Double Life* (Toronto: Macmillan, 1976), p. 97
7 Massey Diary, 21 September 1930
8 Toronto *Globe*, 9 March 1931
9 Massey Diary, 28 November 1931
10 *Ibid.*, 1 December 1930
11 *Ibid.*, 6 December 1930
12 *Saturday Night*, 18 April 1931
13 King Diary, 27 January 1934
14 King to Massey, 13 February 1930. WLMK, vol. 178, p. 151771
15 Blair Neatby, *William Lyon Mackenzie King, vol. 2: The Lonely Heights 1924–1932* (Toronto: University of Toronto Press, 1963), p. 369
16 *Canadian House of Commons Debates*, 30 July 1931, p. 4709
17 Massey Diary, 26 January 1928
18 *Ibid.*, 27 February 1928
19 *Ibid.*, 10 April 1933
20 *Ibid.*, 22 January 1931
21 King to Massey, 21 January 1931. WLMK, vol. 187
22 Massey Diary, 4 August 1931
23 King Diary, 4 August 1931
24 King to Massey, 6 November 1931. WLMK, vol. 187, pp. 159666–70
25 Massey Diary, 1 January 1932
26 J.A. Spender, *Sir Robert Hudson, A Memoir* (London: Cassell, 1930), pp. 64–5

27 King Diary, 6 January 1932
28 *Ibid.*, 14 January 1932
29 Calgary *Albertan*, 7 December 1931
30 Lambert was proposed by Dafoe, but Massey made the actual recommendation.
31 King Diary, 8 March 1932
32 *Ibid.*, 9 March 1932
33 *Ibid.*, 28 March 1932
34 *Ibid.*, 29 May 1932
35 *Ibid.*, 29 May 1932
36 Massey to King, 22 August 1932. WLMK, vol. 192, p. 163842
37 Massey to King, 31 August 1932. WLMK, vol. 192, pp. 163847–8
38 Neatby, *Mackenzie King*, vol. 2, p. 344
39 King Diary, 15 December 1932
40 King to Massey, 21 November 1932. WLMK, vol. 192, pp. 163861–4
41 King to Massey, 28 November 1932. WLMK, vol. 192, pp. 163865–8
42 Massey Diary, 24 March 1932
43 Alice Massey to King, 27 March 1933. WLMK, vol. 192, pp. 167877–8
44 King to Alice Massey, 31 March 1933. WLMK, vol. 192, pp. 167879–80
45 King Diary, 31 March 1933
46 25 January 1933
47 Lambert Diary, 1 May 1933
48 Massey Diary, 11 May 1933
49 Lambert Diary, 17 May 1933
50 *Ibid.*, 8 July 1933
51 Vincent Massey to Violet Carruthers, 13 February 1933
52 'The Significance for Canada of the American "New Deal",' in *The Liberal Way* (Toronto: J.M. Dent & Sons, 1933), p. 195
53 'Liberalism and the Economic Challenge, in *The Liberal Way*, p. 215
54 King Diary, 21 July 1933
55 *Ibid.*, 3 September 1933
56 *Ibid.*, 8 September 1933
57 *Ibid.*, 15 September 1933
58 *Ibid.*, 28 October 1933
59 King to Massey, 3 November 1933. WLMK, vol. 197, pp. 167946–54
60 Robert Caygeon in *Saturday Night*, 22 July 1933
61 *Canadian Forum*, October 1933
62 R.T.L. was Charles Vining. Denton Massey, Vincent's cousin, had achieved considerable popularity by his broadcasts from his men's Bible class in Toronto. He had inherited a good deal of his father's flamboyance and

energy, along with the family allegiance to the Conservative party. Denton became the Conservative campaign director in Ontario in January 1935. His attack on Vincent during the campaign widened the gap between Vincent and the other members of the Massey family. Denton spoke of '... the voice of a man supposedly cultured, a man of education, and the dean of a University, a man of diplomatic training. Yet that man blindly followed his leader to the extent of making statements which he knew, he must have known, were utterly untrue.' Toronto *Mail and Empire*, 27 August 1935

63 King Diary, 10 April 1934

64 Lambert Diary, 10 April 1934

65 *Ibid.*, 7 February 1934

66 *Ibid.*, 28 February, 2 March 1934. Stephen Cartwright, Massey's secretary since October 1932, became editor of the *Canadian Forum* in April 1934. The *Canadian Forum*, founded in 1920, was the leading Canadian journal of left-wing opinion, and, during the thirties, moved close to the CCF.

67 *Ibid.*, 21 January 1934

68 *Ibid.*, 13 June 1934

69 *Ibid.*, 11 September 1934

70 Address at the annual meeting of the Central Ontario Liberal Association, Kingston, 7 August 1935

71 Address at Maple Leaf Gardens, Toronto, 9 October 1935

72 Lambert Diary, 19 January 1934

73 Massey to King, 1 October 1935. WLMK, vol. 209, pp. 179818–23

74 Massey Diary, no date. This is a long retrospective entry on the campaign, and prefaces a volume that deals with his first year in London.

75 Massey to King, 13 January 1935. WLMK, vol. 209, pp. 179781–3

76 Massey Diary, 6 February 1933

77 King Diary, 20 July 1935

78 Neatby, *Mackenzie King*, vol. 2, p. 117

79 Massey to King, 1 October 1935. WLMK, vol. 209, pp. 179813–16

80 Massey to King; no date, but probably 6 October 1935. WLMK, vol. 209, p. 179824

81 King Diary, 22 October 1935

82 *Ibid.*, 7 July 1933

83 The phrase is attributed to Herbert Asquith, who was describing the Balliol man of Jowett's day. Vincent Massey was fond of quoting it too, always for humorous effect.

84 King Diary, 5 December 1925

85 *Ibid.*, 8 September 1932

86 *Ibid.*, 11 January 1927

87 Neatby, *Mackenzie King*, vol. 2, p. 412

88 King Diary, 2 January 1933

89 Brooke Claxton to Vincent Massey, 4 April 1935

90 The book was never published. When he was appointed high commissioner, he decided that it was improper for him to publish a personal account of his views on foreign affairs. There are several bound copies of the page proofs in the Massey College Library. It is written in a clear and lively style, and contains considered arguments for an independent Canadian foreign policy directed towards the preservation of peace by collective security.

91 The speech was given to the Kiwanis international convention in Toronto, 12 June 1934. Before he gave the speech, he sought help from the young registrar of the Ontario Securities Commission, George Drew, who had written on the subject of arms control. Drew wrote to Massey on 21 May 1934: 'It seems to me that the evils are sufficiently apparent that everyone should strike at the continuance in private hands of a business that may not necessarily cause war itself but does undoubtedly stir up the other causes of war by attempts to sell munitions in a market which can only be stimulated by appeals to fear and patriotism.'

92 King Diary, 31 October 1935

93 Massey Diary, 2 November 1935. King maintained that Massey had preferred Lord Irwin to Buchan as governor-general but that he, King, had argued persuasively for the commoner and Presbyterian against the high churchman and aristocrat.

Index